HEALING MEMORIES

LATINX AND LATIN AMERICAN PROFILES

Frederick Luis Aldama, Editor

HEALING MEMORIES

Puerto Rican Women's Literature in the United States

Elizabeth García

University of Pittsburgh Press

Published by the University of Pittsburgh Press, Pittsburgh, Pa., 15260
Copyright © 2018, University of Pittsburgh Press
All rights reserved
Manufactured in the United States of America
Printed on acid-free paper
10 9 8 7 6 5 4 3 2 1

ISBN 13: 978-0-8229-6564-0
ISBN 10: 0-8229-6564-X

Cataloging-in-Publication data is available from the Library of Congress

Cover art: *Melancolia* by Poli Marichal
Cover design: Melissa Dias-Mandoly

To the generations of women in my family

Grandmothers:
Concepción Calde Negrón
Carmen Dalila Ramos Vélez

Mother:
Carmen María Lugo Ramos

Sister:
Julissa García Lugo

Daughter:
Lina María Farías

May their (her)stories never be forgotten

CONTENTS

Acknowledgments

ix

Introduction

"La Cultural Cura": Healing Historical Absences

3

Chapter 1

The Making of a Curandera Historian: Aurora Levins Morales

23

Chapter 2

Double Victory for Puerto Rican Women Too: Nicholasa Mohr's *Nilda*

51

Chapter 3

"Mending Broken Memories": Judith Ortiz Cofer's *Silent Dancing: A Partial Remembrance of a Puerto Rican Childhood*

75

Chapter 4

"Degrees of Puertoricanness": Esmeralda Santiago's *When I Was Puerto Rican*

107

Conclusion

Who Tells Your Story? Situating DiaspoRican Women's Literature

139

Notes

155

Works Cited

159

Index

173

ACKNOWLEDGMENTS

The completion of this book was a long journey filled with many doubts and detours. As such, there are so many people to thank that I'm hesitant to list individual names for fear of forgetting someone. Please take these acknowledgements not as an exhaustive list, but perhaps as what Judith Ortiz Cofer might call a "partial truth" of my journey. This book began as my dissertation for the Comparative Ethnic Studies Department at the University of California, Berkeley. I am grateful to the many faculty of the Department and the affiliated African American Studies Department faculty. In one way or another, they all have influenced the kind of scholar, educator, and mentor I have become. In particular I'd like to thank Jose David Saldívar, who greatly influenced my literary and theoretical training. I also would have never survived the graduate school years without my classmates, especially my hermanos Jason Ferreira, Dylan Rodriguez, and the late and sorely missed Horacio Roque Ramirez. I would also like to thank my friend Vilma Huertas, who I met in California through another good friend Jennifer Leigh, and quickly became an incredible source of personal support. Mil gracias for all of our adventurous escapades.

My first academic job was in the historic Black and Puerto Rican Studies Department, now known as the Africana and Puerto Rican/Latino Studies Department, at Hunter College, CUNY. I thank all of my colleagues for their support of my teaching interests and my research. Teaching at Hunter has definitely been one of the highlights of my career. I so appreciated opportunities to develop new courses especially in the area of gender and women's studies. I would like to particularly thank Felix Matos Rodriguez, former Director of the Center for Puerto Rican Studies, and now President of Queens College, for his wonderful support and encouragement. He was one of the early mentors who guided me through my moments of frustration and doubt. I'll always cherish our lunch meetings.

One of the long detours in my path was my years working at Connecticut College as Dean of Multicultural Affairs. There are very few faculty who get the opportunity to see the other side of higher education, the side that keeps the machine running so to speak. Without a doubt, my years as Dean have made me a much better teacher and mentor. I would like to thank the former Dean of the College, Armando Bengochea, for giving me the opportunity in the first place and for pushing me to take on the role as Coordinator of the Mellon Mays Undergraduate Fellowship Program, despite my many hesitations. It was my time with the MMUF program that first inspired me to return to my scholarly work. Thank you also to Carolyn Denard, who took over Dean Bengochea after his departure, for giving me the opportunity to return to the classroom and teach courses in the History Department. There are many faculty colleagues who were supportive of my work not just as an administrator but who also supported my teaching and scholarly endeavors, including Lisa Wilson, Leo Garofalo, David Canton, David Kim, Ron Flores, and Rosemarie Roberts.

A couple of years ago my husband and I reconnected with an old friend and distinguished scholar, Fred Aldama. When he asked about my book and expressed interest in potentially publishing it as part of his series with the University of Pittsburgh Press, I knew the time had finally arrived. His encouragement and support gave me the energy and motivation I needed to get through the final stages of completion. I am also so grateful to the anonymous reviewers whose careful reading and suggestions have undoubtedly made this a much better book. Finally, I'd like to thank Josh Shanholtzer, editor at University of Pittsburgh Press, for shepherding this work through the publishing process and helping me finally make this book a reality.

I owe a huge debt of gratitude to three women from Connecticut College who were not only colleagues, but also became sister-friends; Cherise Harris, Jennifer Rudolph, and Dulmarie Irizarry. Cherise introduced me to the work of Kerry Anne Roquemore and the National Center for Faculty Development and Diversity. The skills I learned through their Summer Boot Camp program were instrumental in getting me back into writing. More importantly, these three women gave me consistent encouragement throughout the last few years as I focused on completing this book. Cherise and Jen treated me like a scholar when I was no longer sure I could still call myself one. Dulmarie has been an endless well of warmth and love. Whenever my doubts got the best of me, I could always turn to them and know that I would be set back on the right path. There aren't enough words to thank you.

Acknowledgments

One of the components of the Summer Boot Camp program was an accountability group, where you are placed into a group of about four other individuals who are also working on writing projects. Long after the program was over, the four of us have continued to call each other every week for an hour, supporting each other through not just our writing, but also the many challenges of being women academics. I'd like to thank the members of this group—Jessica Millward, Betty Izumi, and Sara Neelon—for the weekly encouragement, for the nudges when I needed them, and for the constant reminder to treat myself after each milestone.

I would be remiss if I didn't also acknowledge my undergraduate mentor Suzanne Oboler. She was the first person to talk to me about the professoriate as a potential career for me, something that, as a first-generation college student, had never entered my mind as a possibility. Thank you, Suzanne, for planting that seed so many years ago. Just look at how it's bloomed!

My work would not exist if it weren't for the amazing Puerto Rican women writers I analyze in this book. Aurora Levins Morales, thank you for creating the "curandera historian" concept and role modeling in your work how to tell history through literature. Nicholasa Mohr, thank you for creating a novel where I finally saw my own life represented. Representation does indeed matter. Esmeralda Santiago, who once after a reading, where I told her about my work on Puerto Rican women telling their histories through literature, agreed that I was on the right track, mil gracias for sharing your memories of being Puerrtoriqueña. Lastly, to the late Judith Ortiz Cofer, thank you for sharing your poetic truth(s).

Finally, I am grateful to my husband Antonio Farias, who more than anyone else has lived through my ups and downs in this journey. The certainty of his faith in me has always been baffling to me. I could not have reached this moment without his consistent "Sí Se Puede" attitude pushing me forward. I finished the dissertation version of this book while my daughter Lina was in the womb. I guess it's only fitting that I'm finally completing it as she's about to graduate from high school and go on to start her own life journey. They have been my cheerleaders every step of the way, for which I will always love them. They are and forever will be the source of my healing.

HEALING MEMORIES

Introduction

"LA CULTURA CURA"

Healing Historical Absences

Reading Nicholasa Mohr's novel, *Nilda*, for the first time, was an overwhelming experience. It was the early 1990s and I was an undergraduate at an elite, private Ivy League institution. I felt the burden of my history as a working-class Puerto Rican woman surrounded by white, wealthy college students and the privileges they represented. I didn't see my experiences reflected in any of the course materials I was reading. The number of faces that looked like mine among the student body was limited. The majority of my professors, except for the rare white female professor, were the prototypical white, heterosexual, privileged male. That is, until I sat in my Latino/a studies course my junior year, the first to be introduced to the curriculum. It was in this course where I first encountered Nicholasa Mohr's novel *Nilda*.

As I read the novel for the first time, I devoured each page thrilled to finally see my life reflected in writing. Yet, with every new hardship I saw the characters endure in 1940s New York City, I was heartbroken, as I realized these were the same struggles I would come to endure over thirty years later. Her description of a crime-infested, poverty-stricken neighborhood in Manhattan reminded me of my early childhood in the Bronx. While I have fond memories of playing in the open fire hydrants during the scorching summers of the 1970s, I also have memories of my mother mopping blood off the hallway floor, left behind after a mentally ill man killed a woman in our building. The dehumanizing experience of the main female characters in the welfare office raised deeply repressed memories of the many long hours my mother and I sat in the small waiting room with its puke green–colored walls, until the social worker finally called our number; only to be told that, once again, we were missing some vital document necessary to process our case.

It was not just my own experiences I saw depicted in this novel. The struggles Nilda's mother endured caring for her children, particularly Nilda herself, always emphasizing the importance of an education in this country as a means through which migrants like herself could escape the conditions of poverty echoed my own mother's constant lectures when I was growing up. She feared I would repeat her mistakes and endure the limitations of her world. I began to hear the voices of the women in my family clamoring for attention, for recognition of their struggles. Their voices have been with me throughout my journey researching and writing this book.

Through Mohr's novel, I learned a history that had been denied me throughout my public-school education. Puerto Rican studies scholars have responded to the exclusion of Puerto Ricans in the nation's history, producing scholarship that documents and tells the history of Puerto Rican migrants in the United States. Yet this history is not widely disseminated in the public-school system. This scholarly work includes the historical studies on the various communities of Puerto Ricans throughout the United States, spanning different periods and locations.[1] The field has also broadened to include studies on political and cultural history.[2] The experiences of Puerto Rican women in the United States as laborers and community members significantly contribute not only to the history of Puerto Rican migrants, but also to the nation's history. Puerto Rican scholars and historians have documented some of these experiences in their historical works.[3] However, unanswered questions about the history of Puerto Rican women continue to exist. For example, how have women experienced periods of war in the United States, such as during the Second World War and the Korean War? How have they experienced migration to different parts of the country? What forms of resistance do women employ against the many barriers they face around issues of race, class, and gender in this society? How have women (re)negotiated and redefined their cultural identities?[4] These questions kept returning me to that first reading of Mohr's novel. If I could relate to this text and the experiences depicted as facts because I too had lived them, then could it be possible that literary works are "fictional" because of their narrative methods, but still factual in content? This question has been the driving force of my research and the way in which I approach literary narratives about Puerto Rican women in the United States.

Reading Nicholasa Mohr's text was the beginning of my own healing process as a young Puerto Rican woman who had no knowledge about Puerto Rican history and literature. I became obsessed with learning more about Puerto Ricans in the United States, and in particular the experiences of women. I craved the validation of my and my mother's existence. I found this validation in the literary works of writers such as Judith Ortiz Cofer, Aurora Levins Morales, Nicholasa Mohr, and Esmeralda Santiago. Not only were these educated women who had differing experiences of being Puerto Rican women in this country, but their texts gave voice to the experiences of women like myself concerning differences in race, class, and gender. These writers were, in essence, documenting the experiences of Puerto Rican women in this country. As Aurora Levins Morales explains in her essay, "The Historian as Curandera," "[o]ne of the first things the colonizing power or repressive regime does is attack the sense of history of those they wish to dominate by attempting to take over and control their relationships to their own past" (*Medicine Stories* 23). The historical narratives created by the colonized through their memory, culture, and oral storytelling traditions, is substituted by a new "origin myth, a story that explains the new imbalances of power as natural, inevitable and permanent, as somehow inherent to the natures of master and slave, invader and invaded, and therefore unchangeable" (Levins Morales, *Medicine Stories* 24). These Puerto Rican women writers, therefore, are using their literary narratives (a written form of storytelling) to rewrite their histories using memory and culture to disrupt the hegemonic and colonizing origin myth created by those in power.

In this book, I focus on the history of Puerto Rican migrant women. I argue that the history of Puerto Rican women has been silenced in the historical narratives of the United States and that Puerto Rican women writers are challenging their erasure through their literary works, documenting their lives and challenging historical methodologies. While one could argue that Puerto Rican men's experiences have also been marginalized in the nation's historical record, this work focuses on the particular experiences of women through an intersectional racial/gendered lens. As Edna Acosta-Belen asserts, "[w]hile men, who tend to be conceived of or conceive of themselves as universal beings devoid of gender, perceive their oppression in U.S. society on the basis of ethnic, racial, or class differences, women additionally endure all the elements of negation and marginalization that come from sexism" ("Beyond Island Boundaries" 990). Puerto Rican women therefore negotiate not only the race and class dynamics that their male peers do, but they must also confront the "patriarchal ideology within the culture of their own group, as well as in the culture of the broader society. As a result, their responses to and strategies against oppression are going to differ from those formulated by men" (Acosta-Belen, "Beyond Island Boundaries" 990). As a response to hegemonic historiographies which have excluded and silenced Puerto Rican history in general (and Puerto Rican women's history in particular) these writers are, as Aurora Levins Morales argues, writing against the historical trauma of silence and erasure. In her essay, "False Memories: Trauma and Liberation," Levins Morales discusses such historical silences as part of the traumatic impact of racist, classist, and sexist oppression endured by people of color in this country. By using the term "trauma", as Bonnie G. Smith states in a different context, "I do not mean to invoke feelings of dismay over victimhood, nor to uphold stereotypical images of Puerto Ricans as pathological, but instead I mean to 'suggest a situation, a social, cultural, and political location' of the oppressed" (38–39). I propose we follow the expanded definition of trauma offered by psychologist Laura S. Brown, which includes "situations of constant coercion, denigration, and inequality, where the announced value of the society is equality" (Smith 38–39). For Puerto Ricans in the United States, where equality is announced as part of its societal values, their exclusion perpetuates a dual trauma. Puerto Ricans not only experience the trauma of being treated as second-class, marginalized citizens of this country[5], but in addition they endure the trauma of having these struggles silenced and their many contributions to the nation's history erased.

Aurora Levins Morales responds to this dual trauma by offering an alternative historical method, which results in both an inclusive and healing historical narrative. Levins Morales provides what she calls a "curandera handbook," which lists fifteen steps the curandera historian must follow in order to produce a medicinal history. These steps will be fleshed out in detail in the next chapter. I situate Puerto Rican women writers of the diaspora within this framework of challenging the absence of Puerto Rican women in the history of the United States by using alternative medicinal methodologies that cross disciplinary borders. If the stories of these Puerto Rican women cannot be found in official historical narratives, we must turn to alternative sources and challenge historical methodologies that privilege certain forms of documentation. This is not to say that these nontraditional sources of history should substitute more traditional sources such as those found from archival research. However, for some historically underrepresented groups such as Puerto Rican women, these sources are either nonexistent or limiting in the amount of information they provide. Relevant information that is absent from these traditional sources can be found in subjective narratives such as those found in memoirs and novels, particularly those written by women authors of color who, at times, conduct historical research of their own. They should therefore be considered additional valid sources for historians to use in their narrative constructions. In other words, I claim that by looking at these alternative sources of history, we can create a healing historical narrative and a more nuanced understanding of Puerto Rican women's historical experiences in the United States.[6]

Challenging Historical Methodologies

Intellectual historians have grappled with the attacks on objectivity by postmodernist theory, trying to reconcile its influential claims with their field's imperative of creating knowledge, which somehow refers to something "real" outside of their narratives. Some historians, like Hayden White, began by embracing certain aspects of the linguistic turn, redefining history as an interpretive art. In *Tropics of Discourse*, White questions the historian's claim to objectivity by demonstrating the ways in which historians use literary techniques in both "interpreting" their archival evidence and in their emplotment of historical narratives into particular stories. Performance studies scholar Diana Taylor has brought the archive itself into question making a distinction between the archive with its "supposedly enduring materials (i.e., texts, documents, buildings, bones) and the ephemeral repertoire of embodied practice/knowledge (i.e., spoken language, dance, sports, ritual)" (19). She uses this distinction to expand "what we understand by 'knowledge'" and to legitimize non-written forms of memory and documentation as legitimate sources of historical knowledge (16). Keith Jenkins and Beverly Southgate, as well as historians of color who have questioned the Eurocentric perspectives of American historical narratives, have further exposed the "subjectivity" involved in the construction of historical narratives, challenging historians to be more subjective about the politics and power relations inherent in the construction of historical narratives (Brooks Higginbotham; Chang; Pesquera and de la Torre). Keith Jenkins, in particular, has suggested that the question to ask regarding historical methodologies is not "What is history?" but "Who is history for?" Beverley Southgate goes even further, demonstrating the multiple agendas behind historical narratives, many of which aim to purposefully uphold the status quo, and suggests that the historian's role in our postmodern tumultuous times is to create "therapeutic, hope-inspiring" narratives (*What is History For?* 125).

As James Loewen argues in *Lies My Teacher Told Me: Everything Your American History Textbook Got Wrong*,[7] historical narratives presented in history textbooks serve to produce model citizens of the nation. In order to produce good patriotic citizens, history textbooks avoid representing the nation in any negative way. Therefore, any historical conflicts, such as those based on race and gender, are minimized or presented as resolved. Similarly, Loewen argues, these texts are said to be objective and therefore not ideological. In other words, objectivity requires that only facts (i.e., names, dates, and events) be presented in the narrative. Anti-racist and feminist ideas are not considered facts, rather ideologies that have no place in objective historical texts. These hegemonic histories serve the colonizing power's objective of writing a new creation myth for the nation that excludes its more problematic subjects.

The historical-colonial relationship between the United States and Puerto Rico, along with the discrimination and marginalization endured by Puerto Rican migrants in the United States, are examples of the kind of history that has no place in such historical narratives of the nation. Puerto Rican communities have existed in the United States since the mid-nineteenth century (Falcón; Andreu Iglesias). These early communities were concentrated in New York City, where the island elite intellectuals organized independence movements for both Puerto Rico and Cuba from Spain's empire. In 1898 the United States acquires Puerto Rico as a result of the Spanish–American war and immediately begins to monopolize the island economy. As a result of the 1917 Jones Act, which grants American citizenship to all Puerto Ricans, the flow of migrants to the mainland increases and Puerto Ricans begin to serve in U.S. wars. The more the United States' goals of perpetual colonization for the island become apparent to the island population, the more we see the rise of pro-independence organizing and movements as evidenced by the creation of the Nationalist Party, with its consequent heavy repression by the government. The Ponce Massacre of 1937 is one of the many examples of the hostility between the pro-independence movements and the island and federal governments.[8]

Puerto Rican migration reached its peak after the Second World War as the island implemented its economic program, Operation Bootstrap, which called for both the industrialization of the island and the migration of Puerto Ricans to the United States to fulfill employment needs on the mainland as a way to depopulate what was considered an overpopulated island. As testimonial accounts and scholarly studies attest, the illusion of the United States and particularly New York as having streets paved of gold, was quickly replaced by the reality of poor social conditions and discrimination (Vega; Colón; Sanchez Korrol; Rodriguez). Since the first waves of the "great migration" of the 1950s, there has been a flow of Puerto Rican migrants back and forth between the island and the mainland, fluctuating according to the economic ups and downs of the United States (Torres; Rodriguez Vecchini; Burgos). This history is evidence that demands a verdict on the actions or at times inactions on the part of the United States in addressing not only the status of the island, but the status of Puerto Rican Diaspora communities throughout the United States (Baker). Including this history into the established model for writing and telling the nation's history would require a critical assessment of the methods used in creating national historical narratives. It requires what Emma Perez calls a "decolonial imaginary" in her work on Chicana history, "a theoretical tool for uncovering the hidden voices of Chicanas that have been relegated to silences, to passivity" (xvi). It requires that, like postmodernists, we question the truth claims made about the nation's history. Such a historical narrative however, must also strive to heal the traumatic effects of oppression and exclusion.

Healing Historical Trauma

Many psychological studies on the effects of prejudice and discrimination on people of color illustrate how the exclusion from historical narrative, as another experience with discrimination, can have negative effects on those excluded from these narratives. Maria Root categorizes systems of oppression such as racism and sexism as insidious trauma. "The effects of insidious trauma are cumulative and are often experienced over the course of a lifetime" (Espin, *Latina Realities* 54). Such insidious trauma can be triggered through the images or messages people receive about their self-worth. As Melba J. T. Vasquez argues about Mexican American women: "If negative messages perpetuated by groups, institutions, and the mass media about one's reference groups are internalized, a Mexican American woman is likely to question her own abilities and appearance, and to have low expectations for entry into powerful positions in the society. Furthermore, if a Chicana grows up perceiving that the people with whom she most strongly identifies (Mexican American women) are not entitled to control of the resources she may internalize feelings of disenfranchisement" (271). This is not to say however, that people of color are not able to cope with the trauma induced by negative representations or complete non-representation of their experiences. Carol T. Miller and Brenda Major discuss various ways through which stigmatized people attempt to cope with their stigmas. These include denial of the stigma, trying to "pass" as white in order to fit into the non-stigmatized or dominant group, and changing their behavior to disprove the stigmas attached to their particular group. Although these coping mechanisms illustrate that the individual does not necessarily succumb to the potential negative results of being stigmatized, there are costs to the various coping mechanisms they employ, including physical symptoms such as hypertension. Although an individual may find other ways to cope with their invisibility in national history and the consequent negative assessment he or she may make based on this erasure on their particular ethnic/racial group—such as conducting their own research or doing extra homework (in the case of the students reading the history textbooks), to learn about their own history—the fact that they have to do this extra work is further indication of their silenced state in this society and becomes an added stressor. Not only are these stressors experienced at the individual level, but because "stigma is linked to a social identity . . . stigma and its accompanying threat are often experienced collectively" as well (Miller and Major 245).

 Levins Morales compares the effects of hegemonic historical narratives on the oppressed to the trauma experienced by victims of sexual abuse. Victims of abuse are disempowered and often silenced by their attackers, fearing reprisals if they come forward. As Judith Herman explains, "in order to escape accountability for his crimes, the perpetrator does everything in his power to promote forgetting. Secrecy and silence are the perpetrator's first line of defense . . . the more powerful the perpetrator, the greater his prerogative to name and define reality" (Levins Morales, *Medicine Stories* 12). The history that we are taught is the "endless repetition of the perpetrator's story" (Levins Morales, *Medicine Stories* 18). Those who have been silenced by the "perpetrator's story" need to reconstruct history. The stories[9] of the abused must be brought to light not only to combat the perpetrators but also to heal the wounds left behind by official history.

The kind of healing evoked by Levins Morales and the other Puerto Rican women authors I discuss is one that challenges Western notions of medicine. Numerous scholars and theorists have challenged the masculinist and oppressive or colonizing foundations of Western medicine. Foucault in *Birth of the Clinic* points to the ways in which power operates in the relationship between the doctor and patient, where the patient's agency disappears and all that remains is the dominating gaze of the doctor on the body (39). As DasGupta and Hurst explain, "[p]rior to the professionalization of medicine, illness was a private experience located within families and traditionally under the dominion of women. With the rise of the medical profession, the illness experience became primarily removed from private suffering to a public experience mediated by physicians" (5). When women search for self-healing within the realm of this professionalized Western medical perspective "we see ourselves as its effects" (Wear and LaCivita 2). Self-healing for women requires turning away from mainstream medicinal methods and returning to a healing that is steeped in their own "culture, identity and environment" (DasGupta and Hurst xii). Furthermore, the types of traumatic pain endured by those who have been erased or silenced by dominant historical narratives, are reminiscent of the kind of pain Elaine Scarry describes as resistant to language. In other words, there is pain for which language or speech is insufficient to fully grasp. However, she argues that "poems and narratives of individual artists" are able to bring pain into speech (9). Women of color authors turn to literature instead of history as a way to speak the pain of historical erasure "because 'what really happened' is often so excruciatingly painful that to articulate these events as American history would be to invite utter disbelief" (Peterson 7). Storytelling by women about their own bodily and historical experiences, Wear and LaCivita assert, "affirms the fluidity of women's corporeality; generates ways of knowing that may take us beyond ourselves—certainly beyond prescriptive medical narratives; and serves as fertile ground for the construction of collective, always shifting realities" (2). Western forms of healing would not be sufficient for mending the physical nor the emotional wounds of historical oppression experienced by Puerto Rican women. Medicinal history places women at the center of their own healing.

Women of color authors have (re)claimed storytelling as a means through which to heal individually and collectively from the traumas of erasure and silence. King-Kok Cheung discusses how the protagonists in *The Color Purple* and *The Woman Warrior*, as women who endure abusive silences, both "proceed to tell all—on paper. Their needs for self-expression are obvious: they hang on to sanity by writing" (163). As Nancy Peterson argues of Kingston's work "[f]acing history as a wound that has not recorded the accomplishments of her people, Kingston turns to literature to shape a narrative that can correct the historical record" (2). Furthermore, bell hooks has asserted in *Sisters of the Yam*, her book on self-recovery and healing, that "writing was always a sanctuary for me in my wounded childhood, a place of confession, where nothing had to be hidden or kept secret. It has always been one of the healing places in my life" (183). This imagery of a wounded history also appears in Gloria Anzaldúa's work where she envisions the border between Mexico and the United States as an open wound of history, one that remains since the time of the Mexican–American War, which created the border. As Peterson argues, for Anzaldúa, "[h]ealing the wounds of history . . . involves not only deconstructing the official story and constructing missing knowledges, but also reconstructing history in such a way that the people will have a useful story to tell themselves—to renew collective memory and to imagine a promising future" (183). Thus, women of color use the literary form to both document their histories and challenge historical methodologies while constructing what Terry Eagleton might call "sources of consolation" not just for themselves individually but also for their collective communities (131). As Gay Wilentz suggests one aim of women authors of various ethnic and racial backgrounds is to "develop a discourse of healing, and on some level . . . create a healing ceremony as part of the novel's structure and content, integrating the storytelling tradition of healing rituals into the consolation narrative of the novel itself" (17).

Puerto Ricans from the diaspora have also expressed the traumatic effects of their oppression as a minoritized, racialized group in the United States, through their writing. A vast Nuyorican literature, particularly poetry, created by Puerto Ricans from New York serves as a space where they uphold their cultural and historical ties to the island while simultaneously creating their own sense of home in the United States. In the 1970s, young Puerto Ricans in New York City, most of whom were either children of migrants or raised in the United States, began to identify themselves as "Nuyoricans," a term that captured the distinct experiences of this generation as "English-speaking children molded in New York" (E. Mohr xiv). Nuyorican literature[10] provides "a means of cultural validation and affirmation of a collective sense of identity that served to counteract the detrimental effects of the socioeconomic and racial marginalization that Puerto Ricans have experienced in the metropolis" (Acosta-Belen, "Beyond Island Boundaries" 980). Through their literature, Puerto Rican women address and attempt to heal the traumatic effects of their socioeconomic conditions and racial marginalization. By discussing the use of writing by Puerto Rican women authors as a way to create healing historical narratives, I am expanding this view of writing as healing to historical writing as well.

Puerto Rican Literature: Ni de aquí, ni de allá

The earliest literary analysis of diaspora literature was Eugene Mohr's *The Nuyorican Experience: Literature of the Puerto Rican Minority*. In this text, Mohr situates Nuyorican literature in the larger literary category of immigrant literature, identifying similarities with the literature of other white ethnic groups where they depict the experiences of the newcomer seeking a better life in America. Yet, he also acknowledged some of the differences he found in this literature. Namely, "its relationship to contemporary ethnic literatures, like those of blacks and Chicanos, which question the traditional insistence on 'Americanization' and often express anger in place of hope or gratitude" (xii). In his work he creates the framework for discussing Puerto Rican diaspora literature that is often still used by literary scholars. He begins his literary history with the works by Bernardo Vega, Jesus Colón, and Pedro Juan Labarthe, who represent the pioneering migrants prior to the Second World War. He follows with those works written by island writers who spent time in New York and who, at times, wrote about the migrant experience disparagingly, in English. He then turns to the works by Piri Thomas and Nicholasa Mohr, in addition to other "barrio writers," whom by now are considered the godparents of diaspora literature, being the first authors to depict the lived experiences of DiaspoRicans. An entire chapter is dedicated to the Nuyorican Poets, given their visibility and centralized presence during the Puerto Rican social movements of the 1970s and the rise of the Nuyorican Poets Café, founded by poet Miguel Algarín. He finally concludes with an assessment of the future of this type of literature, erroneously believing that Nuyorican literature will eventually disappear. Nonetheless, his analytical lens centering the experiences of Puerto Ricans in the United States provided the first framework from which to approach this body of work.

In her essay, "Puerto Rican Writers in the U.S., Puerto Rican Writers in Puerto Rico: A Separation Beyond Language," Nicholasa Mohr (no relation to Eugene) upholds the distinction between Puerto Ricans of the diaspora and Puerto Ricans from the island first asserted in Eugene Mohr's work. The difference, she argued, is not just one of language, but of experience and identity. In her essay she situates her work within the context of North American literature. "When I started to write in 1972, I realized that, except for a book or two that concentrated on the Puerto Rican male's problems and misfortunes, there were no books in United States literature that dealt with our existence, our contributions, or what we Puerto Rican migrants were about" (113). It was the absence of Puerto Ricans in U.S. literature that inspired her to write her works, not the absence of the migrant experience in the island literary canon. While she recognizes that she comes from "an island people who have been colonized from the very onset of their being" she also admits that for the children of migrants "there was no going back; 'home' was here" (113). Nonetheless, Puerto Rican scholars have consistently attempted to find a connection between island and diaspora literatures, insisting on some kind of continuity between the two.

Juan Flores's critical work on Puerto Rican culture and identity is illustrative of this search for connection. In *From Bomba to Hip Hop*, this desire for connection between island and diaspora evolves into the concept of the "trans-colony," whereby he defines a transnational relationship between the island and the diaspora that is still impacted by the colonial relationship between the United States and Puerto Rico. In this definition however, the island is still conceived as the "homeland" of the diaspora, countering Nicholasa Mohr's insistence that the migrants and their children reach a point in their experience where they come to understand that "home" is here in the United States.

A more recent work which continues to seek ties between island and diaspora writers is one by Marisel Moreno. In her study, *Family Matters: Puerto Rican*

Women Authors on the Island and the Mainland, she offers a welcomed focus on the literary works by women providing a gendered analysis of their representations of Puerto Rican culture and history. However, she insists on creating a connection between diaspora and island women arguing that these women are all engaging with and responding to the patriarchal construction of the cultural ideal of "la gran familia puertorriqueña." She begins her text with the unveiling of the Monumento a la Familia Puertorriqueña in Hartford, Connecticut, and reads this event as proof of a connection between the diaspora and the island. As she explains, "I have chosen to begin with this anecdote because I find it encapsulates and brings to life some of the main arguments I put forth in this book, namely, that la gran familia continues to inform notions of Puerto Rican identity both in and outside the island and that the diaspora community has invoked this myth as a strategy to reclaim its kinship ties to the greater Puerto Rican family" (3). While she goes on to recognize in various moments throughout the text that DiaspoRicans, including their literary works, have experienced consistent rejection by the island as not being "authentically" Puerto Rican, she nonetheless insists that there is a connection, and seeks to prove to islanders that the Diaspora still upholds Puerto Rican cultural elements, as evidenced by the monument unveiled in Hartford, Connecticut.[11]

Lisa Sánchez-González's literary history, *Boricua Literature*, boldly challenges this approach to diaspora literature. There is among Puerto Rican Studies scholars, a "reluctance to deal with the diaspora as a distinct constituency in the United States, one that has self-consciously produced its own body of knowledge, based in its own specific assessment of its own unique predicament as a U.S. community of color" (17). Diaspora literature, in her argument, should not be shoehorned into a particular national canon, whether it's a U.S. American one or an island one given their perpetual neglect of this literary work. As she states:

> Tethering Boricua literature to either "Puerto Rico" or "America" as acts of nationalist signification simply does not serve the best interests of Boricua literary scholarship. Clearly the work of Boricua writers and cultural intellectuals is an equally valuable and vulnerable legacy that is routinely hijacked and/or disappeared on either side of the San Juan-New York divide. Reclaiming Boricua literature therefore means attending to this perpetual sequestration and invisibility in a context of forced exile from dual national identities and nationalist intellectual traditions.

> More important, however, it also means tracking and analyzing the diaspora's unique tradition of contiguous dissent and self-articulation, speaking not only of or about but with a community facing its own specific challenges in its own creatively stylized and politicized ways. (20)

Nonetheless, her work still defines Boricua literature in hegemonic political terms, limiting "Boricua literature" to that steeped in a working-class politic. Through her definition of Boricua literature works such as those discussed in this book, by Esmeralda Santiago and Judith Ortiz Cofer, continue to be discussed as assimilationist and not authentically part of the diaspora literary canon. In addition, Aurora Levins Morales's significant body of work is nonexistent in her literary history.

While these scholars have brought analytical attention to a body of literature that otherwise would have remained marginalized and silenced, their situating these works either as part of a continuum between the island and the diaspora or within a particular working-class foundation, limits its analytical possibilities by basing their selections of which literary works to include on some definition of "authenticity." Does connecting the works of the diaspora to island literature make them somehow more "genuinely" Puerto Rican? Does juxtaposing Rosario Ferré[12] with Judith Ortiz Cofer validate the latter's work more so than if we allowed her work to be judged on its own merits? Similarly, how does defining DiaspoRican literature as only that body of work that represents and stems from the Puerto Rican working-class experience limit the possibilities not just of this community's artistic expression but also of its ability to imagine a world beyond poverty and oppression? Lisa Sánchez-González critiques more recent works by authors such as Judith Ortiz Cofer and Esmeralda Santiago for their depictions of upward mobility of the individual narrator instead of proposing advancement for the collective community.[13] Prescribing that these authors depict only certain experiences in collectivist ways in order to be included into the DiaspoRican canon silences certain historical experiences that don't fit this mold and creates one more form of rejection. Not only have these authors experienced the "dual national exile" from U.S. and Puerto Rican literary canons, but they also experience a third exclusion from the literary history of the diaspora.

In this book I expand on the work of Flores, Sanchez-Gonzalez, and Moreno tipping the analytical lens back to where Eugene Mohr set it for us in the first place, in the "here" that is now our "home." Writers such as Aurora Levins Morales, Judith Ortiz Cofer, Nicholasa Mohr, and Esmeralda Santiago provide us with a rich depiction of the many ways in which Puerto Rican women have experienced migration. Their upward mobility provided them with the tools and resources to be able to write their stories and bring the histories of their families (and, by extension, their communities) to light. While their histories stem from an island past, these authors' understanding of their cultural identity was shaped by their, at times, traumatic experiences of oppression and discrimination as part of the diaspora. I therefore situate their works as part of the DiaspoRican literary canon representing their lived experiences in the racialized, classed, and gendered context of the United States.

Puerto Rican Women's Medicinal Historical Narratives

Following Levins Morales's historical methodology, which she describes as "medicinal," I argue that the literary works of mainland Puerto Rican women authors are the alternative, creative, "nontraditional places" where healing narratives of Puerto Rican women's history can be found (Saldóvar-Hull 206). Levins Morales contrasts "medicinal histories" from "imperial history, the history made by people with agendas of domination and used to strip those targeted for domination of hope" (*Medicine Stories* 5). A medicinal history "does the opposite, distilling a legacy of pride, hope and rebellion from ordinary people's lives" (*Medicine Stories* 5). These writers are using their literature as an alternative space in which to document and narrate their histories. Diaspora writers such as Judith Ortiz Cofer, Nicholasa Mohr, and Esmeralda Santiago are historians as they reclaim and write a collective history of Puerto Rican women in the United States. By writing down the experiences of their mothers, sisters, and daughters, they heal the wounds of silence, give agency and power to the voiceless, and contribute to achieving a more accurate understanding of the history of Puerto Rican women in the United States.

Instead of just looking at these texts through a purely literary lens, where we critique the form of the narratives, discuss the ways in which these texts follow or not the characteristics of particular genres, or debate whether they are new forms of the bildungsroman or of autobiographical writing; I propose we also look at these texts through a feminist socio-historical lens where we can find a wealth of possibilities for both literary and historical research. In my analysis of the works, I will therefore refrain from close readings on questions of style, narrative structure, or voice; instead I will use more of a content analysis approach where I focus on certain plot points as evidence of the medicinal historical methodology used by each author.

By discussing these texts as medicinal histories, I also intend to create a healing narrative of my own where the methods used result in a kind of scholarship that introduces the reader to tools and potential skills of personal and collective empowerment. In this sense, I follow in the footsteps of Bettina Aptheker, who in her book *Tapestries of Life* advocated for a more healing historical method and narrative which acknowledges that "the dailiness of women's lives structures a different way of knowing and a different way of thinking" (254). Using the knowledge found in these women's everyday experiences leads to a historical narrative that helps women "heal from the racist and sexual violence that permeates our lives" (7). Aptheker's strategy gives women agency by acknowledging daily coping strategies and methods of survival as forms of resistance. The knowledge embedded in the daily struggles and coping strategies of Puerto Rican women, documented in the narratives of Puerto Rican women writers, is why it is imperative that these narratives be approached and reread through a historical lens.

In this book, I focus on three specific ways in which these writers challenge historical methodologies and rewrite healing historical narratives: First, they offer the literary work as a documentation of the experiences of Puerto Rican women. Secondly, they use memory, with all of its complexities, as a legitimate source of history. And finally, Puerto Rican women writers engage in cultural history, using not only their cultural products as forms of historical revision, but also of passing on the culture as a carrier of Puerto Rican history. Through these alternative sources of history these women construct narratives in which they rewrite themselves as historical subjects, healing the traumatic effects of historical erasure.

In the next chapter, "The Making of a Curandera Historian," I discuss the works of Aurora Levins Morales tracing her beginnings as a curandera historian to her contribution to the pioneering collection *This Bridge Called My Back* (Moraga and Anzaldúa), entitled "And Even Fidel Can't Change That . . ." I analyze in more detail the tenets of the curandera historian as delineated in her collection of essays *Medicine Stories: History, Culture, and the Politics of Integrity*. I look at her previous works analyzing how she develops her medicinal methodology in *Getting Home Alive* and comes to full maturity in her latest work, *Remedios: Stories of Earth and Iron from the History of Puertorriqueñas*. Unlike the other authors analyzed in the rest of the book, Levins Morales's work does not follow the linear structure of a memoir or autobiography. Her work can be best described as creative nonfiction using various forms including essays, poems, and short narratives to create her own hybrid genre. As such, her work defies consistent plot lines and instead pulls together thematic threads that appear throughout her narrative. My analytical approach to her narratives therefore is to pull particular plot themes in order to demonstrate the consistency of curandera tactics throughout her body of work.

In chapter two, "Double Victory for Puerto Rican Women Too," I discuss Nicholasa Mohr's *Nilda* and the ways in which Mohr uses this novel to challenge official historical narratives and heal the trauma inflicted on her by the absence of Puerto Rican women in U.S. history. *Nilda* depicts both the collective and individual experiences of struggle and survival of the East Harlem Puerto Rican community during a time period that is rarely documented in DiaspoRican history, the Second World War era. This novel provides an inside view of how the war impacted Puerto Rican families from the perspective of the women responsible for these families. Therefore, Mohr not only challenges official histories, but offers her narrative as an alternative historical document.

In the third chapter, "Mending Broken Memories," I focus on Judith Ortiz Cofer's *Silent Dancing: A Partial Remembrance of a Puerto Rican Childhood*. In this text, Ortiz Cofer provides fragmented memories of her childhood written in prose and poetry, similar to the sketch format of earlier Puerto Rican writers such as Jesus Colón and Bernardo Vega. Efraín Barradas argues that both the schematic form, as well as the representation of a collective history, are constant throughout the literature of migrant Puerto Ricans. Ortiz Cofer's text also broadens the representation of migrant communities portraying the experiences of communities in New Jersey. In the preface to *Silent Dancing*, Ortiz Cofer invokes Virginia Woolf's *Moments of Being* where she writes about "the problem of writing truth from memory," in order to address the claims against memory as a reliable source. Ortiz Cofer explains that Woolf, "accepts the fact that in writing about one's life, one often has to rely on that combination of memory, imagination, and strong emotion that may result in 'poetic truth'" (Ortiz Cofer 11). Ortiz Cofer claims Woolf as her literary foremother and proceeds to write the "sketches" of her past as she defines her work as "a partial remembrance of my childhood." Her goal is to also present "poetic truth." I am suggesting that within this poetic truth we can find an "understanding of the historical experience" of Puerto Ricans in the same manner that writers such as Toni Morrison find about the experiences of other communities of color.

Finally, Esmeralda Santiago's *When I was Puerto Rican* depicts the traditional linear migration from the island to New York City. Unlike texts from the island and other texts from the diaspora, she also represents the experiences of a migrant family on the island prior to their migration. Santiago has also expressed a concern for the lack of representation of Puerto Rican women like herself in both historical and literary narratives. She has experienced firsthand the sense of not belonging to either historical narratives of the United States or Puerto Rico. She thus purposefully sets out to make the experiences of Puerto Rican women in her narratives visible.

In my analysis of Santiago, I use the medicinal as an interpretive lens, focusing on how she engages in cultural history from a particular gendered perspective. She takes on two cultural binaries within which Puerto Rican women's culture has been defined: a) the American vs. Puerto Rican cultural binary and b) the virgin/whore dichotomy. In response to those who have critiqued her as becoming too Americanized as a result of her time living in the United States, she problematizes the binary that assumes that island culture is somehow pure and unblemished by Americanization. She therefore demonstrates that Americanization, as a result of the colonial relationship between Puerto Rico and the United States, is already present within island culture. She also challenges the cultural icon of the *jíbaro*, which has been defined as a male figure, and takes on this identity for herself as a woman.

Puerto Rican womanhood, as is the case for many other Latinas, has been defined within the binary of the virgin/whore dichotomy. In Santiago's work we see the negative impact this has on the gender construction of young Negi. Santiago not only documents this experience, but also offers alternative definitions of Puerto Rican womanhood that are still steeped in Puerto Rican cultural history. She thus creates in her narrative a healing cultural history for Puerto Rican women.

Paula Moya defines identities as "socially significant and context-specific ideological constructs that nevertheless refer in non-arbitrary (if partial) ways to verifiable aspects of the social world" (13). Therefore, examining individual identities and histories can provide us with insights about the historical experiences of the collective group. The goal of this study is to raise questions and suggest certain theoretical and methodological approaches for thinking about Puerto Rican women's literature and history. The three texts chosen represent the multiplicity of the migrant experience and serve as sample case studies of how to apply an analysis of historiographical narratives and methods.

In the concluding chapter, "Who Tells Your Story: Situating DiaspoRican Women's Literature," I turn to the question of citizenship and belonging. As discussed above, the history of Puerto Ricans is one that is intertwined with that of the United States as a result of their colonial relationship. Yet, even though Puerto Ricans have had American citizenship since 1917, have consistently contributed to the nation through their labor and military service, their history is absent from historical narratives of the United States. While their history has been silenced Puerto Rican women such as the authors analyzed in this work, have resisted their erasure finding alternative ways to tell their (her)stories. Their efforts are part of a larger struggle by other Latinos and people of color, literary authors, scholars, and lay people to challenge and redefine our sources of knowledge. Areas of study such as ethnic studies, women's studies, and queer studies, "have presented major challenges to elite control of knowledge, to what story is told about U.S. society" (Levins Morales, *Remedios* 14). Recent attacks in states like Arizona and Texas on ethnic studies broadly and Chicano/Latino studies in particular, are the contemporary manifestations of this struggle over who controls the story we tell about the United States. As I demonstrate in this book, it is this particular conflict that these Puerto Rican women writers are writing against. Through their literary works, they create narratives that challenges those dominant stories about U.S. history while broadening the methods we use and the sources we turn to in order to create more inclusive national (his)stories.

Chapter 1

THE MAKING OF A CURANDERA HISTORIAN

Aurora Levins Morales

Aurora Levins Morales began graduate school and therapy within two weeks of each other. In her collection of essays, *Medicine Stories: History, Culture, and the Politics of Integrity*, she explains that while she was digging through the histories of Puerto Rican women for her dissertation work, she simultaneously dug through her own personal experiences of abuse and subsequent trauma. This led her to find commonalities between personal abuse at the hands of individual victimizers and the collective abuse of oppression at the hands of a racist, sexist, and classist society. As a result, she creates a unique brand of historical methodology that serves to document and heal the traumas of historical oppression and silence. Through this methodology she (re)defines the role of Puerto Rican historians, in particular, to not only document the consistently silenced history of Puerto Ricans in the United States, but also to create healing narratives.

Evoking the tradition of Puerto Rican and Latina women's roles as spiritual and medicinal healers, Levins Morales creates a culturally grounded historical methodology to heal the wounds of historical oppression and silence. Olivia Espín in "Spiritual Power and the Mundane World: Hispanic Female Healers in Urban U.S. Communities," has investigated the "prominence of women healers" in Latino communities. She argues that the role of the healer allows these women to cross gendered barriers and not be limited to traditional gender roles. Because her powers are perceived as supernatural, healers are able to move beyond some of the gender constraints Latinas endure within their cultures. The role of healer "constitutes, for some, the expression of a sense of self that is strong and competent but cannot be fully communicated in all spheres of life without breaking cultural norms" (162). Thus, Levins Morales defining her historical methodology as medicinal and calling the practitioner of this methodology a "curandera" is significant both for its cultural grounding but also for its specific gendered qualities. Levins Morales documents Puerto Rican women's experiences, accounting for their cultural hybridity and multiplicity of experiences along race, class, and gender lines.[1] Her methodology heals not just the traumas of silence, exclusion, and marginalization but also of disconnection and division by illustrating the fluidity of Puerto Rican identity, documenting the multifaceted experience of being Puerto Rican from various racial, class-based, and gendered perspectives. Levins Morales's concerns with histories of the oppressed and, in particular, that of Puerto Rican women from both the island and the diaspora can be traced to her earliest writings, beginning with her contribution to the groundbreaking anthology, *This Bridge Called My Back* (Moraga and Anzaldúa), entitled "And Even Fidel Can't Change That . . ." In this chapter, I will explain her "medicinal history" methods and trace the making of this curandera historian throughout her literary works. As we will see, Levins Morales's writing defies linearity, consisting of collections of poems, essays, and short creative nonfiction. Instead of focusing on a particular plot narrative, her work takes on a variety of themes including but not limited to culture, gender, language, race, and sexuality. In my analysis, I pull particular themes from her narratives to demonstrate how she employs curandera tactics throughout her work. I employ Tey Diana Rebolledo's approach to literary criticism, where my role as literary critic is "to make the writers known" and "remember our literary history" (349). As she states, "our literature and our cultural production does not need legitimization from the academy... it already is legitimate in itself" (354). As Levins Morales states, "[i]n the market place of ideas, we are pushed toward the supermarket chains that are replacing the tiny rural colmado" (*Medicine Stories* 67). I therefore, shop in Levins Morales's own intellectual colmado for my theoretical grounding in this analysis of her work.

The Curandera Handbook

In her essay, "The Historian as Curandera," Levins Morales provides what she calls a "curandera handbook" listing fifteen steps the curandera historian follows in order to produce a medicinal history. These can be condensed into the following five key areas which appear repeatedly throughout her work: a) giving agency and voice; b) questioning and challenging definitions of historical evidence; c) showing multiple historical perspectives; d) local and global contextualizing; and e) crossing borders. Through these steps, Levins Morales offers a concrete process for the type of postmodernist history theorized by scholars like Hayden White, Keith Jenkins, and Beverly Southgate. As I discuss in a previous article, postmodernist theorists of history have challenged historians to account for the "subjectivity, interpretation, and power dynamics" involved in the production of historical narratives (Garcia, "Medicinal Histories" 254). In *Tropics of Discourse*, Hayden White discussed the interpretive methods used by historians of archival evidence and thus challenged claims to objectivity. Furthermore, Keith Jenkins argued "history remains inevitably a personal construct, a manifestation of the historian's perspective as a 'narrator'" (12). While these theorists challenge historical methodologies and raise provocative questions, they stop short of offering a methodology that can be used to create historical narratives that are consciously and overtly revealing the historian's subjectivity while making visible the many power dynamics across race, class, and gender lines that are always present in historical events.[2] Levins Morales's curandera handbook offers such a methodology.

In the curandera handbook, Levins Morales is first and foremost concerned with giving agency and voice to those who have been historically silenced. This requires "telling untold or undertold stories," (*Medicine Stories* 26), particularly those of women. Once you change the focus of the lens of history, the methodology forcibly changes. For instance, Levins Morales explains, by centering women in her historical narrative, the kinds of questions asked must also change. "We need to ask, [i]f women are assumed to be the most important people in this story, how will that change the questions we ask? How will it change the answers to questions that have already been asked" (*Medicine Stories* 26). In trying to represent the experiences of the oppressed, some narratives end up victimizing their subjects, by focusing on the many injustices and abuses experienced by these groups. Part of giving agency and voice to those that have been excluded from historical narratives entails also illustrating the ways in which the marginalized resist and revolt against their oppressions. "People who are being mistreated are always trying to figure out a strategy. Those strategies may be shortsighted, opportunistic, ineffective or involve the betrayal of others, but they nevertheless represent a form of resistance" (*Medicine Stories* 30). The strategies used for resistance are clearly diverse and complex. Therefore, an added element in giving agency to those marginalized is to "personalize" as much as possible. Levins Morales explains that, at times, the experiences of marginalized groups are summarized into general statements and therefore fail to convey to the full extent the ways certain events are experienced and individualized. Therefore, she argues, historians should personalize their historical narratives by naming individuals. "Using the names of individual real people, and any details we know about their lives, to dramatize and personalize the social condition of a group makes those conditions far more real. When the disenfranchised appear only in crowd scenes, it reinforces a sense of relative unimportance" (*Medicine Stories* 33). Her goal here is to empower women who at times have been portrayed as merely victims. Throughout her work she illustrates and asserts the everyday ways in which Puerto Rican women empower themselves.

Creating a healing history requires that the curandera historian question and challenge definitions of historical evidence. She does this by using alternative sources to written documentation, relying on oral histories, myths, and stories. Yet there are still those moments where very little evidence, whether traditional or alternative, is available on the history of Puerto Rican women. In these cases, the curandera historian must make these absences and gaps visible in her narrative, instead of simply excluding the experiences of these women. One technique Levins Morales suggests is using "what if" questions. For example, she discusses the story of the Taína cacica Guanina, whose life story resembles that of Pocahontas. She falls in love with a colonizer and dies beside him after her people kill him in battle. "The two are buried side by side and the lilies of Spain entwine with the wildflowers of Puerto Rico upon their graves" (*Medicine Stories* 29).

Levins Morales wonders what was most likely to have happened given the historical context of Guanina's time period. She asks what would the story be if we assume that Guanina was not a naive woman and her liaison with the colonizer was intelligent and strategic. Levins Morales's reinterpretation "proposes another possible set of motives and understandings that could explain the known facts of her life and death and leave us with a sense of her dignity and purpose" (*Medicine Stories* 29).

The third key element to the curandera historical methodology is to show the multiple perspectives and angles to particular historical experiences. In addition to addressing the multiple racial, class-based, and gendered experiences of Puerto Ricans, illustrating a multifaceted Puerto Rican history also means showing the various sides or perspectives of a particular historical event. For instance, representations of Puerto Rican militant resistance, particularly through historical figures, such as Pedro Albizu Campos. Although these figures are significant to the history of Puerto Ricans both on the island and the diaspora, one should be wary of romanticizing these movements. Although there is the leftist and perhaps politically correct perspective of the independence movement, there are also other sides to the history of Puerto Rico's status. "Stories of accommodation, collaboration and outright defeat are just as important because they give us ways to understand our position as caused rather than just existing" (*Medicine Stories* 31). Another way of illustrating various historical perspectives is to reveal hidden power relations. For instance, "Puerto Rican liberal feminists of the late 19th century, all those 'firsts' in the arts and education, came primarily from an hacendado class made affluent by the slave-produced profits of the sugar industry" (*Medicine Stories* 31). In other words, we shouldn't let the feminist accomplishments and contributions of these women overshadow the economic privileges, which allowed them, at times, to exploit other women.

Levins Morales has also made it a point to show connections between Puerto Ricans and their experiences and other peoples both locally and globally, by contextualizing Puerto Rican history more broadly. As a Jewish Puerto Rican woman, she consistently makes connections between Jewish and Puerto Rican historical experiences. She also illustrates the ways that race, class, and gender relate Puerto Ricans to other ethnic/racial groups in the United States and in other locations globally. "The fact that General Nelson Miles, who led the U.S. invasion of Puerto Rico in 1898, was also the most prominent military commander of the wars against the Plains Indians is not just biographical information about Miles's career. It connects the stories of peoples affected by U.S. expansion from Puerto Rico to the Dakotas, from Idaho and Arizona to Hawaii and the Philippines" (*Medicine Stories* 36). This also requires contextualizing historical figures within a larger historical framework. She specifically gives the example of Rosa Parks, who has come to symbolize the beginning of the Civil Rights movement. Yet these individual historical contributions are part of a larger context, involving a broader group of people. As Levins Morales explains, "Rosa Parks didn't 'get tired' one day and start the Montgomery bus boycott. She was a trained organizer, and her role, as well as the time and place of the boycott, was the result of careful planning by a group of civil rights activists. Just as medicinal history must restore individuality to anonymous masses of people, it must also restore social context to individuals singled out as the actors of history" (*Medicine Stories* 35). Through such contextualization, we heal the divisions and silences that focusing on national heroes produces. In this manner, the many Puerto Ricans who were instrumental in the everyday practices and/or support of the ideas and movements embodied by such historical figures can also come to the fore.

Finally, the curandera historian is concerned with crossing multiple borders. Related to the fourth point of contextualizing and making connections, this fifth and final component of the curandera handbook requires that we cross racial, classed, and gendered borders so that Puerto Ricans can also gain a better understanding of their multifaceted experiences and heal some of the divisions caused by these differences. Crossing borders also means crossing those geographical borders as well, where we can see those connections between Puerto Ricans and Africans, Latin Americans, Asians, and Europeans. Maria Lugones has defined this kind of border crossing as "'world'-travelling," where women of color are able to constantly shift between "worlds" (i.e., through mainstream culture and their own various cultures) and find ways to function in all of these. Another way of building this capability of crossing borders into the medicinal historian's narrative is to make sure that the narrative is accessible to large audiences. "If the purpose of medicinal history is to transform the way we see ourselves historically, to change our sense of what's possible, then making history available to those who need it most is not a separate process from the researching and interpreting. The task of the curandera historian includes delivery. To do exciting, empowering research and leave it in academic journals and university libraries is like manufacturing unaffordable medicines for deadly diseases" (*Medicine Stories* 37). The role of the curandera historian is not just to heal others but also to heal herself. So, an additional aspect of crossing borders and making the work accessible is to personalize the historical narrative. This means not just naming individuals but also including her own individual voice and experience as part of the collective. The curandera historian, therefore, is a socially committed one, who uses "history, not so much to document the past as to restore to the dehistoricized a sense of identity and possibility" (*Medicine Stories* 24). In essence, Levins Morales is posing a challenging (re)definition of Puerto Rican historiography where our roles as historians is not just to document the history of Puerto Ricans, but to create narratives that heal the traumatic effects of historical oppression and silence.

The Birth of the Curandera Historian

The origins of Aurora Levins Morales's "medicinal history" can be traced to her contributing piece "And Even Fidel Can't Change That . . . ," published in the anthology *This Bridge Called My Back*.[3] This collection arose from a need felt by women of color to give voice to their experiences as historical and multiply identified subjects. "*This Bridge* documents particular rites of passage. Coming of age and coming to terms with community—race, group, class, gender, self—its expectations, supports, and lessons. And coming to grips with its perversions—racism, prejudice, elitism, misogyny, homophobia, and murder" (Cade Bambara vii). The contributors used creative methods of voicing the many concerns and issues that had been brewing for so many years. In this collection are poems, essays, letters, and dialogues in which women of color address their anger and frustration at the historical invisibility of their experiences. They speak about the agonies as well as pleasures involved in negotiating and navigating one's identity through the axis of race, class, gender, and sexuality. Their concerns shape many of the methodologies listed in the curandera historian's handbook. They center on women and focus on untold stories. They challenge traditional notions of what is historical evidence through subjective accounts of their experiences. And they cross borders by making their work readable and accessible to a wide audience.

The writings in *This Bridge Called My Back* were also intended to heal the damage caused by sexist, racist, homophobic, and classist oppressions. The contributors, in particular, address white women and the Anglo-American dominated women's movement for its exclusion of their experiences. The rejection many of them experienced by women in a movement based only on "sisterhood" or gender further contributed to the societal traumas they had suffered as women of color. They are therefore rejecting their usual role as the bridge between white women and women of color and are instead reclaiming a bridge back to themselves, as expressed in "The Bridge Poem" by Donna Kate Rushin, "I must be the bridge to nowhere/But my true self/and then/ I will be useful" and therefore, healed of racist and classist trauma (xxii).

In her earlier works, Levins Morales first addresses the healing of her divided self along racial, class-based, and gendered lines. However, throughout these works we can see evidence of her application of some of the curandera historian's methods. In "And Even Fidel Can't Change That . . . " she begins by addressing the distance she feels from Nuyoricans. She describes the aspects that separate her from her Nuyorican family history as her "points of terror, points of denial" (54), identifying how race, class, and gender are more specifically those "points" that separate her as a middle-class, light-skinned Puerto Rican-Jew who was born and raised until the age of thirteen on the island, from the rest of her Puerto Rican past. "Where I grew up, I fought battles to prove I was Puerto Rican with the kids who called me 'Americanita,' but I stayed on the safe side of that line: Caribbean island, not Portah Ricah; exotic tropical blossom, not spic—living halfway in the skin and separating myself from the dark, bad city kids in Nueva York" ("And Even Fidel" 53).

However, as she goes on to describe those "points of terror, points of denial" she begins to find connections between their differences. The Nuyorican women in her family and their apparent excess (such as their loud clothes, heavy makeup, and contradictory sex talk) are at first some of those elements that she fears within herself. Their contradictory messages about women's bodies, sexuality, and relations with men—on the one hand, her female relatives point out prospective suitors for her, while on the other, warn her of men's evil ways—led her to question how as a feminist she could claim alliances and connections to these women. Yet as she proclaims, "I love these women for facing up to the ugliness there" ("And Even Fidel" 54). Although they appeared to be passing on patriarchal ideologies to the younger women in the room, through these "bitch sessions" they were able to "pool common knowledge," creating community for themselves, offering support and strategies on how to negotiate what they seemed to accept as the limitations of their gender. Here, she practices some of the elements of the medicinal historian as she gives voice and agency to these otherwise silenced women. Even though she cannot claim the experiences of these other Puerto Rican women in her family as her own she still recognizes her connection to these women, who belonged to older generations, her ancestors. As she states, "behind me lies my grandmother," and these stories are also her stories, as part of a collective Puerto Rican experience and history ("And Even Fidel" 55).

This first realization of connection with multiple Puerto Rican experiences spills over into other points of terror and denial across race and class difference. After reading Piri Thomas's *Down These Mean Streets*, which chronicles his sordid street life as a Black Puerto Rican man in Harlem in the 1940s and 1950s, she acknowledges that although her middle-class background and light skin privilege have afforded her many advantages, circumstance has basically saved her from experiencing firsthand the racial discrimination and poverty that so many of her Puerto Rican peers have endured. "The junkies could be my younger brothers. The prisoners could be them. I could be the prostitute, the welfare mother, the sister and lover of junkies, the child of alcoholics. There is nothing but circumstance and good English . . . between me and that life" ("And Even Fidel" 55). Any slight change of path or circumstance such as her mother marrying someone other than her middle-class Jewish father, could have greatly affected her own racialized, class-based, and gendered experience. Because she sees how much of her fate as a Puerto Rican woman is related to her circumstances of class and different skin color, she is able to recognize herself in the experiences of Puerto Ricans, such as her Nuyorican female relatives or Piri Thomas, and connect her past to theirs. "Behind me stands my grandmother. Behind me lie the mean streets. Behind me my little brother is nothing but skin and skeleton" ("And Even Fidel" 55). Through this written piece she practices facing those points of terror and denial and sees the ultimate connections of all of her various parts, linking her past to a broader Puerto Rican community. She further applies the curandera historian's tools as she makes connections and contextualizes the multiple experiences of Puerto Ricans in the United States.

At the end, she returns to the issue of gender focusing primarily on the relationship between mothers and daughters. She argues that one way in which to begin to heal is to repair the relationships between mothers and daughters, where not only mothers can change the experiences of the next generation of women by teaching their past, but also altering the messages the younger generation receives about their infinite possibilities as "'world'-travelers." She calls for at the end, "a revolution capable of healing our wounds. If we're the ones who can imagine it, if we're the ones who dream about it, if we're the ones who need it most, then no one else can do it. . . . We're the ones" ("And Even Fidel" 56). Part of the process of healing and breaking the silence means writing those stories that once distanced her from her own identity. In this preliminary piece she does this not just by addressing the cultural hybridity and multiplicity of her self and by extension Puerto Ricans in general, but the way in which she invokes her own individual and communal healing, previews what she later names as medicinal history. She uses curandera tools such as giving agency and voice to the voiceless, contextualizing and making connections, and thus as a result she crosses borders. By using her skills as a creative writer to document her experiences, she challenges the idea of historical evidence, expanding the definition to include her own subjective experiences. And finally, she provides a history that is communal through her own personal voice and experience, producing a personalized historical narrative. In her next project, *Getting Home Alive*, which she coauthors with her mother, Rosario Morales, she picks up on her own suggestion about the healing and revolutionary potential of the mother/daughter relationship.

In Search of a Healing "Home"

Aurora Levins Morales continues her own search for a sense of a healed completed self, in *Getting Home Alive*. The text is a testimonial written in prose and poetry, in which the coauthors bear witness to their collective history across time and place. The collection includes pieces written by both mother and daughter although the specific writer of each individual piece is not identified within the text. The only marker differentiating the pieces are the very similar type of font used, allowing for a flow between mother and daughter's writing, thinking, and experience—a fluidity and experiential continuity which is directly addressed by the authors through their representations of racialized, class-based, and gendered Puerto Rican identities.

Although *Getting Home Alive* was published in 1986, following the phase of Nuyorican movement poetry of the 1970s and preceding the surge in the publication of Puerto Rican and Latina women's novels in the 1990s, many of which are dismissed by literary critics as assimilationist, this particular text is conspicuously absent from the literary histories of Puerto Rican diaspora literature. As Lara-Bonilla explains, Puerto Rican literary criticism tends to follow a trend of defining diaspora literature in two particular ways, either as oppositional and anticolonial in spirit as in "the nuyorican texts of the 1960s and 1970s, while others establish polarizing distinctions between those earlier works and the literary production of subsequent generations, often considered less political, more in keeping with the commercial expectations attributed to multicultural projects" (1). This type of periodization excludes certain texts, on the one hand, for not fitting into a particular type of aesthetic, "that associated with the early nuyorican movement, which favored portrayals of the 'barrio,' of marginality, of filth and violence . . ." (Lara-Bonilla 1). On the other hand, "it reproduces polarized categories and confines the focus of textual analysis to political intent," dismissing those that do not fit a leftist working-class politics (1).[4] In *Getting Home Alive*, the authors portray a more complex and nuanced experience of Puerto Rican migration and identity that doesn't centralize the Nuyorican barrio nor the island itself as the space of belonging. As the title suggests, home is an allusive place, the journey to which isn't straightforward or always uplifting, but one that will inevitably include dangerous encounters. Borrowing Donna Haraway's term, Jacqueline Stefanko argues, these writers "create hybrid texts in order to 'survive in diaspora,' . . . seeking to heal the fractures and ruptures resulting from exile and dispersal" (50). While Levins Morales and Morales align themselves with leftist revolutionary feminist politics, they do so in critical ways without romanticizing or essentializing any one political identity as inherently Puerto Rican. In this sense, *Getting Home Alive* fails to fit into the periodizing trends of Puerto Rican literary criticism and thus ends up being erased from the literary history of the diaspora. Ironically, while the authors aim to create a text that tells stories that have been silenced and marginalized, their unwillingness to fit into a particular essentialist (and, I would argue, a patriarchal nationalist framework) results in the text itself to be silenced and marginalized by Puerto Rican literary scholars. In order to gain a more complete understanding of the complex nature of Puerto Rican migrant history, one that includes the voices of women, we must return to some of these earlier works with a feminist historical lens.

The text opens with the piece "Wolf" written by Levins Morales.[5] She imagines an encounter with a shape-shifting wolf, symbolic of her true self. "It is changing shape to protect itself from extinction"(Levins Morales and Morales

16). His presence is a warning to the potential dangers that multiple, hybrid beings such as herself may encounter. In the wolf's case the danger lurking overhead is extinction, in her case it is erasure from history. The urgent need to avoid this erasure or extinction drives her to tell her story. "For their survival and mine and the world's, I must make them see the wolf's nature. I must tell them this story" (Levins Morales and Morales 16). The stories she tells are those that follow in the rest of the text.

Throughout the text the two authors document the dangers of extinction and loss as they discuss their cultural transformations and migrations from New York City to the island and back to the mainland for the mother, and from the island to Chicago to California for the daughter. As Rina Benmayor states, "the authors tangle the linear view of the immigrant trajectory" (109). Although their migrations do not follow the expected linear migration between the island and New York City, they do show historical continuity between the island and the diaspora and across generations, in particular gendered ways. In "Kitchens," Levins Morales links her cultural history through her own cooking, to women from the island that she remembers from her childhood in the town of Indiera. "Mine is a California Kitchen, full of fresh vegetables and whole grains, bottled spring water and yogurt in plastic pints, but when I lift the lid from that big black pot, my kitchen fills with the hands of women who came before me, washing rice, washing beans, picking through them so deftly, so swiftly, that I could never see what the defects were in the beans they threw quickly over one shoulder out the window" (Levins Morales and Morales 37). She uses a specifically gendered space such as the kitchen through which to connect her own history to those of other women in her family. As Consuelo Lopez Springfield notes, the kitchen and food are both metaphors that represent a space and a tool used by many women to transfer their culture. But the kitchen is also significant "not only because it has been conceived as a traditionally feminine space—the 'womb' of a feminine culture based on story-telling, female control, and domesticity—but also because the kitchen is where one brews new concoctions, mixing various ingredients to produce a desirable blend," (Bost 201) or healing potion. As a curandera historian in the making, she also brews in her pot healing recipes mixing together the ingredients of Puerto Rican women's lives with her medicinal tools.

Throughout Levins Morales's pieces in *Getting Home Alive*, we repeatedly see an urgent preoccupation with telling untold and undertold histories while always making local and global connections. In "Immigrants" she reminds herself that as someone who left Puerto Rico at the age of thirteen to move to Chicago, she shares certain aspects of the immigrant experience, not only the sense of displacement and the difficulties of adjusting to a new place and culture, but also a deep desire to remember where she came from. "For years after we left Puerto Rico for the last time, I would wake from a dream of something unbearably precious melting away from my memory as I struggled desperately to hold on, or at least to remember that I had forgotten. I am an immigrant, and I forget to feel what it means to have left. What it means to have arrived" (Levins Morales and Morales 22). Given current debates around immigration reform and the consistent attacks on undocumented people, this piece is particularly significant since it problematizes media's assumption that only particular Latin American immigrants, namely Mexicans, are impacted or concerned with these issues. As American citizens, Puerto Ricans are presumed not to have any connections to the debate around immigration. But as Levins Morales's piece attests, the immigration experience isn't just about legal status, nor does one's status necessarily protect one from the anti-immigrant repression and violence. As she describes her own experience adjusting as a new immigrant in the United States, "Learning fast not to talk about it, learning excruciatingly slowly how to dress, how to act, what to say, where to hide" (Levins Morales and Morales 25). Any sense of safety her American citizenship status was supposed to grant was clearly elusive.

In the "Class Poem" Levins Morales once again addresses her class difference but here she takes ownership of her class-based identity as a middle-class Puerto Rican woman. She therefore critiques those who define Puerto Rican identity in essentialist terms where one must be from "the barrio," and of the working class in order to be considered authentically Puerto Rican. She embraces her middle-class identity as an homage to her ancestors who struggled so that her generation could have a better chance at a more comfortable life. She dedicates the poem to the hunger endured by her mother not only physically but intellectually, not having easy access to books and an education, as Rosario Morales herself describes in such pieces as "Destitution" and "Dairy Queen." She also dedicates the poem to her "great-grandfather Abe Sackman/who worked in Bridgeport making nurses' uniforms/and came home only on weekends, for years" (Levins Morales and Morales 215). She engages medicinal tools here as she shows the connections between her Puerto Rican and Jewish pasts. She also dedicates the poem to others like Norma, a young child who suffered the consequences of poverty, dying from inadequate healthcare. Levins Morales deromanticizes popular notions of "the people" or "the community" as only being those who live in poverty.

> This is a poem to say
> My choosing to suffer gives nothing
> to Tita and Norma and Angelica
> and that not to use the tongue, the self-confidence, the training
> my privilege bought me
> is to die again for people who are already dead
> and who wanted to live (Levins Morales and Morales 47).

Instead of holding on to some working-class identity, she acknowledges and represents those Puerto Ricans who no longer live in the barrio and who have achieved access through education to a middle-class lifestyle. Yet, she uses her middle-class privilege to give voice and agency to those less fortunate who have not for example, achieved access to publishing houses. She documents their stories along with her own.

In the now classic piece, "I am what I am," Rosario Morales clearly illustrates the multiplicity and cultural hybridity of Puerto Ricans while contextualizing and connecting her own historical experiences locally and globally, demonstrating that the curandera methods her daughter identifies and uses had early roots in her mother's teachings. In this piece, Morales reclaims her position as a subject of United States' history and challenges hegemonic constructions of history and culture in this country. She states, "I am what I am and I am US American" (Levins Morales and Morales 138). She had not claimed this part of her identity before because, in the context of U.S. hegemonic culture, this affirmation would have meant a denial of her Puerto Rican heritage. She reclaims her identity as a "US American" along with her Puerto Rican, Caribbean, and Latin American identities as she "croon[s] sentimental tangos in my sleep and Afro-Cuban beats in my blood" (Levins Morales and Morales 138). She continues to challenge hegemonic constructions of identity by also claiming her many languages; English, Spanish, and Spanglish. She also claims all those cultures and histories that shaped her identity construction, including Irish and Jewish, representing those groups with whom early migrant Puerto Ricans shared neighborhoods in the 1930s and 1940s. She makes no apologies for this hybridity that avoids easy compartmentalization into neat and essentialist labels such as Latino, Hispanic, or even Nuyorican. As she states at the end of her piece, "I am what I am Take it or Leave me alone" (Levins Morales and Morales 139).

This defiant tone is found in their overt discussion of the challenges of working in solidarity. Presaging the curandera historian's tenet of showing multiple perspectives and not romanticizing movements or heroes, Levins Morales and Morales present bold pieces where they reveal the hidden power dynamics of solidarity work. In "Letter to a Compañero," Levins Morales challenges those men in leftist movements who use the argument for solidarity in their pursuit of female conquests. She addresses her critique to a particular *compañero*, who simultaneously pursues three different women, including the author. The damage this behavior causes to leftist movements is at times long lasting and results in the loss of potential women leaders. "There are women who were leaders, who worked night and day, defeated not by foreign policy, but by the sexual politics of solidarity, bitter now, unable to work anywhere near you" (Levins Morales and Morales 155). Similarly, in "I am the Reasonable One," Morales proclaims her voice among white women, confessing to her role in enabling her own silence. "You know me to be reasonable, to be rational. You know me to be almost white, almost middle class, almost acceptable . . . I am the Puerto Rican you can ask, 'Why don't they learn English?'" (Levins Morales and Morales 147). She was allowed among white women because she was perceived as non-threatening, as the exceptional "minority" that won't be offended nor will she offend in her responses to their ignorance. In this piece, however, she calls an end to her silence. "But now I tell you reasonably, for the last time, reasonably, that I am through. That I am not reasonable anymore, that I was always angry, that I am angry now" (Levins Morales and Morales 148). This piece reveals the traumatic effects of always being the "reasonable one." Her consistent accommodation of her voice and repressing of her anger in her interactions with white women in the name of solidarity, have taken a toll on her psyche to the point where she can no longer remain silent and finally uses her writing to speak back to those people that would have her continue to subvert her own voice for their comfort.

In "The Ending Poem," the two authors bring together the many elements of the medicinal historian continuing to make those necessary historical contextualizations through their poetically personalized historical narrative. The authors clearly depict the multiplicity they are claiming as their historical and cultural identity. They reiterate their different migrant trajectories as they claim geographical identifications with Puerto Rico, New York, and California. They position Puerto Rican history in a broader global context as they define themselves as Caribeña and also of Latinoamerica, "rooted in the history of my continent" (Levins Morales and Morales 212). They reclaim their racial hybridity composed of African, European, and Taino descent further contextualizing in the larger global history of conquest and diasporic displacement. They also centralize women in their narrative. "I am a child of many mothers/They have kept it all going/ All the civilizations erected on their backs. All the dinner parties given with their labor" (Levins Morales and Morales 213). As they close the poem and their hybrid text they claim their "newness," a direct result of the global history they portray. "We are new . . . born at a crossroads" (Levins Morales and Morales 213). However, their hybridity is not fragmentary or divisive. They refuse to choose a particular side or to melt into the hegemonic cultural pot. Empowered in their multiplicity they assert, "And we are whole" (Levins Morales and Morales 213). "Getting home alive" means surviving the many barriers and struggles en route to this home they have found at the crossroads of their multiplicity.[6]

The Curandera Historian's Healing Narratives

It is not until her most recently published works, *Medicine Stories* and *Remedios: Stories of Earth and Iron from the History of Puertorriqueñas*, that Levins Morales names the methodology she has been using in her works all along and directly defines her work as medicinal history. As mentioned earlier, the catalyst for this work was her own personal search for healing from her traumatic experiences of sexual abuse. The first part of the collection of essays, *Medicine Stories*, includes those where she defines and describes the curandera historians' handbook. The essays that follow continue to address her earlier concerns with the cultural hybridity and multiplicity of the Puerto Rican experience, but more directly implement the curandera historians' methods.

For instance, in "The Tribe of Guarayamín," she discusses the pitfalls of binary constructions between oppressor and oppressed which do not allow alternative visions of being to flourish. She argues that people of color, in their zeal to overcome their status as oppressed, end up adopting the behavior and ideologies of the oppressor. In this essay, she discusses the recent trend among some Puerto Ricans who have claimed to be direct descendants of Taino natives. She explains, how the quest for nationalist self-affirmation has resulted in the construction of a historical heritage that perpetuates the same hierarchies of dominant society. In this particular case, most of those who are leading the movement toward the adaptation of Taino lineage, are men who have all claimed themselves to be caciques.[7] Where are the Tainas, and the descendants of the rest of the Tainos who were not caciques? This kind of self-affirmation also ignores the more complex history of racial mixture, appearing as a denial of both African and European ancestries.

She further solidifies her point on the complexities of Puerto Rican history through her series of essays on language and its function as a tool of silence. "On Not Writing English," discusses how her works have been subjected to editorial abuse as female editors of various journals have critiqued her use of language. Some have criticized her for using grammatically incorrect English. Others have complained about her use of Spanish. Both uphold claims to some kind of "pure" language, which ignores the natural changes and evolution of languages as more people come into contact and share the nuances of their respective languages, such as dialects and accents. "Forked Tongue: On Not Speaking Spanish," addresses the other side of the purity debates on language. Here she addresses islanders who criticize diaspora Puerto Ricans of supposedly corrupting their pure Spanish. She offers more complex understandings of culture and language from both the island and the diaspora.

Her vision of an alternative method of doing history and healing trauma comes full circle in her last section where she offers a sense of wholeness found in the life of the activist. In "Circle Unbroken: The Politics of Inclusion," she addresses the need to commit to justice for everyone, not just the victimized. She believes that part of understanding how issues such as race, class, and gender affect those victimized by the oppressions perpetrated along these axes of power, is to offer healing to those who participate as perpetrators. As she explains, "it is a call for a politics of inclusion that abandons no-one, and begins with those it is hardest for us to think about with compassion—the professional perpetrators of atrocities" (*Medicine Stories* 8). She brings this collection to a close, affirming her vision for healing both at a personal and collective level. This vision led to her creation of what she calls a radical history, a medicinal history, which has widened the possibilities for historiographical work, producing empowering narratives not only for the excluded, but for those who have blindly accepted the exclusions and their subsequent positions of privilege.

Remedios: Stories of Earth and Iron from the History of Puertorriqueñas serves as an in-depth example of a curandera historian's narrative. While following a chronological historical order, she does not present a singular narrative of history. The narrative consists of a collection of brief pieces, each focusing on a particular historical figure, event, or moment. As Julie Fiandt explains, she shares "untold and 'undertold' stories, individual and collective, of women in history" (573). The historical narrative becomes a global story as she connects the history of Puerto Rican women to women throughout the world, across time and space. Although she continues to address issues of race, class, and gender; in this text, her priorities shift. Whereas before these issues were her primary concern as she strove to heal her multiple identities along these axes while indirectly applying her medicinal tools; here, her conscious use and goal of presenting a curandera's history of Puerto Rican women takes center stage. As she explains in the preface, her goal in this text is "to unearth the names of women deemed unimportant by the writers of official histories" (*Remedios* xvii). Interspersed throughout the episodic historical narratives are short pieces where she describes different medicinal herbs and foods, which are symbolic of the healing properties of the narratives that follow those sections. In this manner she treats historical erasure and hegemony as diseases, which a curandera historian can heal through her "home-grown" herbal history. For instance, the preface to the text is entitled "Yerba Bruja": "Its common name 'witch,' refers to its resistance to even the most cruel treatment that can be inflicted on it" (*Remedios* xxiii). In her essay, "Nightflying: Transforming Traumatic History," Levins Morales laments the lack of scholarly work on the history of the persecution of "witches," most of whom have been women healers of some sort. The persecution continues in our contemporary culture where the term "witch" still appears as a derogatory term hurled at women for all manner of supposed "deviant" behavior. "Popular culture continually reinforces the image of the dangerous old woman dressed in dark peasant clothing and a medieval peaked hat who wants to kidnap, torment and eat children, while the few 'good witches' are invariably young, beautiful and richly dressed. We are taught to fear women elders, and 'witch' is still an epithet of contempt for a strong-minded assertive woman" (*Medicine Stories* 48). Not to mention the "good witch" and "bad witch" are usually racialized, the former depicted as usually white while the latter always signifies a person of darker skin (i.e., Wizard of Oz). Among the many evils "witches" were accused of during their persecution was the act of nightflying, "the ability to change shape or endow a household object, a pot or a broom, with magical powers and soar above the landscape of daily life, with eyes that can penetrate the darkness and see what we are not supposed to see" (*Medicine Stories* 49). Yet it is exactly this kind of power that we must reclaim and hone. As Irene Lara argues, we must assert what she calls a "bruja positionality," where Latinas reclaim their own "spiritual conocimiento, re-membering and creating powerful knowledges for personal and community healing" (26). For Levins Morales, this means that the curandera historian engages in the willingness required of nightflying. "Nightflying requires a willingness to leave the familiar ground and see what is meant to be hidden, a willingness to be transformed. If we are to know and understand the landscape of our history, we must be willing to do this: not only to look upon the horrific, the night shadowed, and bear witness to it" (*Medicine Stories* 49). It is no surprise then that she opens *Remedios* with "yerba bruja" as the guiding medicinal herb to her curandera historical narrative. The histories that she portrays in the rest of the text demonstrate the strength and resistance of Puerto Rican women and their ancestors, just like yerba bruja.

Keeping to the tenets of a curandera historian, Levins Morales incorporates her own personal history into the text. While writing the narrative she engages in two tasks: "digging up the histories of Puerto Rican and related women and their responses to the often brutal conditions of their lives; and recovering the buried memories of my own experience of, and responses to, brutality" (*Remedios* xxv). Following the traditions of Jesus Colón and Bernardo Vega she writes a communal, collective historical autobiography. Efraín Barradas has discussed the autobiographical nature of Colón and Vega's texts arguing that these sought to represent a collective "I." In other words these texts are actually communal autobiographies as the authors represented not only their individual lives but also that of their communities.[8] Yet Levins Morales's goal is not just to represent the untold histories of Puerto Rican women and their communities. Her community also includes the larger human race, indicating a universal usefulness of her medicinal history and methodology. "I am moved by an urgent sense that in order to find those paths that lead to the continuation of life on earth, we must come to understand the nature of these blows: how and why they fell, what was lost, what was hidden away and sacred, and, most of all, what we, the majority of humans, have learned from the long process of resisting, surrendering, accommodating, and transforming ourselves so that we could live" (*Remedios*, xxvii). By including her personal experiences, contextualizing these along with the histories of Puerto Rican women and positioning these within a broader universal context, she employs the curandera tenets of both personalizing and local/global contextualizing.

In the introduction, entitled "Revision," she establishes her own revision of Puerto Rican history by refuting the hegemonic constructions of Puerto Rican historiography from both the island and the diaspora. She centralizes women by arguing "Puerto Rico was a women's country" (*Remedios* xxi). She also asserts Puerto Rico as both a multiracial society, and one where the majority of the people were poor. She immediately repositions the historical lens away from narratives that have privileged the experiences of those who had access to power (i.e., the Creole elite, the Europeans, and men). Instead, she centralizes the experiences of multiracial, poor and/or working-class women. She establishes a continuity with her earlier works as she defines the particular untold story she here sets out to tell along race, class, and gender lines. However, as we move throughout the text it becomes clear how conscious she is about demonstrating the curandera historians' method.

Beginning with the section she calls "Bisabuelas," or great-grandmothers, she employs the first key element of the curandera historian, centralizing women and giving them agency and voice. She begins Puerto Rican women's history in the year –200,000, with the African mother of all humanity. She relies on the mitochondrial DNA research resulting in the "Eve theory," which argued that all human beings have one common female ancestor, living in Sub-Saharan Africa 200,000 years ago (*Remedios* 3). She continues reclaiming Puerto Rican women's great-grandmothers throughout the world. "Women of the Yams," refers to the African great-grandmothers. She re-imagines these women's lives creating place and home around fire, and centralizing their key roles as those in charge of finding "medicines in the trees and herbs" (*Remedios* 5). She establishes her own medicinal role as a historian as a trait passed on from her female ancestors. "Women of Bread" covers the Mediterranean female ancestors of Puerto Rican women. She reclaims these European foremothers along with her African and Native foremothers in order to heal the wounds of self-hatred. "How do we love what is pale-skinned in us? Listen, daughters of Spain, inheritors of ancient Europe: once there was a time before war. Once upon a time, it was Europe that was free and flowering, Europe that was indigenous, Europe where women were honored, nature respected, the hoop unbroken" (*Remedios* 10). Finally, "Women of the Yuca," are the native female ancestors of the Americas. Here we see how she establishes continuity across time and space, in the piece "City Girls-Teotihuacan, Mexico." She compares the "city girls" of Teotihuacan, their experiences and interests, with contemporary ones from Los Angeles and New York City. "All you big city girls with hearts that sing to the bustle of crowds, let me tell you, it didn't begin in Manhattan, didn't start in L.A. Teotihuacan may not have had subways or Central Park, but you could walk for hours around the rim of that lake. . . . There were no department stores, but who needed them with all the crafts people's quarters where you could shop for obsidian mirrors, jade jewelry, feather garments, and polished beads?" (*Remedios* 25). Contemporary metropoli like New York City and Los Angeles are not the only ones in the world nor have they been the only ones in history. She debunks western hegemonic notions of "Third World" societies and their histories as backward and uncivilized. She demonstrates that our present conditions are part of a larger and broader context, across space and time, employing the additional elements of contextualization and crossing borders of the curandera historian's methods.

We see an example of how she deals with the issue of questioning accepted forms of evidence when she addresses the unavailability of documentation of Native American women's lives. Instead of perpetuating their silencing by not writing about them, she documents the absence and self-reflexively discusses the limitations of the historian's task. "Here I sit, a storyteller looking back across places that have been altered beyond recognition, looking for the lives of women in a splinter of bone, a single hair, a shard of pottery. The bone suggests the graceful movements of an arm, the hair the sound of someone breathing in their sleep, the shard, the curve of a vanished bowl. But perhaps the arm was clenched in anger, the hair shaved from an enemy's head, the shard from a chamber pot" (*Remedios* 34). Echoing postmodernist theorist arguments about the historian's subjective role as interpreter, she makes "reading" an obvious part of the historian's task, as she suggests the many possible interpretations of the evidence she finds. Similarly, in "1515: Naborias—The Names of the Captives" she reveals the limitations of archival evidence, describing a roster filled with the supposed names of indigenous women, yet, as she explains, the names were those given to these women by their Spanish captors and thus do not adequately represent anything other than these women's position as slaves, their subjectivity and agency completely buried. In her piece, the author employs the curandera tactic of asking speculative questions in order to balance the archival "evidence": "At night, after the work was done, what did they say among themselves speaking the soft sounding languages of the islands? How did they find consolation? What did they hope for sitting in the warm evening, watching the stars fall into the sea?" (*Remedios* 86). In this section, she gives examples of the medicinal historian's methodologies such as self-reflexivity, showing agency, questioning evidence, and making absences visible.

Another one of the methodological rules of the curandera historian she employs is illustrating power dynamics and not romanticizing historical heroes or heroines. For instance, she depicts the history of María Bibiana who was a poet in Puerto Rico, in 1833. She first praises her as "the first published poet to speak in a Puerto Rican voice, a criolla voice" (*Remedios* 149). However, she also illustrates her privilege as a slaveholding woman. "Sitting at her desk, she reaches absently for the cup of coffee handed to her by her slave and never sees the woman's shadow fall, leaving no trace, across the page" (*Remedios* 150). Although she is one of the first poets to write as a Puerto Rican woman, the experiences of her slave women are not part of her imaginary, and hence remain in the shadows. Similarly, in her two pieces depicting Queen Nzinga of Angola, she aims to strike a balance between acknowledging the significance of this historical figure, as a woman leader who successfully kept Portuguese conquerors at bay for many years, while simultaneously demonstrating the Queen's ruthless disregard for her slaves, as made evident in the piece "1618: Nzinga's Stool—Angola," told from the perspective of the slave woman. "Queen Nzinga sends musicians playing instruments before her and walks in surrounded by her servants. She sees that solitary seat of power and she is angry, but anger never interferes with her cunning. She summons me with a gesture, and before the astonished eyes of the Portuguese officials I fall upon hands and knees, making of my body a throne for Nzinga. Balanced on my ribs, she meets the governor face to face, as his equal" (*Remedios* 108–9). She simultaneously captures the intimidating power of the Queen against her would be oppressors and her complete disregard for her own oppressive actions against her slave, overtly turning her body into an object, a throne.

A clear depiction of personalizing historical narratives appears in the section entitled, "Discovery" which serves as the transition between the historical period prior to 1492 and the history that ensues as a result of conquest. In this piece, she juxtaposes her own personal history of violence and physical conquest with the history of her Native American female ancestors who also were victims of violence and oppression as a result of "discovery": "In the violated places of my body I find the voices of the conquered of my island. When I seek their voices among the yellowed manuscripts, I find my own bad dreams. In a time of personal nightmares and hours spent in archives I wrote these words to break both silences and embarked on the work of a people's historian, a wounded healer. I thank the spirits of the invaded who accompanied me" (*Remedios* 55). The simultaneous experiencing of digging through both personal and collective histories are blended here for the curandera historian who because of her methods is able to see the connections between the exploitations of her body and those of native women.

In the section that follows, "Huracán: 1492–1600," she documents the terrors experienced as a result of "discovery" and prefaces the section with the herb "Bitters." "Eat bitterness and speak bitterness and share bitter herbs upon your bread, for in bitterness we empty ourselves of poison. . . . But if you take these stories as bitters, your own pain will dissolve into the larger stream of pain and you will find comfort with these women, for the poison they suffered and died from is the same poison, and if you eat bitters, drink bitters, speak bitterness with them, you will be cleansed. You will be healed" (*Remedios* 64). Here the author makes explicit not only the connection between these women's experiences of oppression and violence and our own in contemporary times, but also the potential healing power that knowing these stories has on the reader. These stories of discovery are bitter ones, but keeping them in silence is just as poisonous as that which they died from. Speaking, or in other words, documenting and narrating these histories is the path toward healing.

In "1513: Flames-Puerto Rico," she continues to contextualize while personalizing her historical narrative as she documents the presence of Jews in Puerto Rico. Specifically, she documents the repression of Jews in Christian Puerto Rico, where a woman and her brother by the name of Morales were hung from a cross on the wall and whipped when they were suspected of being secret Jews. "No one remembers her name or the exact date of her death. Only that under torture she confessed what they asked her to confess" (*Remedios* 101). In a chilling connection between past and present she illustrates why we must remember those who came before us. "I am a Jew. . . . If I had been there, if someone had told on me, I would have burned. You would never have known my name" (*Remedios* 102). She points to our own vulnerability to the dangers of historical erasure. If we do not actively participate in documenting our own experiences and bear witness to the terrors and atrocities of our own lifetime, these too can be erased by those who hold the power to dictate what constitutes national history. Bearing witness to traumatic histories recalls the work of scholars like Rothberg, Laub, and Feldman, who in their studies of the Holocaust grapple with the simultaneous limitation and necessity of representing the Holocaust. Michael Rothberg in particular argues for the need for "traumatic realist texts," which "search for a form of documentation beyond direct reference and coherent narrative but do not fully abandon the possibility for some kind of reference and some kind of narrative" (100–101). The necessity to bear witness to the experiences of these Jewish people in Puerto Rico is more important to Levins Morales than any limitations she may have to be able to fully represent this event. Creating "some kind of narrative" is significant if we are to avoid complete historical erasure.

Included in her curandera narrative, she fills gaps in the national historical narrative, documenting little known historical moments or contributions made to significant historical events by Puerto Rican migrant women. For instance, she discusses one of the earliest histories of migration of Puerto Ricans to Hawaii as sugar workers for plantation owners. In "1901: The Death Train," she not only depicts the arduous journey that began on ships from Puerto Rico to the Southeast, continued on trains along the southwest until they reached the West Coast, where they once again boarded ships to Hawaii, but along that journey illustrates the connections made with other marginalized groups, such as the African American men working on the trains. These men notice the harsh traveling conditions endured by these migrants on the trains where, "[b]y day they sit, doors shut in the desert, guarded by armed men. Inside the stifling iron boxes of the freight cars, people die of the heat, and infections pass from breath to breath" (*Remedios* 166). The men witness this abuse and upon arriving in Los Angeles report the death of a young boy, "leaving the only official news of the passing of this train" (*Remedios* 166). Because of these African American men daring to speak up and report this incident, a historical record exists for her to discover and be able to narrate a little known historical moment in the broader migration history of Puerto Ricans. Thus, she not only fills a historical gap in migration history, but also crosses racial borders connecting the histories of Puerto Rican migrants to that of African Americans.

The contribution of Puerto Rican women to the needle trade industry both in Puerto Rico and in the United States has been documented by many historians[9]. In her piece, "1909: Lessons," however, she fills another historical gap, demonstrating how school girls were exploited through the colonizing educational system in Puerto Rico, where they were socialized into the needle trades industry enduring lessons in school. While the pieces they created were sold by Philadelphia manufacturers, their labor went unpaid. Young women workers were also lured to the garment industries of New York during the 1920s answering the call from ads asking for "[y]oung women wanted to sew ladies' blouses, to sew dresses and suits" (*Remedios* 176). She thus contributes to the migration historians that have taken a masculinist approach where men's experiences as migrant laborers are prioritized. Finally, in "1934: Needleworkers," she connects the histories of these women to other migrant women who have replaced them, "Chinese women, Haitian women, Vietnamese, Salvadoran, and Laotian women," demonstrating the continuity of experiences among immigrant women workers from different parts of the world (*Remedios* 185).

Levins Morales also fills gaps in our national war histories documenting the unseen ways in which Puerto Rican women have contributed to war efforts of this country. This is a theme that we will later see again in the works by Nicholasa Mohr and Judith Ortiz Cofer. In "1917: War Effort" and "1918: Lavanderas," she portrays how women supported the war effort through their labor whether they worked washing the uniforms of soldiers in businesses dedicated to this service or distributing homemade guava jelly "for the wounded soldiers returning from the battlefields of France" (*Remedios* 172). She not only highlights their contributions but also documents their forms of resistance. The washerwomen, for instance, organize a strike against their bosses and state in their demands "we, who give our sons for the war, cannot consent to the owners enriching themselves by exploiting our blood" (*Remedios* 173). She also depicts the experiences of migrant women in New York during the Second World War where they experience the impact on their domestic lives of the rationing system of certain goods, like olive oil and sugar (*Remedios* 192). "When the war is over, we inherit distant graves, wounded veterans, in-laws from a dozen countries, and a simmering resentment just this side of rage" (*Remedios* 193). While historical war narratives tend to focus on the service of the predominant male soldiers and their sacrifices, the impact of these wars on the women they leave behind whether they be wives or mothers is rarely affirmed. By centralizing the focus on women's perspectives, Levins Morales broadens the meaning of service and sacrifice during wartime to include these women and the impact of war not only during but also after the men return.

In the last piece "1954: Transitions" she celebrates her own births, both physical and intellectual, resisting those who have tried to stop these, telling her "no nascas." In this piece Levins Morales evokes the governmental population control policies of the 1950s that essentially sent the message "no nascas" to every unborn working-class child. In an effort to control the supposed overpopulation problem of Puerto Rico, an aggressive policy was instituted targeting poor women in particular, encouraging sterilization. By the 1970s one third of the Puerto Rican female population had been sterilized.[10] Therefore, in this context, every birth is a form of resistance. Levins Morales imagines herself on the other side, on the threshold of birth surrounded by her ancestors giving her last-minute advice before she embarks on her journey, in 1954. "Ancestors crowd around me, giving me advice, shouting last minute instructions about life on earth" (*Remedios* 205). Yet the piece also documents other moments of birth. For instance, she experiences rebirth in 1964 during a childhood moment of freedom, stealing tangerines from a neighbor's yard in Puerto Rico with her friend Tita. She is born again in 1988 when she gives birth to her daughter. Finally, her latest moment of rebirth in 1996 as she comes to the end of her book and to her self-healing, "pushing myself forward through the narrow opening carrying all these voices I have called to me, wrapped in my skirts. Carrying my own voice, leaving behind skins that only hamper me now. I am in transition, pushing myself out of myself" (*Remedios* 207). This final rebirth is also a collective one, symbolic of her broader Puerto Rican community's continuous rebirth into history. "We are pushing into history, we are coming out of the corners, we are gathering our spirits, we are taking up the challenge, we are living in this heartbeat, we are deciding . . . venga lo que venga, to be born" (*Remedios* 208). She's not only speaking about those who have already been born but also those future generations that, as they carry this same ancestral history she has gathered in this text, continue the history of resistance and healing of historical trauma.

Conclusion

Aurora Levins Morales's trajectory as a medicinal historian began with her first piece in *This Bridge Called My Back*, where she began her search for a sense of wholeness. Her exploration of using literary forms as a way of telling and documenting Puerto Rican women's history continues in *Getting Home Alive* as she joins her mother Rosario Morales in documenting the hybrid nature of Puerto Rican culture as well as the myriad experiences of migration and struggle along race, class, and gender lines. Although the primary concerns in these earlier works appear to be the search for "home" and an identity that was encompassing of her multiple ways of being Puerto Rican, there is evidence that, whether consciously or not, she was already employing curandera methods in her search for healing. In *Medicine Stories*, after receiving her PhD as a historian, she creates her own empowering methodology steeped in Puerto Rican women's traditions of oral storytelling and *curanderismo*. Levins Morales offers historians a new method that both documents the experiences of many who have thus far been excluded from historical narratives of the United States and heals the consequent traumas of these exclusions. She particularly focuses on centering the lives of women, giving agency and voice to them by telling their untold stories. She expands the definition of historical evidence using alternative sources and when even those are nonexistent, asking "what if" questions making those absences visible. The curandera historian's work contextualizes and shows local and global continuities, crossing not only geographical and cultural borders, but personal ones as well as she must include herself within the (his)stories. Levins Morales uses the educational tools her middle-class privilege has made available to her, to create a historical methodology that gives agency and voice to those who have been oppressed, suffering the traumatic erasure and silencing of historical narratives. With *Remedios* she puts the tools of her curandera medicinal bag to use and demonstrates the rich historical narrative created by using her medicinal historian's methods.

Throughout her body of work, however, we also see common preoccupations found in the works of other women writers of the Puerto Rican Diaspora. She shares with Nicholasa Mohr, an urgent desire to document the experiences of these women who have been invisible in national historical narratives both in the United States and the island and employs the literary space as one in which to create this documentation. Over and again she discusses the significance of memory in both creating historical narratives and sustaining a healthy sense of self in a context filled with the dangers of forgetting, as we also find in the work of Judith Ortiz Cofer. We see this for instance in the herb she chooses to open the first section, "Bisabuelas," of *Remedios*, Gingko. "Gingko remembers. Gingko restores, Gingko for stroke, for loss of memory, for bringing back that which is too old, too far gone, too deep in the past to find any other way" (*Remedios* 1). Finally, she shares with Esmeralda Santiago, an identity as a cultural historian, or as she specifically calls herself, a "cultural activist," responsible for creating narratives that celebrate and pass on Puerto Rican culture to future generations, while using a feminist critical lens that reveals the patriarchal aspects of the culture that must be questioned and redefined in order for Puerto Rican women to be able to reclaim a kind of Puertoricanness that is empowering. In the chapters that follow, I turn to these three writers and their versions of medicinal histories as each focuses their work on these historical preoccupations.

Chapter 2

DOUBLE VICTORY FOR PUERTO RICAN WOMEN TOO

Nicholasa Mohr's *Nilda*

The Second World War was called the war of the "Four Freedoms—freedom of speech, freedom of worship, freedom from want, and freedom from fear" (Takaki 7). Yet these freedoms were denied to people of color in the United States, many of whom continued to experience segregation and discrimination throughout the country. This inconsistency led African Americans claiming that there were two wars in which their communities were involved with: one against foreign enemies and one against the continued injustices they experienced at home, beginning what came to be known as the Double Victory campaigns: "The first V for victory over our enemies from without, the second V for victory over our enemies from within" (Takaki 20).

This experience of a dual struggle however, was not limited to the African American community. Mexican Americans, who also experienced segregation throughout the Southwest, faced the apparent contradiction of shedding blood in defense of principles that were not applied to their communities. Puerto Rican families in the East Coast and on the island, found themselves also contributing the lives of their sons to the war effort, while continuing to experience colonization and discrimination. Although there has been some documentation and scholarship dedicated to the dual struggle of African Americans and Mexican Americans, the experiences of Puerto Ricans on the mainland during World War II have not been sufficiently documented or examined.[1] In this chapter, I look at Nicholasa Mohr's novel, *Nilda*, set entirely during the Second World War, as an alternative source documenting the experience of the Puerto Rican community of Spanish Harlem during this time period.

By using a literary space to document her history, Nicholasa Mohr joins literary and historical theorists who have exposed the role of subjectivity and creativity in the construction of historical narratives. Feminist literary narratives by women of color have consistently used literary spaces to document their historical experiences. By representing the lives of people during particular periods of history, authors such as Alice Walker, Maxine Hong Kingston, Gloria Anzaldúa, and Louise Erdrich, have inadvertently retold the history of women of color.[2] As Elliott Butler-Evans states of Walker's work, "[g]enerally covering four or more decades in her novels, Walker evokes specific historical events and personages, and her metaphorical and metonymical representations of the experiences of Blacks as oppressed people reflect historical consciousness" (125). In works such as these, "the individual's story and experience express the untold histories of black Americans" (Willis 7). In these narratives, the individual characters become metaphors for their respective communities and their historical experiences.

Loosely autobiographical, *Nilda* was intended to transcend the experiences of an individual and "express an experience that would be not only what [Mohr] felt, but what [her] sisters felt, and above and beyond what [her] people have felt in a society that has oppressed them" (Acosta-Belen, "Conversations" 38). Many critics have discussed Mohr's work as a form of bildungsroman, a coming-of-age novel of self-development. However, these critics have also noted that Mohr redefines this novel form by making the focus of the novel a young woman and by disrupting the notion that self-development occurs as an internal and individualistic process removed from the impact of the historical moment or social power dynamics. As Fernandez Olmos notes in the works of Puerto Rican authors such as Mohr, "the evolution of the individual is closely interlocked with particular sociohistorical and political considerations" (59).[3] In this sense, then this novel is an example of a medicinal historical narrative. Mohr is centralizing the experiences of those who have been excluded from the various narratives about the nation's involvement in a significant historical moment as is the Second World War and therefore provides an alternative healing narrative. However, examining such a text does not only provide the curative effects for its Puerto Rican readers, for instance, who have not been exposed to this part of their historical experience in the United States. This text, when juxtaposed against the larger narratives of the nation's experience during the Second World War allows us to get closer to a more accurate historical account of this period.

The novel is told from the perspective of a young girl growing up in New York City during the Second World War. From Nilda's viewpoint, we see the many struggles that her family and her mother, in particular, endure during this time period. Although the chapters of the novel are demarcated by various chronological dates that clearly indicate the story is taking place during this great national historical event, the daily experiences of Nilda and her family take precedence over the war itself. While most historical accounts of this time period emphasize how the war and its home front effects (such as the elaborate rationing system and the changing face of the labor force) were major influences on people's everyday lives, in this account the war appears more as a backdrop to the more central survival story of the women in this family. In other words, as Christine Bold states about Toni Morrison's novel *Paradise*, she displaces "recognizable public history to its margins" (22). Mohr's central concern is to "document what it was to be poor, female, and Puerto Rican" during this time period in New York City (Mohr, "Journey" 84). She particularly chronicles their living conditions, financial hardships, educational experiences, and struggles over national identity. These are all part of Nilda's, and her mother, Lydia Ramirez's, larger struggle over family unity and survival, while the nation focused on its struggle over national unity.

The oddly marginalized position of the war itself in the narrative could be explained by the young age of the story's narrator. Yet, other accounts of the war illustrate that children were not only very aware of what was going on in their surroundings during the war, but personally experienced the hardships and traumas of the war (Tuttle). Instead, I suggest that the apparent distance between Nilda's focal point and the war itself echoes the ambivalence felt by African Americans and Mexican Americans toward this war, where on the one hand they believed in the principles the war was being fought for, but on the other hand resented the fact that these same principles didn't seem to apply to them.

In Ronald Takaki's *Double Victory* we learn how members of various communities felt when they heard the news of the bombing of Pearl Harbor. "Nine-year-old Patty Neal was sitting with her family around the radio when the news broke. She was 'chattering away,' and her mother asked her to be quiet. 'I kept on talking,' she recalled, 'and my mother, who NEVER spanked me, slapped me, and said, "Patty, you will remember this day"'" (10). A Japanese family recalls being in church when they learn the news of Pearl Harbor. Mary Tsukamoto remembers how stunned she was. "And suddenly the whole world turned dark" (10). Filipino Americans worried about their loved ones back home, while Korean Americans rejoiced. "Every Korean felt that the long dream for national independence would soon become a reality" (11).

Meanwhile, in Nicholasa Mohr's semi-autobiographical account, ten-year-old Nilda is on her way to meet her friend Benji on the evening of this day in December 1941. She's looking forward to visiting the Pentecostal church with Benji's family and getting a chance to witness one of the occasional outbursts that Benji always recounted. Specifically, he had told her about one man who would burst into the church, drunk, in search of his wife. He would curse and end his enraged performance by pulling out his penis and urinating in the Church floor. When she arrives at Benji's house everyone was talking about Pearl Harbor, "my mother and abuelita was crying" (93). Nilda wondered if the church services would be cancelled with the announcement of the war. But the war was just one more reason for the Pentecostals to gather in prayer. As Benji's father explains to him, "We need the meeting because it is sin and the devil that causes war and we got to pray and fight evil" (94). Clearly the adults are aware and have been greatly impacted by the news of Pearl Harbor. To Nilda however, the possibility that the news of war might jeopardize her chance to see Mr. Justicio's performance is of more pressing concern. In other personal accounts people who experienced this day as children remember a sense of instability, insecurity, and fear (Tuttle). Among Nilda's childhood friends, we don't perceive the same kind of experience. Although the war's presence is felt throughout the novel in various ways, it consistently functions as a backdrop to Nilda's everyday experiences of struggle and survival as a Nuyorican girl living in poverty. The Second World War enters her life episodically, while the war at home against discrimination and poverty that the second V in the struggle for Double Victory implies, is experienced by Nilda daily.

Throughout the text the war makes its presence in various ways. At the Pentecostal Church, the minister begins his sermon, quickly turning it into a patriotic call for the support of the country during this time of need. "Our country is in danger. . . . What do we do? Live in sin" (105). From the pulpit the minister situates this migrant community as part of the nation claiming the United States as "our country" and his congregation as citizens with a responsibility to serve it in moral ways. However, the minister's voice is just part of a larger chorus surrounding Nilda's childhood world rallying the nation's citizens into patriotic support of the war effort. When Nilda turns on the radio hoping to hear her favorite program, "The Lone Ranger," she instead hears news announcements. "Yes, this is a massive war effort by the entire nation. Americans are rallying to the call. Fathers, mothers, sons, uncles, and cousins. Americans and patriots all!" (127). In every advertisement around the city citizens are encouraged to "Buy an extra war bond. You'll be glad you did" (67). As William Tuttle explains, "The government, the schools and the media were constantly urging children to buy stamps and bonds" (125).

The war propaganda became more prevalent in the rallies that included burning effigies of Hitler, Tojo, and Mussolini. One of these rallies takes place in Nilda's neighborhood. Congressman Vito Marcantonio, who was in fact a prominent Congressman whose district included Spanish Harlem and was very vocal in his support of Puerto Rican independence and of the Puerto Rican community in New York, participates in this rally (Sanchez Korrol). He encourages his constituents to buy war bonds. "Ladies and Gentlemen, fellow Americans. We are fighting a war not just to defend our homeland, but to wipe out Fascism. . . . We have to pull together and show the world that we care about ending this menace to all mankind" (189). Music blared, war bond trucks were parked along the street, making themselves easily accessible. War bond rally workers called out to the onlookers to support the war. "Buy war bonds, they identify you!" (192). On the one hand Puerto Ricans were courted as "Americans" and are asked to demonstrate their loyalty by buying war bonds. Yet on the other hand, their daily experiences consistently remind them of how they were excluded from the nation.

The propaganda was successful at convincing some Puerto Ricans to do their patriotic duty and enlist for military services. Conflicts between wanting to be accepted as an American while at the same time enduring racism and exclusion from the nation are evident when Nilda's brother Victor announces he will be joining the army after graduation. An argument with his brother Jimmy who doesn't believe in the national fantasy of the American Dream ensues. Jimmy warns Victor not to be a "sucketa" and questions why he's made such a decision. Victor responds, "Because I believe in my country and I believe we should defend it" (132). Jimmy continues to press him on his loyalty to this country given that he was actually born in Puerto Rico. However, Victor emphatically insists that he is an "American" while Jimmy responds, "Oh yeah? . . . You're a spick. You can call yourself an American, all right. But they are gonna call you a spick!" (132–133). As Lisa Sánchez-González argues about this scene, "[t]he brother's argument reflects the two options young Puerto Rican men faced at the outbreak of the Second World War, that is, to support the 'democratic mission' of the rising U.S. military-industrial apparatus or to invent some other belief system" (129). However, the belief system Jimmy espouses captures the racializing process that Puerto Ricans were experiencing where they were being defined as an "other": always foreign, always an inferior group. From Jimmy's perspective, no amount of military service or purchases of war bonds would ever change the dominant racialized perspective of Puerto Ricans. Sánchez-González ends her analysis stating, "[n]either brother wins the argument in this episode, ostensibly because neither has really come up with a convincing position" (129). However, she stops short of the intervention of the mother, Lydia. As the argument becomes more heated both men get off their chairs threatening physical violence. Lydia jumps in and reclaims the family unity over national unity as she exclaims "'I mustn't have this. You hear? You mustn't do this. My children cannot fight like this. You are a family'" (133). By giving family unity overriding importance compared to the national rhetoric of unity, Lydia refutes the myths symbolically present through the war rallies in her neighborhood. These rallies may temporarily blind Marcantonio's Puerto Rican constituents who conform to the national image of unity and show their loyalty to the nation, but Lydia is not fooled. She never loses sight of the fact that her home is the only space deserving of her loyalty and the only safe place in a nation that otherwise excludes her and her sons. Should they succumb to the destruction of their family, they would have lost everything that is truly theirs in a country where they are denied full existence. She thus offers an alternative option to the two posed by the warring brothers, one that disrupts the seemingly binary between either succumbing to the pressures of the war or those of the street which we later see Jimmy fall victim to.

The exchange between the two brothers also symbolically depicts the historical struggle Puerto Ricans have had over national identity. Are we Americans as our citizenship status both on and off the island implies? Or is this citizenship meaningless when it is attached to brown bodies? As these two struggle over national identity, Lydia asserts her agency and resists the oppressive trauma that this national rhetoric and war propaganda has had on her sons by making family unity predominant over national unity.

Victor does represent, however, the many Puerto Ricans who sought respect from their fellow Americans by joining the armed forces. "Thousands of Puerto Rican men and women, whether residents of New York or of the island, served in the armed forces, often with distinction" (de Roman 36). According to historian Arturo Morales Carrion, "a total of 65,000 Puerto Ricans served in the U.S. armed forces during World War II" (257). Men such as Anibal Irizarry and General Pedro Del Valle served and made their families proud with their courageous contributions to the success of the war. Anibal Irizarry captured eight prisoners in North Africa while the General, a marine, distinguished himself at Guadalcanal. Although patriotism may have been the reason for some to join the military service, for others, poverty and racism at home became the actual reasons for many Puerto Ricans and other men of color to join the armed forces. As Nilda's brother Paul later asserts, "If I join the Navy, I can learn me a trade, man. . . . And help Mama out and the family" (180).

While her brothers served as soldiers, Nilda and her mother Lydia fought the war at home against the same discrimination and poverty that pushed these young men into the war effort. Although the war was clearly present and directly impacted the Puerto Rican community of El Barrio, Mohr gives precedence instead to the everyday experiences of Puerto Rican women. Mohr illustrates how institutions such as schools, welfare offices, and the police posed as the battlefields where the war at home was being fought by Puerto Rican women, represented in her narrative by Lydia and her daughter Nilda.[4]

Poverty and Welfare

In 1948, the Welfare Council of New York City published a report on the problems afflicting Puerto Rican communities. Among the needs listed for areas such as East Harlem there were: "(1) need of houses, (2) need of care for children, (3) need of recreation centers, (4) need of more special teaching and handling of school children" (Welfare Council of New York City 16). The Council studied the living conditions of several families. One family of nine lived in an apartment of four rooms, all of which were used for sleeping. "One room has a double bed and one folding bed which is opened up for the night and closed during the day. When the beds are opened, in order to get into them it is necessary to step into one to reach the other . . . one boy sleeps on the couch" (Welfare Council of New York City 17). Nilda's living situation was not different from many of the other Puerto Rican families in New York City. In Nilda's home there are at one point, nine people living in a six-room apartment. The household is constantly rearranged depending on the number of people in the household. For instance, when Sophie, Nilda's sister-in- law, moves in with her newborn baby, Nilda's mother shifts "things in the apartment so that Sophie and the baby could have a room to themselves. Frankie now shared a bedroom with Victor and Paul, but slept on the sofa in the living room. Nilda had Frankie's cot in her parents' bedroom" (72). In addition, the family has to eat dinner in shifts since only four people at a time fit in the kitchen (80).

As the family's financial hardship worsens with her stepfather's continued illness, Lydia decides to apply for welfare assistance. Through the depiction of Lydia and Nilda's encounters with the welfare system, Mohr brilliantly illustrates the traumatic effects that class and racial oppression have on the oppressed. Nilda accompanies her mother to the welfare office since Lydia hated going to these places alone. While at the office, Nilda notices the condescending and irrelevant posters in the walls, indicating the overall oppressive environment of the office itself.

> The one nearest to Nilda had a lifelike drawing of a young, smiling white woman, showing how well she was dressed when she went to look for employment. The reader was carefully informed about proper clothing, using this figure as the perfect model.
> The second poster was a large faded color photograph of a proper breakfast. The photograph showed fresh oranges, cereal, milk, a bowl of sugar, a plate of bacon and

eggs, toast with butter and jelly. The reader was warned that it was not good to leave the house without having had such a breakfast first. Looking at the food, Nilda began to remember that she was hungry. She had eaten her usual breakfast of coffee with boiled milk, sugar, and a roll. (63–64)

By juxtaposing Nilda's own breakfast against the supposed proper one, Mohr illustrates the economic discrepancies between middle-class America and that of Puerto Rican women living in poverty. The posters message of a proper breakfast that is unaffordable placed in an office where the poor come seeking assistance, creates dissonance between middle-class expectations and the realities of the poor. The message portrayed in the poster becomes one more reminder for Nilda of how far removed her reality is from this ideal. After hours of waiting, Nilda and Lydia are finally called in to speak with one of the officers about her case. The welfare officer interprets Nilda's presence as the mother's lack of English language skills. When Lydia asserts that she does speak English, the officer then proceeds to question her decision to bring Nilda to the welfare office on a school day. Lydia responds, "she wasn't feeling well so I kept her with me" (66). Nilda looks at her mother surprised since she was feeling just fine. The officer continues judging Lydia's skills as a parent arguing that if she's sick she should be home in bed. The officer moves on with her interrogation of Lydia to assess her financial needs. She notices that Lydia's sons have a different last name and asks if Nilda is her second husband's child. Lydia "sat up straight and answered, 'Yes.' Nilda glanced at her mother. Surprised and confused, she knew that she had been almost three years old when her mother married her stepfather" (67). Through these subtle lies Lydia asserts her agency in a situation that is otherwise oppressive and humiliating. The officer may insist on intruding in their lives in exchange for a pittance of assistance from the government, but Lydia will control exactly what information they are allowed to have.

This kind of limited agency has been discussed by Frances Negrón-Muntaner, Ramón Grosfoguel, and Chloe Georas as "jaibería": "Within the Puerto Rican usage, jaibería refers to collective practices of nonconfrontation and evasion . . . of taking dominant discourse literally in order to subvert it for one's purpose, of doing whatever one sees fit not as a head-on collision . . . but a bit under the table, that is, through other means" (30–31). This is one practice through which colonized subjects can have a voice and agency within the limitations of their colonial situation. Jaibería becomes a "tactic" as defined by Rey Chow, used by people to negotiate and survive within colonial confines (25). Living in the belly of the imperial beast, Lydia engages jaibería practices at the welfare office in order to ensure the economic survival of her family, withholding information that may otherwise prevent her from receiving the economic assistance she needs to support her family. As Barbara Roche Rico states, "[e]ven as Mohr's texts represent the migrants as within what other writers have termed 'a colonized space,' her work also challenges any representation of migrants as entirely passive 'victims,' subjects whose identities are shaped wholly by the environmental, cultural, and institutional forces that surround them" ("Rituals of Survival" 169). By allowing Lydia some agency, Mohr also employs the historical methods of the medicinal historian, refusing to portray women like Lydia as mere victims of the system.

After a long and arduous interrogation, the welfare officer suddenly addresses Nilda who had fallen asleep, demanding to see her hands. "You have got filthy nails," she exclaimed and questioned Nilda about her bathing habits. In anger Nilda responded, "I take a bath when I need it! And I clean my nails whenever I feel like it!" (69) affirming her own voice against the racist assumptions that Puerto Ricans are dirty and are ignorant about proper hygiene. The officer was shocked by her "impertinence" and "bad manners." She then gives Nilda a nail file for her to use in the future to clean her nails.

When they finally leave the office, Nilda angrily questions her mother's apparent disregard of the welfare officer's insults. Lydia responds, "I had to say what I did, that's all. I have to do what I do. How do you think we're gonna eat? We have no money, Nilda. If I make that woman angry, God knows what she'll put down on the application. We have to have that money in order to live" (70). She was willing to endure the humiliation not only of herself but of her daughter to ensure the security of her family. Here we see the presence of silence in its dual role "as both a disabling force and one that accords the speaker a special kind of control" (Roche Rico, "An Island Like You" 207). On the one hand the family's desperate need for economic assistance silences Lydia disabling her from speaking back to the welfare officer in protection of her daughter, at the same time however, through her selective silences she controls, albeit with some limitations, the welfare officer's intrusions into her private life.

The humiliating process of applying for welfare assistance continues when the social worker comes to visit the family's home. The stressful effect of this whole procedure is seen in Lydia's constant nervousness and the "worried look . . . that seemed almost permanently fixed" (114) on her face. She coached everyone in the family on what to say and how to behave during the investigator's visit. "Nilda and her brothers were instructed to answer with polite yes-and-no answers and, when asked about personal family matters, to say only 'I don't know' and not another word" (114). Her nervous behavior is indicative of the kinds of stressors experienced as a result of her marginalized position as a poor Puerto Rican woman. These stressors have long-lasting traumatic effects which the marginalized experience living in a society where they endure constant inequalities while being exposed to a rhetoric of equality, freedom, and justice. Yet Mohr does not just illustrate the trauma and its causes, but also, in a medicinal manner, depicts how one woman copes with these stressors for the overriding goal of survival. Once again Lydia is aware of the limitations of her situation, yet she holds on to some semblance of agency and control.

The social worker finally arrives and does a thorough inspection of the entire family. She questions Lydia about her Aunt Delia and insists that if she receives a Home Relief check she needs to contribute toward rent. Lydia anxiously agrees. As she continues walking through their apartment she meets Nilda and is impressed with how well she speaks English. Lydia, offended, responds, "She was born here, Mrs. Wood." Lydia's anxiety is further exacerbated when her husband mistakenly mentions his intention of returning to work when she had specifically stated that he would be doing no such thing (122). Finally, the investigator makes her way out the door not making any promises to Lydia and leaving the family behind feeling helpless, at the mercy of this white woman's judgment.

In *A Welfare Mother*, Susan Sheehan conducts a study on one Puerto Rican woman's welfare experience in the 1960's. In this account we see startling similarities with Lydia's encounter with welfare officers. Like Lydia, this woman, Mrs. Santana, would assert her agency and control by giving wrong information. When her purse was snatched and she lost the thirty-five dollars she had, she went to the Welfare office and claimed she had lost the entire proceeds of her check "because a friend had told her the department wouldn't replace small amounts" (Sheehan 18). Mrs. Santana also employs jaibería practices with the welfare office, asserting her limited agency as a colonized subject. She also would take one of her children with her to the welfare office. In addition, she was subjected to similar reprimands from her welfare officer on the cleanliness of her children. In one of their reports one case worker who had "a penchant for referring to himself in the first person plural," wrote "our client does not keep a clean house" and proceeded to offer her advice on how to keep her home and children clean (Sheehan 21). The caseworker buttresses his own power by taking on the power of the institutional identity, referring to himself in the plural "we" throughout his report, illustrating how this institution functions to uphold consensual identities. The institutional "we" also illustrates that the prejudices implied in the individual caseworker's report are not just his own, but those of the government institution itself.

The stressful process of asking for government assistance appears when Mrs. Santana requests funds in order to move to another apartment. She arrives with her son Gabriel at the office at 9:45 a.m. By noon she was still sitting, waiting to see a caseworker. "Mrs. Santana gave Gabriel some money to go out and buy himself a sandwich. Mrs. Santana was low on funds, so she went without lunch" (Sheehan 60). Finally, at two in the afternoon she is called in by a caseworker. After waiting for so many hours and explaining her request the caseworker informs her "that no one had been able to find her case record, that the rent sounded excessive to her, and that she should return in a few days with some valid reason for moving" (Sheehan 61). She returns to the office another day to endure another long wait. A different caseworker sees her this time. He disagrees with the previous caseworker and does not believe the rent is excessive. Now she is asked to bring in a two-year lease for the new apartment. That afternoon she returns once again with the required paperwork. A third caseworker calls her in to the office only to request more paperwork, a copy of the broker's license. At her fourth visit she is asked once again for another piece of paper at which point she explains to the man that this is the fourth time she's had to come to the welfare office on the same matter. The worker responds "in a nasty tone, 'I don't care if you have to come here fifteen times. It's not my problem. You people always think you can get something for nothing'" (Sheehan 63). Reminiscent of Lydia and Nilda's previous experiences with the welfare officers we see again the hostility directed at Puerto Ricans who are simply trying to make ends meet. The similarity between Mrs. Santana's account and the experience represented by Nicholasa Mohr in her narrative, even though the former takes place twenty years later, is disconcerting to say the least, as it demonstrates a pattern and continuity in the experiences of Puerto Rican women living in poverty who have to navigate the systems in place that are intended to help them and to which they are entitled to as citizens.

Susan Sheehan's narrative, however, is unfortunately tainted by her own assumptions and judgments about Puerto Ricans. In the afterword she concludes her narrative by sealing Mrs. Santana and her children's fate. "As for where it will end, it is not easy to foresee Casilda's daughter finishing high school and getting a decent job. It is, alas, far more likely that Helen will drop out of school, get pregnant at an early age, and become the third generation of Mrs. Santana's family on welfare" (144). In the end she is no better than the earlier caseworker who implies that all Puerto Ricans are looking for a free ride. Nowhere in her account does she provide any in-depth explanations about what factors may be contributing to the drug addiction of Mrs. Santana's son and the teenage pregnancy of her daughters. One is to assume that these are the inevitable results of being on welfare. Nicholasa Mohr's account fills the gaps in this account. She corrects the stereotypes, demonstrating the complexities that determine the choices her characters make and so works toward creating a more healing and empowering historical narrative.

Education

As a response to her experiences with poverty, Lydia constantly emphasizes the importance of education to her children. Education is perceived as the only means through which her children can reach success in this country. As she states in one of her lectures to Nilda, "You do as the teacher says and learn, so you can be somebody someday. Amount to something. I don't want to hear no complaints, because it'll be much worse for you here with me. Comprende? I only got to the fourth grade; I never had the advantages you got here in this country. You want to be a jíbara when you grow up? Working in a factoría? Cleaning houses? Being a sucketa for other people?" (60). Lydia's belief in the educational system, however, is undermined by its inherent racism as we see through Nilda's numerous experiences with her public-school teachers. One of these teachers, Miss Longhorn, would abruptly close her supply closet after milk and cookies time saying to the class, "Don't tempt a thief. . . . That's how it all starts; first it's just a pencil, then perhaps a fountain pen" (51). She tries to impart honesty to students she has already judged as criminals. She would also lecture her students on the greatness of the nation's forefathers. "Brave people they were, our forefathers, going into the unknown where man had never ventured. They were not going to permit the Indians to stop them. This nation was developed from a wild primitive forest into a civilized nation. Where would we all be today if not for brave people? We would have murder, thievery, and no belief in God" (52). On numerous occasions Nicholasa Mohr has shared her own very similar experiences with the educational system. As a child she was eager to learn how to read and was taught by her older brother. She was excited to enter kindergarten, but recalls her first day as a bitter disappointment.

> I had been warned to 'be a good girl and do exactly as you are told.' With happy anticipation I sat at my desk watching my teacher with a sense of awe. What mysteries would teacher reveal and what new worlds of wonder was I about to discover? I was so eager that when my teacher asked the first question I shot up my hand, desperate to show her all that I had learned. She asked that I count to ten. I stood and counted beyond ten, for I could count as high as 100! Teacher interrupted me and told me to come to the front of the class, then warned that I was not to take it upon myself to speak out of turn or offer information that had not been requested. I still can feel the humiliation as she dug her index finger into the middle of my shoulder blades before she sent me back to my seat. (Mohr, "Freedom to Read" 14)

In a matter of minutes Mohr's enthusiasm for learning was diminished by the teacher's authoritarian control over learning where the students are not allowed ownership over their own education. Obeying arbitrary classroom rules is more important than nurturing a young child's enthusiasm for learning. Mohr has also endured skewed historical narratives throughout her educational experience. "Schools provided either nothing or a distorted sense of our own history. . . . I learned in the public schools in New York City that it was the benevolent Americans who saved us from the cruel Spaniards, and in a sense adopted us. We in turn should be grateful, speak only English and strive toward total acceptance" (Mohr, "Journey" 82).

In essence, the schools function to socialize Puerto Rican children to be good citizens for the nation by teaching them American middle-class values. "Psychologists and political scientists have found . . . that the grade schools are the primary agents of citizenship training" (Tuttle 113). Eugene Bucchioni in his study of Puerto Rican children in elementary schools illustrated how this socializing role is experienced in the daily lives of Puerto Rican students in U.S. schools. In "The Daily Round of Life in the School," he portrays one typical day in the school life of Puerto Rican children in the 1960s. The children begin their day with nationalist rituals that are meant to incorporate them into the nation regardless of nationality, language, or race. Two children are chosen to be Mr. and Mrs. America and lead the class in the "Pledge of Allegiance," singing of the national anthem, and the approved school prayer (Bucchioni 287).

> These rituals, however, become especially important when lower class children or children of differing ethnic backgrounds are in attendance. The salutes to the flag and the singing of a suitable patriotic anthem help to promote a sense of identification with the society as a whole. Puerto Ricans as well as other children participate into this unifying ceremony together, without regard to race, color, religion or culture. In this manner, the ritual functions to overcome, to some extent, ethnic group divisiveness. This ritual also tends to obscure economic differences. Even those who are poor are Americans. They too salute the flag and sing the National Anthem in a ceremony that renders homage to the nation, a nation in which even the poor are important participants. (Bucchioni 303)

Similar to the rallies and other propaganda witnessed by Nilda which tries to include Puerto Ricans into the nation, participation in these rituals provide these children with a sense of belonging. Yet, the teachers' behaviors throughout the rest of the school day remind these children that they are always "foreign" and therefore excluded.

When Nilda's stepfather dies she misses three weeks of school to be with her family during this time of mourning. She returns to school with a note explaining her absence. Her teacher, Mrs. Fortinash responds, "You people are the limit! No wonder you don't get anywhere or do anything worthwhile with these kinds of customs. People pass away every day—you're not the only ones, you know! Your mother will have to come in and explain that custom and what tribe you belong to!" (212). Similarly, in Bucchioni's example, when two students walk in late to the classroom and attempt to explain that their alarm clock was broken, their teacher, Mrs. Dwight, responds, "Please, Dolores. We've taken enough of the class's time for this. Furthermore, if it's not your alarm clock, it's having to go to the store, or helping dress your brother or some other excuse. You will have to learn to come to school on time. You too, Jesus! You have been coming to school long enough to realize that one of the important rules is to be early in the morning. And another thing, you are to bring a note each time you are late or absent" (Bucchioni 287). Like Mrs. Fortinash, this teacher is also frustrated with having to constantly explain "American" ways to these children. In her response, she implies that these children are lying, are always "making up" excuses, and are irresponsible, reinforcing the necessary lessons about bravery and honesty that we see Mrs. Longhorn giving earlier to Nilda's class. Although these teachers are frustrated and some are outright hostile to teaching these students, as some of the teachers in Bucchioni's study made clear when in their teacher's lounge one complained, "The Puerto Ricans seem to learn absolutely nothing—either here or at home," (Bucchioni 286) they are still fulfilling their socializing role as cultural transmitter, passing on to her students the "cultural traits [and] values of the middle class group to which she belongs" (Bucchioni 305).

With fierce hostility, Mrs. Fortinash continues to lash out at Nilda for her supposed "customs" demanding that her mother come to school and explain their ways. With the generic "you people" she calls Nilda and her family irresponsible as she continues in her seemingly never-ending rampage. "Well, you are not the first ones to be allowed into this country. It's bad enough we have to support strangers with our tax dollars" (212). Here Mrs. Fortinash conveys to her Puerto Rican students the clear message that they are not part of the nation. The "we" that is supporting strangers through tax dollars does not include Puerto Ricans. Thus, the school functions as a space where students are exposed to a definition of national belonging that contradicts the one portrayed at the many political rallies taking place in their neighborhoods reminding them to buy war bonds. Nor does Mrs. Fortinash's definition of who belongs to the nation include Nilda's brothers serving in the military during the war. Meanwhile Nilda is paralyzed by the teacher's anger. All she can do is wait and hope that Mrs. Fortinash will end her tirade soon.

Nilda's reaction is consistent with Bucchioni's study twenty years later, where he found that Puerto Rican children implement survival methods that allow them to continue to endure their experiences in schools where their "ego is threatened and weakened by constant and often derogatory reference to [their] culture" (Bucchioni 315). Similar to Nilda's quiet response to Mrs. Fortinash's rampage, Bucchioni found that Puerto Rican children were usually very quiet, and extremely polite and courteous. "The excessive courtesy helps the child avoid further attacks upon his social and cultural status by this teacher, for teachers are less likely to reprimand or attack those who are polite and who accord them the proper deference" (Bucchioni 315). While Mrs. Fortinash continues to attack Nilda's "customs," Nilda quietly waits, hoping that her silence will also at the very least shorten the duration of her abuse.

Even in her Spanish class Nilda faces discrimination against her Puerto Rican culture and language. Señorita Reilly, her Spanish teacher, mostly spoke to her students in English. When she did speak in Spanish her accent was so bad that many of the Spanish-speaking students in the class could not understand her. Yet her arrogance allowed her to talk down to her students and criticize their Spanish as impure. She wants her students to speak the "real Spanish," Castilian Spanish. "None of that dialect spoken here. If only you could hear yourselves chat chat chat! Like a bunch of Chinamen!" (214). In one racist sweep she not only insults and degrades the Spanish language of her students but also shows her prejudices against another racial group, Chinese Americans. The students however still found ways to rebel against her racism. One student, for instance, writes on the blackboard in Spanish, "Miss Reilly is in love with a Spanish matador who fucks with a Castillian accent!" (215). The teacher simply erases the words from the board seemingly not understanding what they meant. It was the students' way of countering the torturous in-class reading assignments where they were to lisp, imitating a Castillian accent. By allowing the students to undermine the teacher's authority Mohr once again documents how Puerto Rican students resisted the daily abuse they endured in schools. For many of these students, their native language served as both a unifying cultural tool and a weapon against their perceived enemies. As Ana Celia Zentella explains in her study of bilingual Puerto Rican children in New York, "the grammar skills [these children] had in two languages and [their] knowledge of two cultures were not sufficiently understood, rewarded, or developed. Indeed, they were often blamed for [their] lack of progress and that of [their] community. Yet, many children who stopped speaking Spanish did not get far in the outside world, and they severed important links to their families and culture" (1). For these children then, upholding their own language, their own version of Spanish, within an educational system that consistently undermines their culture and native language, is a way to maintain some agency in an otherwise oppressive environment.

Bucchioni found numerous moments where Puerto Rican students reverted to speaking in Spanish in the presence of the non-Spanish speaking teacher. Although in some of these instances, children were trying to help each other by translating what the teacher was saying for those students who had difficulties comprehending certain words in English, at other times students used Spanish to express their own frustrations against the teacher. In one instance when the teacher reprimands one of the children named Antonio, he responds with a Spanish obscenity. When she demands to know what he said, none of the children translate. They just explain he has used an untranslatable curse word. Bucchioni explains this use of obscenities in Spanish as "the defiance of a child who can no longer accept what he views as intolerable" (312). In this example, we also see however how through language the students disrupt the previously established sense of national unity through the nationalist rituals with which they began their school day. In this moment the solidarity the students have with Antonio as they refuse to translate the obscenity recreates a unity based on culture and language. As Bucchioni explains,

> Spanish is, for these Puerto Rican children, a symbol of their solidarity. As a means of communicating, the use of Spanish assists Puerto Rican children in sharing their experiences and thoughts with one another. But as a symbol of solidarity, the language helps to define the social situation in the classroom. It establishes a degree of rapport among the Puerto Rican children present physically in the classroom. Its use symbolizes the cultural understanding and unity of Puerto Rican pupils, especially when confronted by an outsider, one who is not a member of the group, and one who represents the imposed authority and control of a superordinate group. (312)

Thus, when Mrs. Reilly's students write the offensive statement on the board, they are also creating a sense of unity and solidarity through language responding to and resisting Mrs. Reilly's undermining through her Spanish lessons of their Puerto Rican culture. Using Ernesto Laclau's "notion of populist rupture," Ellen McCracken suggests in her analysis of Mohr's work, that Mohr uses her literary works not only as a recounting of "instances of populist rupture in U.S. Latino communities," but that the texts themselves "constitute moments of populist resistance" (204). Analyzing one of Mohr's short stories, "The English Lesson," where we see the interactions between adult immigrant students and their English language instructor, McCracken states, "antagonism is established between immigrant students who want to obtain the power of language that learning English in the U.S. will allow and an oppressive teacher who uses her knowledge of English, her position as the classroom authority and her desire to control, to maintain power over the subordinates. We see the numerous ruptures with which she must contend and her attempts to maintain order" (205). Similarly, these students in Señorita Reilly's class, are disrupting in their own limited ways, her authority in the classroom and her hegemonic discourse about language purity.

In "Puerto Rican Students in US Schools: A Brief History," Sonia Nieto provides a survey of the historical educational experiences of Puerto Rican students in the United States. As she demonstrates, Puerto Ricans have had a long struggle with the educational system fighting against the types of abuses depicted by Nicholasa Mohr and Eugene Bucchioni. By writing her narrative, Mohr not only acknowledges the many, like herself, who endured such abuses in their own educational experiences, but offers a healing narrative documenting their struggles and resistance. As Mohr argues, "[t]he making of these United States was accomplished by many different kinds of people and unless they share an equal place in history, our books and curriculum will remain exclusionary and incomplete" ("Freedom to Read" 19).

Police Brutality

In *Race, Police, and the Making of a Political Identity*, Edward Escobar documents the experiences of Mexican Americans with the Los Angeles Police Department between 1900 and 1945. He explains that the role of the first police departments was to "control the burgeoning working class in industrializing northeastern cities. As the police institution spread and evolved throughout the rest of the nineteenth century and into the first decades of the twentieth century, it continued to concentrate its efforts on maintaining order in the working-class sections of urban America" (11). Among the many encounters between Mexican Americans and the police, the one that stands out as a historical event occurred during the Second World War. Known as the Zoot Suit Riots, this event epitomizes how institutional racism functions within the police system. On June 3, 1943 in Los Angeles, a disturbance occurred between Mexican Americans and sailors who were on shore leave. It escalated to the point where sailors left their ships and raided Chicano neighborhoods attacking young Mexican American men and women, stripping them of their clothing and beating them. The commanders in charge of the sailors did not do anything to stop them. The police arrested Chicanos, accusing them of disturbing the peace. The riots lasted for a week before the navy declared Los Angeles off limits to its sailors. Nine sailors were eventually arrested but released immediately without filing charges, whereas 600 Chicano youths were arrested, the police labeled this preventive action (Acuña).

African American communities were also erupting into uprisings primarily as protests against police brutality. One example of many, occurred in 1943 in New York City's Harlem, when army private Robert Brandy was shot by police officers, after he attempted to protest against what he perceived to be the unfair arrest of an African American woman. "When word of the shooting hit the streets, Harlem roared like a bonfire. It looked as if the war had come home: 6 people lay dead, 550 had been arrested, 1450 stores had been damaged or burned to the ground" (Kelley 34).

Nicholasa Mohr depicts a similar hostile relationship between the police department of New York City and the Puerto Rican community. On a hot summer day in El Barrio, the grocer Jacinto offers a reprieve from the oppressive heat by opening up the fire hydrant. "People plunged right into the onrushing water with their clothes on, arms outstretched, mouths open, drinking the cool liquid" (4). Moments later the police arrive and close the hydrant. "One policeman held a large wrench, the other had one hand placed on his gun holster and the other hand wrapped around his nightstick" (5).

Frustrated with the crowd's lack of response to their questioning, the officers lecture them on their supposed irresponsible behavior. From the crowd someone responds "Coño, leave the water on man. It's too hot here! Have a heart" (5). The use of the Spanish curse word "coño" illustrates not only their resistance but that their protest is expressed in their own language, again distancing themselves from a national rhetoric which, given their mistreatment at the hands of police (i.e., a national authority) excludes them from the nation. The officers escalate their hostility and engage in verbal brutality with insults, calling them bastards, animals, and spicks. As Escobar explains, "[p]robably the most common type of police misconduct was verbal abuse, in particular the use of racial slurs" (172). Finally, the officers leave with a stern warning.

As Nilda witnesses this confrontation she tries to create some distance between herself and the policemen. Nilda begins to fantasize about her summer camp wondering what it might be like "with all kinds of trees and grass and maybe a lake. These thoughts helped erase the image of the two big white policemen who loomed larger and more powerful than all the other people in her life" (7). Unfortunately, this would not be her last encounter with police authority nor the only occasion where we see her escape into her imagination as a strategy for dealing with the everyday racist abuses she endures. Mohr has admitted to using this strategy herself as a child. For instance, when she would be punished by being sent to sit facing a wall by her teachers for speaking out of turn or speaking in Spanish in the classroom, she would stare at the walls "searching for discoloration in the paint, a crack in the plaster or shadow on the surface, I'd visualize trees, a waterfall and, in one spot, I imagined the profile of a horse. My humiliation, my embarrassment and anger at teacher was ameliorated by this game that somehow helped ease my punishment. I now recognize that it also sharpened my sense of imagination and provided yet another survival skill to be used under oppressive circumstances" ("Freedom to Read" 15). The level of hostility experienced by this community from the police is most clearly depicted in one particular moment in the story when there have been rumors in the neighborhood of a "rumble" between warring gang members. On this fateful day, Nilda is on her way back from her friend Sylvia's house, when she runs into Benji's brothers, Chucho and Manuel, who offer to walk her back home. A police car speeds past them, stops abruptly and returns to where Nilda, Chucho, and Manuel are standing. The police officers ask why they are hanging outside at night. The policemen, hands firmly grasping their nightsticks, asked the boys where they lived. When Chucho responds the policeman says, "That's quite a few blocks from here. What the hell are you doing way up here, God Damn it!" (226), demonstrating their aggression toward them. Once again, we see how the police function not to serve and defend citizens but to discipline subjects into good citizenship. When they see Puerto Ricans outside of the parameters of their own space (i.e., their neighborhood), these policemen become agitated and demand that Nilda and her friends conform and accept the boundaries of their racialized spacial containment.

The officers begin to question Manuel and Chucho, who are both members of the Pentecostal church and not involved with any gang activity, asking about other boys their age. When the boys explain that they know nothing about any gang or a rumble the policemen become frustrated. One of them picks up his nightstick and swings it "hard at Manuel. Nilda heard a thud and saw blood coming down the side of Manuel's face as he reeled over" (227). The policeman kept hitting him until the other officer finally stepped in and controlled him. "Nilda had heard loud screams; only now, as she cried quietly, feeling the hoarseness in her throat, did she realize that it was she who had been screaming" (228). As a crowd began to gather, the police officers put Manuel and Chucho in their car to drive them to the emergency room and sent Nilda home on her own.[5] While her brothers defend democracy and the four freedoms overseas, she is subjected to harassment and violence by members of the local armed forces who in an instant can strip Puerto Ricans of the "Americanness" bestowed upon them by officials such as Vito Marcantonio and through their purchases of war bonds, redefining them once more as the enemy.

By the end of the novel, Lydia has struggled to maintain family unity. She has made unfortunate and failed attempts to protect her children from crime. She's endured humiliations to ensure at least food and shelter for her family. She loses a husband, has a son in jail, and another son wounded in the war. In the meantime, her daughter Nilda comes of age during a time of battle both at home and abroad. She experiences the consistent conflicting messages from the educational system, the welfare officers, and the policemen, who remind her that she will always be "foreign" regardless of how much her family contributes to the war effort. The purpose of Mohr's narrative however, is not just to document the ways in which Puerto Rican women were victimized by racism, poverty, and war. She creates a medicinal historical narrative by recording the historical experiences of this community during the Second World War, a period of history that is rarely discussed in the histories of Puerto Ricans in the U.S., but more importantly documenting their strategies of resistance.

Throughout the text we see the many counter strategies used by members of this community and in particular by the women. We repeatedly see Lydia's strategic negotiation of the welfare system in order to ensure economic survival for her family. We see her standing up to her husband and her sons reminding them of the importance of family unity in the midst of so many threats to their safety and security. We also see Nilda, drawing from her mother's lessons, and finding her own strategies of resistance against the consistent messages she receives, undermining her culture and history. As Lydia's body succumbs to cancer at the end of the novel, there is still one more lesson that she must pass on to her daughter. In the last conversation between Nilda and Lydia, the mother tries to leave her daughter with some advice that might protect her from a life of financial and emotional hardship. Other than her children, Lydia feels she has had nothing in life that was all her own. She warns Nilda of how, much like her cancer, the dominant institutions and racist society will slowly kill those who are poor, uneducated, and Puerto Rican. She encourages Nilda not to let the same thing happen to her.

> "Do you have that feeling, honey? That you have something all yours . . . you must . . . like when I see you drawing sometimes, I know you have something all yours. Keep it . . . hold on, guard it. Never give it to nobody . . . not to your lover, not to your kids . . . it don't belong to them . . . and . . . they have no right . . . no right to take it. We are all born alone . . . and we die all alone. And when I die, Nilda, I know I take nothing with me that is only mine." She paused and said, "You asked me something, didn't you? . . . oh yes . . . Am I happy? . . . I don't know . . . But if I cannot see who I am beyond the eyes of the children I bore . . . then . . ." turning her head, she looked directly at Nilda for a moment ". . . it was not worth the journey . . . and I might as well not have bothered at all." (277)

In one final moment, the mother summarizes living as a Puerto Rican woman in a racist, patriarchal, poverty-stricken society. She feels she has no agency, nothing of her own, nothing outside of the confines of the system. Even her children seem like something that she doesn't own, because she can't control their destiny. "How is that possible? That there is this life I have made, Nilda, and I have nothing to do with it? How did it all happen anyway?" (277). Lydia is thus a casualty of the war at home. And yet, even though Lydia herself isn't able to recognize her own agency, however limited, or the significance of her life, Mohr ensures that these are visible to her readers.

Conclusion

Historical accounts document how different groups of color worked at home and abroad to win the war for double victory, whether by serving in the military, working in the defense industries, or protesting against racism. Nicholasa Mohr demonstrates another way in which the war for double victory was fought by

Puerto Rican women. While they contributed the lives of their sons to the fight abroad, they fought the battles at home against the violence of policemen, racist educators, and welfare officers.

Mohr experienced the traumatic effects created by official historiographical discourses first hand as a student in the public schools of New York City. While enduring this process of assimilation she wondered about the history of Puerto Rican women. "Where were the rest of us? Where were my own mother and aunt? And all those valiant women who left Puerto Rico out of necessity, for the most part by themselves bringing small children to a cold and hostile city" (Mohr, "Journey" 83). It was this invisibility in the national historical narrative which "compelled [her] to produce a body of work that would confront the reader with the truth of [her] existence and [her] community's impact on the larger society" (Mohr, "Journey" 83). As an author then, Mohr intentionally created literary narratives that "recover a more authentic view of history" (Roche Rico, "Rituals of Survival" 166–167).

In her view of history, we see evidence of the curandera historical tactics at work. She uses her literary space as an alternative historical document in order to archive the historical experiences of Puerto Rican women during the Second World War. She centers women in her narrative focusing on the everyday experiences of struggle and resistance of Puerto Rican women in New York. She makes evident the dissonance experienced by Puerto Ricans as American citizens subjected to the propaganda of national belonging and unity while enduring consistent reminders of their always being "foreign in a domestic sense."[6] Yet while she fills historical gaps documenting these experiences, she defies representing Puerto Rican women as victims of their circumstance. She demonstrates their agency representing the many ways that these women resisted the stereotypical narratives created by institutions of power and how they held on to their dignity and honor amidst hostile intrusions into their daily lives. Mohr thus creates a medicinal historical narrative and counters hegemonic historical methodologies.

Chapter 3

"MENDING BROKEN MEMORIES"

Judith Ortiz Cofer's *Silent Dancing:*
A Partial Remembrance of a Puerto Rican Childhood

In the preface to her memoir, *Silent Dancing: A Partial Remembrance of a Puerto Rican Childhood,* Judith Ortiz Cofer shares the concerns of many historians over "the problem of writing truth from memory" (11). Yet, as I will illustrate in this chapter, Ortiz Cofer addresses this concern by creating a medicinal historical narrative that is self-reflexive in its methodology. While she relies on her memories to create her narrative she consistently questions these and juxtaposes them against those of other members of her family. She evokes Virginia Woolf's concept of a "poetic truth," one that captures not just the particulars of an historical event but also the emotional experience and psychological effects of those events. As she explains, "I think literature has a truth that has something to do with the dictionary definition of truth. I think there's factuality and there's truth. I can say to you, 'My father was in the Cuban missile crisis,' and tell you the dates, but that is not as meaningful as the fact that we lost contact with him for six months and thought he was dead. The truth is what I felt about my father disappearing, not that he was actually on a ship in Cuba at that time" (Ocasio, "Speaking" 145). She proposes a radical definition of truth and one that poses a significant challenge to our understanding of what constitutes history. Historical accounts of factual events are incomplete if they don't also include the affective experience of those historical moments. These affective experiences are the historical gaps filled by authors such as Judith Ortiz Cofer in memoir writing.

She turns to Virginia Woolf as a model for her memoir writing because, as she explains, Woolf was the only female author she was exposed to during her own education.[1] In "Sketches of the Past" Woolf pieces together her early life from different moments from her own childhood, having lost her mother at a young age. "And she does so not to showcase her life, extraordinary as it was, but rather out of a need most of us feel at some point to study ourselves and our lives in retrospect; to understand what people and events formed us (and, yes, what and who hurt us, too)" (Ortiz Cofer 11). Ortiz Cofer thus situates her own memoir work in this broader human need to understand ourselves and the context from where we come from. Yet, her own context, as a Puerto Rican woman shaped by two locations, the island and the U.S. mainland, particularizes this universal need into that of the Puerto Rican migrant woman. Her journey to self-understanding also includes those people and situations that have caused pain. She recognizes writing from memory then as both a way to understand our histories as well as the traumas experienced. Writing becomes part of the process of achieving greater understanding and healing from trauma.

In her study of the writing of Puerto Rican women, Marisel Moreno discusses the significance of memoir writing or, as she calls it, "self-life-writing" for Puerto Rican diaspora writers. Their invisibility in historical narratives in the United states, "partly fueled their desire to write and thus participate in a process of historical recovery. . . . Therefore, in writing their own stories they are often writing the history of their community" (Moreno 97). Moreno addresses the resistance from both historians and scholars of "traditional autobiographical studies" for whom autobiographies are about the individual and not the community. Nonetheless, as Moreno demonstrates, "scholarship focusing on ethnic and female self-life-writings" such as those by Martin Japtok and Nelli McKay, have challenged the resistance by the aforementioned scholars who see "the connection between self and community as a distinctive feature of women's and minority autobiography" (Moreno 100). Thus, it's no surprise then that Ortiz Cofer and other Puerto Rican women writers have used memoirs as a form not only to write their own individual stories, but through these stories document a collective history of the Puerto Rican migrant community.

While she affirms her reliance on memory to create her narrative, Ortiz Cofer nonetheless wrestles with its reliability and legitimacy. In an interview with Rafael Ocasio she confesses being "afraid to begin writing this autobiographical work, thinking, 'How can I trust my memory? They will call me a liar because what I remember is not necessarily what other people remember" (Ocasio, "Infinite Variety" 732). It was Woolf's example that gave her the confidence to accept her own memories as legitimate. She echoes postmodern theorists' suggestions on the creative and interpretive role of the historian. "I faced the possibility that the past is mainly a creation of the imagination" (Ortiz Cofer 12). Yet she also acknowledges that there are forms of evidence available to research in order to confirm one's memories. "There are birth, marriage, and death certificates on file, there are letters and family photographs in someone's desk or attic; and there are the relatives who have assigned themselves the role of the genealogist or family bard, recounting at the least instigation the entire history of your clans" (Ortiz Cofer 12). However, as we will see, she consistently problematizes the reliability of these sources of the past, illuminating what is beyond the margins of the archival evidence and filling in the gaps left there.

Focusing on her own Puerto Rican childhood might suggest an individualistic history relevant only to her particular experience. Her prefacing quote suggests however an interest in proposing her narrative as a more collective historical narrative. She quotes Virginia Woolf's "A Room of One's Own": "A woman writing thinks back through her mothers." And it is indeed through her own mother's stories and memories that the author creates her historical narrative. Throughout the text, Ortiz Cofer incorporates the experiences of her mother and grandmothers as Puerto Rican women through the stories they share. "My literary ancestry comes from the oral tradition of these women. They were strong. They might have played submissive roles because that's what society demanded, but when they were running the house, making the decisions and telling the stories, they were powerful matriarchs to me" (Ocasio, "Infinite Variety" 733). By incorporating the experiences of other women within her own memoir she attempts to "connect myself to the threads of lives that have touched mine and at some point converged into the tapestry that is my memory of childhood" (Ortiz Cofer 13). She thus situates her own history as part of a collective historical experience of Puerto Rican women.

By using this kind of poetic truth to document her individual and collective history, she creates a healing historical narrative that accounts for the dual traumas of being a Puerto Rican migrant woman in the United States and having these experiences excluded from national memory. In *Silent Dancing* she practices "medicinal history" as she tries to heal the traumatic effects of her constant moving back and forth between the island and the mainland and the consistent sense of displacement she experiences in both places. She explains, "the shifts were abrupt and always traumatic" (Ocasio, "Puerto Rican Literature" 45). By writing this experience not only as her own history but as part of a larger, collective, migration history, Ortiz Cofer remembers the shifts for their positive influences in her construction as a Puerto Rican woman and therefore "heals," in the sense discussed by Levins Morales, the original trauma the movements inflicted on young Judith. As Frances Aparicio asserts, *Silent Dancing*, is a "profound reflection on the power of memory, which has the potential to sustain and nurture someone throughout the difficult situations that result from change and displacement" (62).

Similar to Levins Morales, Ortiz Cofer uses both poetry and prose in the creation of her healing historical narrative, providing multiple perspectives on the same event at times. Through her "poetic truth," Ortiz Cofer recognizes that knowledge is always theoretically mediated yet still affirms that some kind of knowledge is attainable by exploring the seemingly subjective experiences of the women in her family. In this chapter, I illustrate the various ways through which Judith Ortiz Cofer addresses the concerns over memory, while still reclaiming these memories to create a historical healing narrative that through its multiple perspectives gives us a better understanding of the histories of Puerto Rican women in the United States.

Ortiz Cofer's Healing Legacy

Finding medicinal methodologies in her narrative is less surprising when we learn of Ortiz Cofer's healing legacy from her grandparents. When describing her maternal grandmother's bedroom, she recalls all of "Mama's symbols of power" that lay upon her dresser. "[T]here were jars filled with herbs: yerba buena, yerba mala, the making of purgatives and teas to which we were all subjected during childhood crises" (24). Reminiscent of the opening pieces to each section in Levins Morales's *Remedios*, prevalent among the grandmother's belongings are herbs used to create healing concoctions for ailing bodies. Levins Morales describes yerba buena as a "hardworking herb" that can be used for multiple conditions. "It will settle your stomach, clear your headache away, soothe you to sleep, calm your nerves, stimulate and tone and sweeten the air" (Levins Morales, *Remedios* 143). It's a multipurpose herb, much like Ortiz Cofer describes her grandmother's stories, which consist of staple stories, the details of which she changes to accommodate the particular audience or lesson she is trying to impart. As she explains in an interview about her grandmother's storytelling, "[s]o I would hear her tell one story for my aunts in a particular way and assure us that it was absolutely true and then tell it to us in a different way to make a different point. What I learned about art from her was that it wasn't so much the facts as the poetic truth that was being made" (Kevane and Heredia 116). Thus, she learned about creating poetic truth from her grandmother's storytelling.

In addition to her healing herbs, the grandmother's room also consists of her collection of objects and photos sent to her from relatives in New York. "Each year more items were added as the family grew and dispersed, and every object in the room had a story attached to it, a cuento which Mamá would bestow on anyone who received the privilege of a day alone with her" (25). Her collection serves as an archive of family migration history whose story can only be completed by Mamá's interpretation and narration of the story behind each object. Thus, in this room which the author remembers as symbolic of her grandmother's matriarchal power, we find the tools, her herbs, and sources of family (his)stories that she uses to heal whatever is ailing her family members whether physically or emotionally.

Her grandfather on the other hand, was a spiritual healer. In "Talking to the Dead" she describes her grandfather's role as a mesa blanca spiritist, and his gift of clairvoyance. Members of the community came to him seeking healing from the painful loss of loved ones. "What Papá performed in his room was a ceremony of healing. Whether he ever communicated with the dead I cannot say, but the spiritually wounded came to him and he tended to them and reassured them that death was not a permanent loss" (32). His form of healing was one where he sympathetically listened to those who came to him and used his faculties to see beyond the margins of reality into the world of the spirits. Similarly, Ortiz Cofer through her search and creation of poetic truth, sees beyond the margins of historical evidence, and fills in the gaps of history creating a healing historical narrative for herself and other Puerto Rican migrants.

In an interesting reversal of gender roles, it was the grandmother who was skeptical of her husband's spiritist abilities. In their household it was the woman who had the dominant position, contrary to usual Puerto Rican custom, where "the man is considered a small-letter god in his home. But, Papá, a gentle, scholarly man, preferred a laissez-faire approach. Mamá's ire [about his spiritual work] could easily be avoided by keeping his books and his spiritist practice out of her sight" (31). On one occasion, however, the grandmother's role of family archivist and her husband's skills as a spiritist would combine to solve a moment of crisis when one of their sons goes missing in the United States.

At the age of eighteen, the son had been recruited to work in the United States and offered a "free ticket." The grandfather had premonitions that something bad would happen. Nevertheless, Hernán left "and was not heard from again for months" (33). His mother frantically searches for her son, asking relatives and friends located in the United States to look for him. She consults with various authority figures such as lawyers, police officers, and writes to the Governor requesting any information that might help her find the whereabouts of her son. Her worries increase when she receives a letter from the government stating, "that the recruitment of Puerto Rican laborers by mainland growers was being investigated by the authorities for the possibility of illegal practices" (33). Then one day Papá has a vision. "He is in a place far north. A place without a name. . . . Here, they are growing things. Fruit, maybe" (34). Mamá sifts through her many memories of relatives and friends who had migrated to the United States, and recalls that one of her nephews had also been recruited to work in upstate New York to pick strawberries and did not like the job. She immediately called her nephew in Buffalo, New York, who successfully finds Hernán and puts him in contact with his family.

In this story we see the medicinal methodology used by her grandparents to find their son. Mamá sifts through her own memories recalling stories shared by neighbors and family members in her search for a possible location for her son. However, it was the gaps filled by Papá's abilities as a spiritual healer, his vision of a particular place, which finally leads Mamá to her nephew in Buffalo, New York. Their combined skills as storytelling and spiritual healers succeed where legitimate authority figures such as lawyers, the police, or even the government fail to assist in the search for their son. Ortiz Cofer demonstrates the limitations of more established forms of evidence as represented by the officials Mamá turns to for help, and suggests the alternative methods used by her grandparents, as more effective in providing solutions and healing in moments of crisis. Her grandparents assert their own agency using their skills to find their son instead of remaining victims to the illegal labor recruitment and consequent labor oppression endured by their son and other Puerto Rican farm workers like him. Her grandparents are thus early role models for her in using medicinal methodologies and pass on to her their skills of listening, memory, and storytelling for healing purposes.

The Dangers of Forgetting

Although Ortiz Cofer recognizes the questions surrounding the reliability of memory as a source of history, a more pressing concern for her are the dangers of forgetting. Should the potential unreliability of memory eliminate it as one of many useful sources in the construction of historical narratives? Whose history do we risk forgetting if we don't use memory? In her poem "El Olvido" Ortiz Cofer captures and warns against the dangers of forgetting. The narrator speaks about the significance of remembering one's place of birth and "the voices of dead relatives," which represent the contextual foundation of one's history. Rejecting symbols of one's past such as clothing, and religious symbols, "the plaster saints before which your mother kneels praying with embarrassing fervor," in order to fit into a new place, what she calls a "forgetting place," alluding to the United States, is dangerous for it has the potential of resulting in a lonely death, disembodied from anything that connects one to community or history (68). Dying alone in a room "with no pictures on the wall," means dying anonymously, particularly if this room is located somewhere in the United States, where the experiences of Puerto Ricans have been silenced from dominant historical narratives.

Diana Taylor has studied the significance of photos to memory in her analysis of how these are used by two protest organizations in Argentina, the Mothers of Plaza de Mayo and more recently the HIJOS organization, which are the children of the disappeared. Both of these organizations have used the photos of their loved ones disappeared during Argentina's Dirty War in order to remember the existence and the "voices of their dead relatives." Not only were the bodies of these people disappeared, but government officials would also confiscate from their homes all photos in order to disappear all evidence of the person's existence. The Mothers of the disappeared would wear small photos of their loved ones around their necks during their marches, in essence turning "their bodies into archives, preserving and displaying the images that had been targeted for erasure" (177). The story of the disappeared in Argentina demonstrates the dangers of forgetting, where if the mothers and children of the disappeared had succumbed to the dangers of forgetting, the existence of thousands of political dissidents would have been erased from national memory. Ortiz Cofer's warnings against the dangers of forgetting therefore are part of a larger historical experience where colonization, imperialism, and repression have worked to erase our histories throughout the Americas, but have also been met with resistance.

The imagery of a lonely death as part of the Puerto migrant experience is also reminiscent of Pedro Pietri's classic poem, "Puerto Rican Obituary" where he also lamented the death of five typical Puerto Rican migrants in New York City whose life of survival in the margins of the metropolis result in pathetic deaths without ever experiencing the kind of affirmation that awareness of ones communal and collective history can provide. While Ortiz Cofer does not position herself within the Nuyorican poetic tradition, represented by Pietri and his generation of diaspora writers, she nonetheless follows similar common themes, documenting the traumatic impact of experiencing a marginalized and silenced existence in the United States.

When asked in an interview by Marilyn Kallet why "not forgetting" was important to her as a writer, Ortiz Cofer responds, "Many people of my parents' generation felt that if we assimilated, if we learned to live within the culture, it would be easier for us. I can see that as an economic survival technique, but as an artist I discovered that assimilation is exactly what destroys the artistic—to blend so well that you forget what makes you unique" (68). Thus, writing is both a way to remember and to challenge assimilation as the only answer to survival in the United States. In her poem she historically contextualizes the choosing of assimilation, represented by the replacing of past symbols in order to fit into one's new environment Yet, she also alludes to what is lost as a result of assimilation, an understanding of one's particular history. Her imperative as a writer, then, is to reclaim what has been lost.

Forgotten histories are the result of silencing the experiences and stories of Puerto Rican migrants. Ortiz Cofer addresses how Puerto Rican migrants are silenced in a number of pieces in her memoir including the titular essay, "Silent Dancing." The first time she evokes the imagery of silent dancing appears when she describes driving past cane fields and observing the cane workers. "I was distracted by the hypnotizing motion of men swinging machetes in the fields. They were shirtless, and sweat poured in streams down their backs. Bathed in light reflected by their blades, these laborers moved as on a ballet stage. I wondered whether they practiced like dancers to perfect their synchronicity. It did not occur to me that theirs was 'survival choreography'—merely a safety measure—for wild swinging could lead to lost fingers and limbs" (77). While on the one hand she recognizes the beauty of their synchronicity, as if they were on a "ballet stage," she quickly situates their movement within the context of their position as laborers for American sugar plantation owners. Their synchronized movements become "survival choreography" that ensures their safety and another day's earnings in their context as colonized subjects with limited economic agency. The beauty Ortiz Cofer sees in their movements is marred by the silenced and marginalized condition of the laborer's bodies. Her documenting of this memory however, is one way through which she challenges their silencing, juxtaposing the ingenuity in their survival choreography amidst inequitable labor conditions determined by the colonial economic relationship between the United States and Puerto Rico.

The performance of their survival movements represents the kind of embodied knowledge Taylor argues can't be found in historical archives but can only be found in the realm of the repertoire, the unwritten forms of producing and passing on of knowledge (20). The "survival choreography" Ortiz Cofer witnesses in the context of the cane fields along with the knowledge it imparts about the survival strategies that develop from the necessity of arduous labor conditions, is one that no archival document could have provided to her. As Taylor explains "[t]he repertoire requires presence: people participate in the production and reproduction of knowledge by 'being there,' being a part of the transmission" (20). Ortiz Cofer enacts the possibilities of both archive and repertoire by documenting within her, albeit partial, remembrance both the performance and its historical significance.

Ortiz Cofer further challenges the silencing of Puerto Rican migrant history in the titular piece, "Silent Dancing," where she juxtaposes her memories against the physical evidence of a silent family movie, featuring members of her Puerto Rican migrant family in New Jersey. The first image we come across in the silent movie is of three women, her mother, her cousin's girlfriend who recently arrived from the island, and her more Americanized girl cousin, all dressed in red. The girlfriend is shy and reserved in contrast to the Americanized cousin who is wearing a tight dress, has highlights in her hair, and smokes a cigarette. The author describes her mother somewhere along the continuum of Puerto Rican womanhood represented by these two women, "halfway between the poles they represent in our culture," referring to the opposing poles of the virgin/whore dichotomy (90). One of the key cultural tenets dictating women's roles is that of *marianismo*. As Maria Perez y Gonzalez explains,

> Traditionally, a Puerto Rican woman's identity is rooted in the function she plays in the family—housekeeping, childbearing, and child rearing. She is socialized to adhere to the cultural concept known as marianismo, which emphasizes virtues attributed to La Virgen Maria (the Virgin Mary): obedience submission, fidelity, meekness, and humility. The expectation is that women will remain virgins until they are married, after which they will bear children without any recourse to contraceptives and will show little interest in and enjoyment of sex—that is the function of a mistress or prostitute—una mujer de la calle (a 'street' woman). (19)

When migration and consequent Americanization are superimposed over these gendered definitions of Puerto Rican womanhood, a woman's value is measured by how closely she adheres to these traditional island definitions. Thus, in the film, the girlfriend who has just arrived from the island, with her shy and demure body language, represents the as yet untainted traditional Puerto Rican woman, the pure *Mariana*. The Americanized cousin on the other hand, with her more brazen look and demeanor, alludes to the "mujer de la calle." This woman engages in premarital sex, has no qualms sleeping with married men, and is generally perceived as a threat to the domestic and wholesome family life of the Mariana. Ortiz Cofer challenges this dichotomous definition of Puerto Rican womanhood by situating her mother in the middle of these two polar extremes, suggesting more of a continuum of Puerto Rican womanhood than two binary roles. As I will discuss later in this chapter, Ortiz Cofer further problematizes the virgin/whore dichotomy by giving agency to both women providing their own perspectives on their lives.

The men appear next in the movie playing dominoes in one corner of the room. "In 'Leave It To Beaver,' the Cleavers played bridge in every other episode; in my childhood, the men started every social occasion with a hotly debated round of dominoes" (92). Juxtaposing the image of the men playing dominoes against the image represented in the popular media of the idealized middle-class American family, Ortiz Cofer makes evident the nuanced ways the Puerto Rican migrants cultural experience does not fit into the American middle-class ideal. She further fills the gaps that are beyond the frames of the video with her own sensory memories of what cannot be seen, "[t]he thick sweetness of women's perfume mixing with the ever-present smells of food cooking in the kitchen" (94). At the end of the movie people are dancing in a circle, filing past the filmmaker. "It is both comical and sad to watch silent dancing. . .people appear frantic, their faces embarrassingly intense" (95). In an interview she explains why she chose this particular scene as the collection's title. "I chose *Silent Dancing* mainly because it went well with the idea of the silent movie and I thought it was both poignant and slightly absurd to see people dancing without music. To me that had symbolic meaning for the life of the immigrant. We are trying to recreate island life in a hostile environment. That's a crucial essay for me because it reflected the sort of sad paradox of the Puerto Rican in the city" (Kevane and Heredia 117). The silence of the people in the film juxtaposed against their awkward facial and body expressions captures the absurdity of Puerto Rican migrant life. On the one hand the festive environment recreated in this New Jersey apartment suggests agency in the migrants' attempts to hold on to their culture, with their domino playing and the mixed aroma created by the women's perfume and the Puerto Rican food cooking in the kitchen. On the other hand, their silence undermines their agency reflecting their actual marginalized conditions in the United States.[2]

Yet, the author refuses to leave them in their silence. She describes similar scenes haunting her dreams. "[F]amiliar faces push themselves forward into my mind's eye, plastering their features into distorted close-ups. And I'm asking them: 'Who is she? Who is the woman I don't recognize? Is she an aunt? Somebody's wife?'" (95). These "familiar faces" that are demanding to be seen and recognized in her dreams are reminiscent of the "dead relatives" she is forewarned not to forget in the poem "El Olvido." Those silent faces in her dreams and those in the film are disturbing reminders of the many silenced (his)stories that are clamoring to be told. While the images in the film remain silent, Ortiz Cofer (re)imagines a chorus of voices telling their own lives, thus liberating them from the constraints of their silence.

The Americanized cousin speaks at first confidently repudiating cultural traditions. "I do what I want. This is not a primitive island I live on. Do they expect me to wear a black mantilla on my head and go to mass everyday? Not me. I'm an American woman and I will do as I please" (96). While at first this appears as an assertion of her place in the Puerto Rican virgin/American whore dichotomy, the rest of her story problematizes the linear progressiveness insinuated by the cultural and gendered dichotomy where Puerto Rican womanhood is primitive and acquiring a more Americanized form of womanhood is deemed as progress. Another voice intervenes, that of "your great-uncle's common-law wife—the one he abandoned on the island to marry your cousin's mother" who tells a more gruesome reality of the Americanized cousin's story, a pregnant girl who aborts the fetus, "inserting something into herself" when she realizes that the father, "a teacher at her school with a house in West Paterson that he was filling with real children, and a wife who was a natural blond" would have nothing to do with her (97). Her dreams of being swept away by a white man into the mainstream American world removed far away from the so-called primitive island ways, are dashed as she finds herself situated as the "other," both as mistress and racialized "other." Ironically, the teenage girl is sent to a remote village in Puerto Rico where she becomes known as *la gringa*. "La Gringa, they call her . . . La Gringa is what she always wanted to be . . ." (97), mocks the narrating voice of her great-uncle's common law wife. In this scene we have examples of both traumatic memory and narrative memory as defined by Pierre Janet and discussed by Jacqueline Doyle in her analysis of *Silent Dancing*. Traumatic memory refers to "trauma locked in the body and manifested in physical symptoms, flashbacks, and nightmares" (Doyle 47). The trauma of being silenced that is captured in the absurdity of the silent film has also been part of the author's own experience and manifests itself in her nightmares of women silenced clamoring for voice. Ortiz Cofer is haunted by these images because they represent the dangers of forgetting that she is also subjected to. Michael Rothberg explains, a traumatic event is "an event that was not fully experienced at the time of its occurrence and that thus repeatedly returns to haunt the psyches of its victims" (12). In this case, however, we are not talking about a specific event such as the Holocaust in the case of Rothberg's study, but a collective trauma which results from being subjected to pressures of assimilation and the erasure or silencing that results as represented in the silent film. By giving voice to these women, including the voice of the great-uncle's common law wife, Ortiz Cofer employs narrative memory, "the ongoing resolution of trauma through story, witness, and contextualization" (Doyle 47). Ortiz Cofer narrates the lives of these otherwise marginalized women and through her narration seeks to heal the trauma of marginalization. She provides a testimony to these women's experiences, but as Felman and Laub argue in order to testify to traumatic experiences, "texts that testify do not simply report facts but, in different ways, encounter—and make us encounter—strangeness" (xv). Through her representation of the absurdity of the silent film and juxtaposing the multiple voices of the women in her nightmares, Ortiz Cofer creates just such an encounter.

This silent dance also recalls the "dance" of the cane workers whose simultaneous swinging machetes were a form of "survival choreography." She creates another form of "survival choreography" by writing their stories into a new dance, one that is not silent. Her memoir becomes the place where she creates a dance of words documenting the lives of Puerto Rican women as varied as the three women in red and a familial, communal culture upheld in the face of "Leave it to Beaver," retold in a Puerto Rican version. She therefore pulls partial remembrances, which together create both a healing and more accurate picture of Puerto Rican women's history.

In "The Looking-Glass Shame" Ortiz Cofer returns to the dangers of forgetting illustrating how the past symbolized by your ancestors, does not allow itself to be easily forgotten as it lingers, always haunting. She recalls Virginia Woolf's frightening experience when she looks into a mirror and sees "something moving in the background. . . . She never forgot that 'other face in the glass' perhaps because it was both alien and familiar" (124). She compares Woolf's experience with her own "cultural schizophrenia," constantly having to perform a cultural balance between the island and the mainland, and their respective definitions of cultural authenticity as either a Puerto Rican or an American. In her looking-glass shame, she is constantly haunted by her cultural "other." When she is in Puerto Rico she is haunted by her American cultural self, on the mainland it is her island "other" that appears over her shoulder. She remembers her mother and father while they lived on the mainland and wonders what their "others" looked like. Did they see the same shadows she saw in her mirror?

She recalls how her mother did not allow American cultural influences to come into the little island world she created in her apartment during their stays in Paterson. Her mother "kept herself a native" and "carried the island of Puerto Rico over her head like the mantilla she wore to church on Sunday" (127). Her mother preferred "the familiar noises of Spanish arguments and loud music" (64). In this unfamiliar and somewhat sterile environment, she would lapse into silence and anxiously wait for the call from the Navy that meant she would return to her beloved island for the rest of the year. Ortiz Cofer imagines that in her "looking-glass" her mother is haunted by the possibility of never returning home. She sees "another face, an old woman nagging, nagging, at her—Don't bury me in foreign soil" (128). Her father, on the other hand, was a man "who rarely looked into mirrors" (129). She wonders what he was afraid of seeing if he looked up while combing his hair. "Perhaps the monster over his shoulder was his lost potential. He was a sensitive, intellectual man whose energies had to be entirely devoted to survival" (129). Unlike his wife who desperately holds on to an island way of life, he does the opposite, distancing himself from Puerto Rican communities on the mainland, always struggling against being marked as "different." For instance, when searching for housing for the family when they moved to New Jersey, he found them an apartment "outside Paterson's 'vertical barrio,' the tenement Puerto Ricans called 'El Building.'" He had to convince the Jewish owner that they were not "the usual Puerto Rican family" (63). Her father's fair skin and unaccented English convinced people such as the Jewish landlord that he was different from the darker, and louder Puerto Ricans who lived in El Building. He brought his daughter along during these occasions, displaying her as a model child, always dressed "as if for church and held firmly by the hand" (63). Her father sought assimilation as a form of survival as she discusses in the interview referenced above. The "lost potential" that haunts him refers to the many paths not available to him as a Puerto Rican migrant man with limited options, regardless of his many efforts to inconspicuously fit into American society. Ortiz Cofer, on the other hand, is trying to find a balance between the two poles represented by her parents. Referring to this cultural balance as "cultural schizophrenia," however, suggests her own distinct traumatic experience as a consequence of striving to achieve such a balance. As Teresa Derrickson suggests the significance of this reference to "cultural schizophrenia" "is the admission that there are costly stakes involved in the process of navigating dual cultural identities . . . the toll on one's mental health can be considerable" (132). While the author follows this admission "suggesting that one's survival depends on one's ability to fit in: to pick up on the social 'rituals' of each territory and learn to play along" (Derrickson 132), she nonetheless demonstrates throughout her memoir that even this approach has a lasting and haunting impact that she is trying to heal, as she alludes to in her poem "Common Ground."

In this poem we finally see a glimpse of what the author sees in her own looking-glass.

> . . . I see
> my grandmother's stern lips
> speaking in parentheses at the corners
> of my mouth of pain and deprivations
> I have never known. I recognize
> my father's brows arching in disdain
> over the objects of my vanity, my mother's
> nervous hands smoothing lines
> just appearing on my skin,
> like arrows pointing downward
> to our common ground. (161)

The shadows lurking in the corners of her mirror are those of her ancestors who, as we saw in "El Olvido," continue to protect her from its dangers by becoming her constant "other," always reminding her of their common history. Following her grandmother's footsteps therefore, Ortiz Cofer uses her storytelling "powers" to heal the traumatic experiences of assimilation (like her father), isolation (like her mother), and her own cultural schizophrenia. Individual memory becomes communal as she carries their fears for them and transforms their experiences into a medicinal history.

Reinscribing National Memory

To combat the "forgetting" by United States mainland histories of its Puerto Rican subjects, Ortiz Cofer remembers historical events from particular Puerto

Rican perspectives. Similar to Nicholasa Mohr, she shifts the lens on certain historical events, focusing on the experiences of Puerto Rican women. In the chapter "Talking to the Dead," Ortiz Cofer remembers the many Puerto Rican migrant farm workers who faced dire conditions in their labor camps, through the story of her uncle Hernán who was recruited to do this kind of work in Buffalo New York. As discussed above, employing their own agency through their skills as storytellers and healers, her grandparents were able to find the location of their missing son who had been subjected to illegal labor recruiting methods. The author describes Hernán's labor conditions in the following way:

> The situation was very bad. The workers had been brought there by an unscrupulous farm worker who kept the men (most of them very young and unable to speak English) ignorant as to their exact whereabouts. They lived in tents while they waited for the fruit to be ready for picking. Though they were given provisions, the cost was deducted from the paychecks, so by the time they were paid, their salary was already owed to the grower. The workers were told that mail was not picked up there and it would have to be taken to the nearest city after the harvest. (35)

Many scholars have documented the experiences of contract laborers who were brought to various parts of the United States to do agricultural labor.[3] In New Jersey, for instance, workers were recruited by the Glassboro Grower's Association beginning in the late 1940s to work in numerous farms throughout that state. In one such farm in New Jersey, "Seasonal laborers are housed on the property [of] the farmer whose land he or she works, or, in some cases, in a labor camp run by a crew leader near the farmer's fields. Such labor camps are deep within the confines of the farm, obscured from view, and inaccessible except to the laborers and the owner. . . . The typical labor camp houses ten to fifteen workers. Some are little more than wooden shacks in total disrepair, while others are cinder block structures with bare cement floors" (Bonilla Santiago 17). We can see the similarities between Hernán's working conditions and those discussed by Bonilla Santiago about the farmworkers in New Jersey. These laborers are provided very little or inadequate information about the work they are agreeing to do. Agreements about working conditions and pay are broken. They live in isolated places and are completely dependent on the farm owners. Ortiz Cofer's memory of her uncle's experience inscribes the lives of workers like him, both men and women, into the historical memory of the nation. However, her narrative goes further by including the experiences of the families left behind, their anguish at not knowing the whereabouts or conditions of their loved ones, as well as their resourcefulness in challenging the inequitable conditions of the labor recruiting system that had been offered by the government as a response to the lack of economic opportunities on the island. Ortiz Cofer thus employs practices of centering the voices of the marginalized and showing agency in her account of these historical experiences of Puerto Rican migrants.

Ortiz Cofer also takes on the historical gaps in the narratives about war and whose experiences are typically highlighted. In "Black Virgin," Ortiz Cofer illustrates the experiences of women during the Korean War who had no other recourse but to sit at home, wait, and pray for their loved ones to return safely from war. During these years her pregnant mother stayed with her mother-in-law and sister-in-law awaiting the birth of her first child and the return of her husband who was serving in the Navy. In the meantime, the author's paternal grandmother, Mama Nanda, turns to her religious beliefs, which helped her feel she could protect her sons from afar. She makes a *promesa*, a "promise or vow," and "went to early mass every day at the famous Catholic Church in our town, the site of a miraculous appearance by the Black Virgin during the Spanish colonial period" (43). She climbed the one hundred steps to the shrine of the Black Virgin on her knees once a week, "along with other women who had men in the war" (43). Climbing those stairs gave her a sense of agency in a situation where she had no control at all. As the author states in an interview, "[i]n a world where women could not keep their men from going to war, could not save their sons, could not do anything else, they could still go upon their knees to a sanctuary and ask this powerful woman behind the throne, Mother Mary, to intercede for them" (Crumpton 102). By depicting how Puerto Rican women experienced the war, she not only fills the gaps of the historical narrative about the Korean War, but she also demonstrates how these women used whatever limited agency they had, given the colonial relationship between the United States and Puerto Rico, where they had no say on what wars (if any) their men would be involved in. Their turn to their religious beliefs brought these women some comfort, as their sons were God knows where fighting "in someone else's war" (Ortiz Cofer 44).

Among the many troops fighting in the Korean War, were the members of the 65th Puerto Rican Infantry Regiment. This unit has a long history of combat, dating back to 1899 when it was called the "Puerto Rico Battalion of Volunteers of Infantry" ("Puerto Ricans Now In Korea"). Although Ortiz Cofer does not specify whether her uncles were fighting as members of the 65th Infantry, through her story, she invokes the experiences of these Puerto Rican soldiers who again and again demonstrated their courage. One patrol of the 65th ran across an open field in order to draw enemy fire away from another regimental patrol which was "pinned down on the frozen bank of the Imjin River, with four men wounded and the escape route covered by exploding enemy shells" ("Puerto Rico Raiders"). The second patrol successfully escaped thanks to the heroic efforts of these Puerto Rican soldiers. Of the total U.S. army in Korea, eight percent consisted of Puerto Rican soldiers from the island. In addition, there were from "1500 to 2000 other Puerto Ricans attached to other U.S. divisions" ("Puerto Rico Officer"). By the end of the war the 65th came home with "four Distinguished Service Crosses and 155 Silver Star medals among the well over 900 combat awards and Purple Hearts" ("Army Set to Assign"). Mama Nanda's sons returned from war, wounded but alive. Her "knees bore the scars like medals received in many wars and conflicts" (Ortiz Cofer 46). Thus, Ortiz Cofer not only inscribes into national memory the experiences of Puerto Rican soldiers, but also counts among the casualties, the women who also sacrificed their sons, their peace of mind, and their knees to the larger war effort.

While she (re)inscribes historical moments from the perspective of Puerto Rican migrant women, she also problematizes mainstream historical methodologies, thus employing another of the tenets of the medicinal historian. In particular we see her problematize the limitations of photos as evidence of past events when she discusses her family's experience of the Cuban Missile Crisis. In the poem "Christmas, 1961" her mother aims a camera at her while she's dressed as an angel for a school Christmas play. The photo will be sent to her father, one of the many documenting the childhood he was missing during his deployments. The photos are meant as proof to the father that she was a well-cared-for and happy child. Marianne Hirsch, in her study of photography, argues that family photos serve to uphold particular narratives of the cohesive modern family. Family photos serve to uphold a particular ideal of family relationships. "The particular nature of the familial gaze, the image of an ideal family and of acceptable family relations may differ culturally and evolve historically, but every culture and historical moment can identify its own 'familial gaze'" (11). In the case of this childhood photo, the intention of the photograph is to capture the ideal of a happy childhood as evidence for her father that his absence has in no way negatively affected his daughter. However, Ortiz Cofer's poem goes beyond the frame of the photograph challenging the "illusion that photographs simply record a preexisting external reality" (Hirsch 51). As she describes in the poem, the photo depicted

> a fake angel
> superimposed on a fake Eden,
> as suspect as the hand-colored photogravures
> in National Geographics during the war years,
> showing "emerald forest and azure seas." (59)

The image is a deception attempting to create a narrative for the father that hid the reality of the fear and worry her mother was going through during this global crisis. Her mother held a letter in her pocket, reassuring her that what the world feared would not occur and she would once again see her husband. The author however remembers the not so innocent images in that child's mind of what might have been.

> "Look at me," she says, and I am nearly blinded
> by her radiance. That day she had swallowed the
> sun.
> I lower my eyes to the box camera aimed at me,
> and in the eye of the lens I can see
>
> a tiny world burning. (60)

She later recalls how this fearful event affected her family,

> That year our father returned to us a changed man too. The six months isolated on a ship circling Cuba—unable to communicate with us, frightened for our lives and for the world—had locked him inside himself. He had grown old. And I too had changed while waiting to know about my father, listening to the President speak about the "threat to the free world" from the grainy screen of our TV; pleading with

strangers to listen to me, a skinny Puerto Rican child; taking my mother from office to office: "Where is my father, her husband? Where is he?" (121)

Ortiz Cofer uses her poetic license to remember what this historical event meant to her as a Puerto Rican child in the United States, to her mother who didn't know for the duration where her husband was, and to the rest of Americans who feared the world would burst into flames. "Ortiz Cofer is able to combine 'how it felt at the time' to the child with the new historical perspective of the adult" (Doyle 224). She thus provides the poetic truth of both the historical event and the affective experience of her family.

Another similarity to Mohr's novel *Nilda*, is her shared concern over the role of educational institutions both on the island and in the United States in socializing children into national definitions of race. The author's schooling began in Puerto Rico during one of the many six-month periods her family spent on the island while her father was called away by his naval duties. Because of her status as the daughter of a military man, she was different from the rest of the students whose parents were mostly workers in the local sugar cane fields. She soon became the teacher's pet because of the teacher's own bias favoring her privileged status. Lorenzo was a fellow student who also vied for the special status of teacher's pet. Unlike the author, he was black and very poor. "His pants were too big for him—hand-me-downs—and his shoe soles were as thin as paper" (57). He achieved the teacher's special attention but only because he would do anything to be accepted. She recalls overhearing a conversation among her teachers who were discussing which student was better suited to host the upcoming PTA show. One teacher said of Lorenzo, "He is a funny negrito, and, like a parrot he can repeat anything you teach him. But his Mama must not have the money to buy him a suit" (58). The other teacher offers to lend Lorenzo one of her children's first communion suits, to which the first teacher responds laughing, "in that suit, Lorenzo would look like a fly drowned in a glass of milk" (58). Lorenzo's efforts to be a good student were overshadowed by his race and class position. The teachers decide to give the coveted role to young Judith since she could speak English and would therefore be able to say a few lines in both Spanish and English to please the American superintendent. When she goes home that afternoon she asks her mother what it meant "to be a 'mosca en un vaso de leche,' a fly in a glass of milk. Her mother laughs at the image, explaining that it meant being 'different,' but that it "wasn't something I needed to worry about" (58). Her mother's response situated the author as part of the racial and classed mainstream in Puerto Rico. She wasn't marked by the kinds of "differences" Lorenzo had, and thus wouldn't need to worry about racism or classism. However, when the family returns to the United States, young Judith finds herself having similar experiences of difference.

In "One More Lesson," she turns to Patterson, New Jersey, where they would spend the other six months of the year when her father would return from the sea. Enrolling in school in New Jersey always required an adjustment period as she reacquired her English skills having lost these during her tenure in the island. One day as she urgently needed to go to the bathroom, and the substitute teacher was across the hall tending to her other class, a fellow student misinformed her that the note the teacher had written on the board stated she could leave the classroom as long as she wrote her name on the board. She begins to make her way to the front of the classroom, when suddenly she feels a book striking her on the back of her head. "Startled and hurt, I turned around expecting to find one of the bad boys in my class, but it was Mrs. D. I faced. I remember her angry face, her fingers on my arms pulling me back to my desk, and her voice saying incomprehensible things to me in a hissing tone. Someone finally explained to her that I was new, that I did not speak English. I also remember how suddenly her face changed from anger to anxiety. But I did not forgive her for hitting me with that hard-cover spelling book" (66). Reminiscent of Nilda's racist experiences with her teachers, we see how as a Puerto Rican in the United States she embodies a similar kind of racialized difference as Lorenzo's black body held in Puerto Rico, albeit this time marked not only by physical but also by language differences.[4] By writing about her educational experiences both on the island and in New Jersey, Ortiz Cofer demonstrates that "[w]hile the systems differed as to the ways in which they normalized dominant ideologies of race, class, language, and social norms, both of the educational experiences offer evidence of the ways in which a colonial education was implemented among Puerto Ricans" (Aparicio 63). She therefore furthers Nicholasa Mohr's documentation and critique of the educational system as experienced by Puerto Rican migrants by demonstrating the continuity of some of these experiences between the island and the U.S. mainland.

In her memoir, Ortiz Cofer documents historical events such as the Korean War, and the Cuban Missile Crisis, as well as systemic discrimination endured by Puerto Rican migrants such as the recruitment of labor from Puerto Rico and the experiences of children in the colonizing educational systems of both Puerto Rico and the United States. In her documentation of these historical events, however, she goes further than traditional historical narratives, not only by centering women's experiences in her narratives, but also by problematizing the methodologies used to tell these histories. She incorporates the affective experiences of those impacted by these historical events into her narrative, providing both voice and agency to those who typically are excluded or invisible from the mainstream narratives about these types of historical events.

(Re)Inscribing Puerto Rican Gender Roles

Ortiz Cofer's challenges to historical methodologies continue in her depictions of how young Judith was socialized into gendered roles. She juxtaposes the lessons passed on through her grandmother and mother's storytelling with her own revisions of these stories. In "Casa," the author defines her grandmother's home as a space where the women gathered at the side of their matriarch and listened to her stories. These stories "were parables from which to glean the Truth," about what it means to be a Puerto Rican woman. She shares the story of "María La Loca" who was driven insane when she was left at the altar by her fiancée. Mamá told these stories for the benefit of the younger women in her audience who were waiting for their boyfriends to return from New York where they had gone with hopes of making a quick fortune and returning home, to marry their sweethearts. "That day Mamá told of how the beautiful María had fallen prey to a man whose name was never the same in subsequent versions of the story. . . . We understood that the name, and really any of the facts, were not important, only that a woman had allowed love to defeat her" (20). A significant element of remembering through storytelling is that the stories are not necessarily fixed. The stories can change and shift depending on when, where, and who is doing the telling. Shostak calls this element of storytelling, "transformation." "Memory and invention are the supreme authorities, and no version caries greater truth value than another" (Shostak 236–237). Along with Mamá's version of María La Loca's story, therefore, Ortiz Cofer offers her own alternative version. In the poem "The Woman Who was Left at the Altar" the woman is not the "character" she first remembers Mamá speaking of, who "walked and moved like a little girl," spoke to no one, and sold meat pies with her mother (17). Instead she is a woman aware of her womanhood, exposing her breasts in church "to show the silent town what a plentiful mother she could be" (22). Instead of meatpies, she sells live chickens, which she hangs from her waist, and takes symbolic revenge on the man who left her at the altar, every time she kills one of her chickens, taking the knife to him "time after time" (22). Ortiz Cofer transforms her grandmother's story to imagine a more empowering image of María La Loca where she has more agency. By transforming Mamá's version of Maria La Loca's story, Ortiz Cofer is resisting dominant forms of history through what Adrienne Rich calls "re-vision," "the act of looking back, of seeing with fresh eyes, of entering an old text from a new critical direction" (35). Ortiz Cofer thus revisits this old story with "fresh eyes" and re-envisions a version where even though the woman still suffers the social consequences of her supposed failure at marriage, she nonetheless does not remain the shy and quiet woman from Mamá's story but instead exposes literally and figuratively the injustices of a patriarchal system where a woman's value to the community is only measured by her roles as wife and mother.

Contrasting the story of María La Loca is the legend of María Sabida who cleverly tames the most vicious thief in town. María Sabida "watched the chief ladrón the next time he rampaged through the pueblo. She saw that he was a young man: red-skinned, and tough as leather. Cuero y sangre, nada más, she said to herself, a man of flesh and blood. And so she prepared herself either to conquer or to kill this man" (70). María Sabida challenges the power of men dismissively pointing out his humanity, just another man made of flesh and blood. She sneaks into the thief's lair, where no woman had set foot before, "no casa is this, but a man-place" (70). She infiltrates this man-place through the kitchen, convinces the cook that she is the thief's fiancé, and proceeds to cook a stew laced with sleeping powder. The men arrive and eat everything ravenously. When the thief learns of this deceit and runs to his bedroom where she awaited him, "María Sabida beat him with the paddle until he lay curled like a child on the floor. Each time he tried to attack her, she beat him some more. When she was satisfied that he was vanquished, María Sabida left the house and went back to town" (72). A week later the thief returns to town and claims María Sabida as his bride, but as she rides with him on his horse, she feels the blade hidden beneath his clothes and knows that her conquest isn't complete. While alone on their wedding night, she creates a life-sized doll of herself filled with honey. When the thief enters the bedroom he stabs the figure believing it to be his wife. "Honey splattered his face and fell on his lips. Shocked, the man jumped off the bed and licked his lips," and begins to cry with remorse, "If I had known she was so sweet, I would not have murdered her" (73). María Sabida comes out of her hiding place and her husband, overjoyed to see her alive, promises never to steal again. The irony of this story is in the location where Mamá tells it, under the mango tree located on "land that belonged to 'The American,'" owner of the sugar plantation where, as already discussed, the men of the town labor in exchange for their economic survival. By daring to trespass into this "forbidden" land and tell such stories as María Sabida around the mango tree (native to the land yet owned by foreigners) Mamá reclaims this space as a Puerto Rican woman's space, and symbolically returns the land to those cane workers whose sweat makes the land profitable for someone else. This story also provides another alternative to María La Loca. In this story the woman does not allow herself to be defeated by the patriarchy but instead uses its prescriptions of women's roles to her advantage. Entering through the kitchen, a typically defined female space, which Suzanne Bost defines as "the 'womb' of a feminine culture based on story-telling, female control, and domesticity," in order to begin her plan of conquest, she re-envisions the domestic sphere as one of power instead of submissiveness (201). By including the stories of these different Marías, Ortiz Cofer follows medicinal historical methodology, providing multiple perspectives to the established story of women's roles in Puerto Rican society. As Patricia Montilla explains in her reading of the María stories, Ortiz Cofer demonstrates how on the one hand the stories uphold gendered narratives of women's traditional roles. María La Loca suffers because she never married and was left at the altar, while María Sabida, although rebellious, is so within the traditional confines of marriage. However, by juxtaposing these two stories Ortiz Cofer "underscores . . . a woman's means of survival" using the limited agency they have within the patriarchal system (Montilla 207).

Ortiz Cofer not only problematizes the image of Puerto Rican women as submissive, but she further challenges the virgin/whore dichotomy dictating Puerto Rican women's sexuality. Here we return to the binary she alludes to when describing the three women in red in the silent film filled with haunting and familiar images. In "More Room" she challenges the role of the "virginal" wife as one who submits to her husband's sexual desires but is not allowed to enjoy her own sexuality. Mamá would always announce her pregnancies to her husband requesting that he add on another room to the house. After her eighth pregnancy, however, she "perceived that if she had any more children, her dreams and her plans would have to be permanently forgotten, because she would be a chronically ill woman" (27). She makes another request for a new addition to the house, to which her husband happily obliges assuming he was building a room for his ninth child. When he announces to his wife that the room is finished, she replies "good, it's for you" (28). "By claiming the bedroom—the epitome of intimate space—the grandmother achieves a degree of intimacy previously denied to her and her actions demythify the stereotype of the 'submissive' woman prevalent in Puerto Rican culture" (Moreno, "More Room" 440). Claiming a separate intimate space for herself was the only means of birth control available to a woman of her grandmother's class standing. "She gave up the comfort of Papa's sexual love for something she deemed greater: the right to own and control her body" (28). In this instance, the grandmother's sexual desire is acknowledged, contrasting the definition of the wife's role as one who submits to her husband's sexual desires but doesn't enjoy them herself. In a context where women's agency over their reproduction is limited, where women's reproduction was controlled by the government through sterilization, often times targeting poor and uneducated women and using deceptive methods to get them to agree to the operation, Mamá's sacrifice of her sexual desires for her husband in order to regain some control over her body, has significant implications.[5] Not only will she no longer succumb to unwanted pregnancies but she will also not submit to the government sanctioned methods for controlling her reproduction.

In her poems, Ortiz Cofer takes on the earliest socialization of young girls into the virgin/whore definitions of Puerto Rican womanhood. For instance, in the poem, "They Say," she describes how patriarchy immediately defines a girl's body as soon as she is born. She explains how on the day she was born, the midwives had to wrap her little body because she was bleeding from a mistaken cut in her umbilical cord. "The midwife sewed and the women prayed as they fitted me for life in a tight corset of gauze" (49). The Victorian image of the corset suggests that even though her birth takes place amidst a circle of women they are unable to protect her from patriarchal society. She follows this poem with another "moment of being," her fifteenth birthday. In the poem "Quinceañera," she describes the transition from young girl to young lady and the societal rules over this transformation. "I am to wash my own clothes/ and sheets from this day on, as if/ the fluids of my body were poison, as if/ the little trickle of blood I believe/ travels from my heart to the world were/ shameful" (50). She reclaims her blooming body as something beautiful, a gift, instead of a curse, as it is usually regarded. She further challenges the hypocrisy of patriarchy where women's blood is less valuable than men's. "Is not the blood of saints and/men in battle beautiful? Do Christ's hands/not bleed into your eyes from His cross?" (50). If the blood of men in battle or in spiritual sacrifice is considered beautiful, then why not the blood that indicates a woman's ability to bring life into the world. Through these two poems, Ortiz Cofer gives voice to young girls who experience the repressions of patriarchy through their bodies but rarely if ever have the opportunity to speak back against it, to vocalize the physical and emotional trauma endured in the process of being socialized into Puerto Rican womanhood.

Finally, Ortiz Cofer gives voice to the "whore" of the virgin/whore dichotomy through the characters of Fulana and Providencia, providing multiple perspectives for understanding those women who are maligned for undermining the defined role of women in a patriarchal society. Fulana is that woman young girls are warned about whose real name is never mentioned in their presence, and so her name is the generic "fulana." Yet in Ortiz Cofer's version of Fulana, she is not the promiscuous girl too mature for her own good. She is a liberated woman who grows up "careless as a bird, losing contact with her name during the years when her body was light enough to fly," (86) when she is young enough to claim her sexuality without a care in the world. But as she gets older and is pulled down by gravity "to where the land animals chewed the cud of domestic routine," (86) she loses her name and becomes "Fulana." Although Fulana is the one maligned by those land creatures, members of a society that disparage women who rebel against patriarchy, it is those impressionable little girls who we are left to pity. Following the proprieties of society will turn them into wingless birds who may never know "how the houses of their earth-bound mothers, the fields and rivers, and the schools and churches would look from above" (86). She takes her grandmother's lessons of claiming one's own body to another level, daring future generations to question societal views which turn women who assert their agencies and claim their own freedoms into pariahs.

While Fulana is a stand in for a particular female archetype, Providencia, was a woman who lived in her neighborhood in Paterson, New Jersey, who had many children, all from different fathers, and who was disparaged by the other Puerto Rican women in the neighborhood for her seemingly out-of-control sexuality.

"Providencia was the whispered joke told by women in their kitchens, she was the social worker's nightmare and a walking threat to the ideals of marriage and fidelity" (111). While she overheard the way other women in the neighborhood spoke about Providencia as the "desgraciada'—the woman who brings shame," she is nonetheless fascinated by the woman who appears oblivious to the criticisms of the other women. "Perhaps she was truly possessed of spiritual calm; her face usually wore the beatific smile I was used to seeing on the visage of Mary and other female saints in religious paintings" (112). Contrary to how the neighborhood women position Providencia, the author sees in her the epitome of the Virgin Mary, as the loving mother of so many children. Ortiz Cofer follows Levins Morales's curandera strategy of asking "what if" questions and fills in a plausible context for understanding Providencia's history in the poem "Why Providencia Has Babies." In this piece she (re)imagines a past filled with trauma, where as a young girl, "Providencia had been left alone/in dark, unheated rooms while her mother/worked the streets" (114). She proceeds to speculate on how this past might explain her current circumstances.

> I imagine her loneliness,
> tangible as breath on a cold night,
> and how she talked to the shadows
> Moved by streetlights. Perhaps the first
> time was a result of violence,
> and as she listened to her body's new pulse
> she felt less alone . . . When Providencia
> first felt the stirrings of life deep inside—
> below the ribcage, under the heart
> where a woman's soul nests—her life was resolved.
> She learned a lesson she would never forget:
> That as long as she lived,
> She need never be lonely again. (114)

In ways similar to Mamá's reclaiming of her body to no longer have any more children, Providencia uses the power of her reproduction to heal from the loneliness felt as a child giving birth to as many children as her body will allow. If her first sexual experience was indeed a result of violence and its subsequent result was her first pregnancy, she chooses to see the birth of that first child as a blessing instead of a cursed reminder of her abuse. She reclaims her body and sexuality from those that would use it to their own ends. This reimagining of Providencia's life and motivations creates an empathic picture of the "whore" who is as much a subject of patriarchy as the other women in the neighborhood who position her as their "other" in order to fit into the binary definitions of Puerto Rican womanhood.

In Search of More Accurate Truth: The Incident

The elements of a curandera historian's narrative are most evident in Ortiz Cofer's work in her constant revisiting of a particular incident from her childhood which comes to be known as "the incident." The event takes place during the celebratory party welcoming her father back after an extended period of absence while stationed in Panama. Just two years old, young Judith is placed inside the new crib her father has brought her to keep her safely away from the pit where a pig was being roasted. "The story varies with the telling and the teller, but it seems that I climbed out of my tall crib on my own and headed for the party in the backyard" (46). She prefaces the next sequence of events in the story stating, "I may have imagined this," shrouding a veil of suspicion over the accuracy of the memory she's about to narrate. "I see myself slipping through the crowd and into flames. Immediately, I am pulled out by a man's strong hands. No real damage: my abundant hair is a little singed, but that is all" (47). The details of this event become a source of contention between her mother and herself, as each remembers the events of the evening differently. "Did I sleep between them that night because my mother had finally realized that I was not a rubber dolly but a real flesh and blood little girl? When I ask, she says that she remembers only staying awake listening to me breathe" (47). While the adult Judith incorporates into her memories potential explanations as to why her mother allowed her to sleep in her parents' bed, which alludes to the youth and inexperience of her teenage mother, her mother "only" remembers the fear she felt about her daughter being harmed. Neither memory necessarily negates the other. The mother doesn't deny that she was young and inexperienced and perhaps was indeed recognizing the kind of responsibility she had now as the mother of a "real flesh and blood little girl." She simply doesn't acknowledge remembering this. However, what placing both "partial remembrances" together allows is for a more coherent understanding of both the events that took place that night and how these affected mother and daughter.

In "The Last Word," a more mature Judith revisits the details of "the incident" with her mother, fascinated "to hear her version of the past we shared, to see what shades of pastel she will choose to paint my childhood's 'summer afternoon'" (162). She questions her mother about the events of that evening, when her father returns after two years of absence. "I want my mother to tell me that what I remember is true" (163). That she did indeed fall into the pit of fire in order to get the adult's attention. But her mother shakes her head in denial turning to photographic evidence to refute her daughter's memory. "Does that look like a child who was neglected for one moment?" (164). The photos are from a birthday party her father had apparently spent a fortune on to throw for her, shortly after his return. Although everyone in her family seems to have photos from this event, which they all pull out as evidence of happy times, the author notes, "I am not smiling in any of these pictures" (164). To her mother, it is imperative that the photo serves its function, as discussed by Marianne Hirsch, of upholding the idealist image of a happy child, a happy family. However, Ortiz Cofer's observation of the unsmiling child suggests the location of the photograph as situated "between the myth of the ideal family and the lived reality of family life" (Hirsch 8). Furthermore, juxtaposing her memories against her mother's photographic evidence not only brings into question documented evidence as the sole source of truth, but by inserting her own interpretation of what she notices in the photographs versus what other family members notice, she suggests the subjectivity of interpretations of historical evidence.

In her mother's version of the story what fell into the pit of fire was not the child but a new book that the child had dragged and thrown into the pit. As "the Keeper of the past. As the main witness of my childhood, she has the power to refute my claims" (164). The mother has the power to cast doubts over her memories. Seeking some acknowledgement from her mother that at least her memory of being neglected that day was true, she asks her mother for her interpretation of her toddler's behavior. Her mother responds, "Why do children do anything they do? The fire attracted you. Maybe you wanted attention. I don't know" (164–165). Although hesitant, the mother does allow for the possibility that the child wanted attention, acceptance of which does implicate a certain level of neglect, however momentary, on the part of the mother and the other adults on that day. Here we see the particular pressure the family gaze of the idealistic family particularly places on mothers who are held responsible for the welfare of their children. "If there is a hegemonic familial gaze, imposing rigid familial ideologies, then mothers are most cruelly subjected to its scrutiny" (Hirsch 154). We can therefore understand the mother's hesitations. However, now she must contend with the now adult child who has acquired her own subjectivity and her own gaze through which to interpret not just the photographic evidence but her own memories. Ortiz Cofer ends the piece asking her mother if her version of the incident is indeed what really happened to which her mother responds, "Es la pura verdad" (165). But Ortiz Cofer has the last word, exclaiming, "but that is not how I remember it" (165). She therefore, illustrates both perspectives to demonstrate how the same event can be remembered and inscribed in history differently depending on one's standpoint. By juxtaposing both perspectives she offers a challenge to allegations made by traditional historians who hold on to hegemonic and complete notions of objectivity and truth.

Her final step in her challenge to historical narratives and methodologies appears in her closing poem "Lessons from the Past," a synopsis of her family's history from her particular perspective. Here she documents her memories of her parents without their individual memories present to refute her particular version of truth. She remembers her birth during the years when her father was at war, learning "to march in step with other men" (166). She remembers how her birth defined that young teenager that was her mother as a legitimate married woman with a child, economically privileged compared to those around her who did not receive military checks. Finally, this piece being the "last word" of the memoir, (re)inscribes her version of "the incident." In the poem however, she adds another memory, of her mother crying in the kitchen as she waited for her husband to return on some nights when he didn't. In the same way that she provides alternative readings of other women throughout her memoir, like Fulana and Providencia, she inserts another motivation for her mother's pastel-colored remembrances of her childhood, a possible avoidance of her own traumas as a young mother and wife. This poem being "the last word" also (re)inscribes her own final authority as the author of the text. She thus makes evident the power of those who are narrating history in dictating whose truth is told. However, because she has incorporated throughout the text prior to this final word, the multiple versions and voices of Puerto Rican women's historical experiences, her final word itself is really just one more version added to the collective history she has presented and thus fits Levins Morales's methodology of a curandera historian.

Conclusion

National historical memory has excluded the experiences of many groups of people of color. In the United States, writers of color are "increasingly confronting the need to construct alternative histories to those of the dominant culture in order to combat the appropriation and oppression of marginalized cultures" (Dehay 26). Writers of color use their literary narratives to resist the dangers of forgetting that this kind of appropriation and oppression creates. Furthermore, they respond to the consequent traumas that their erasure and silence has caused them.

In *Silent Dancing*,[6] Judith Ortiz Cofer responds to the trauma of the historical erasure of Puerto Rican women by taking on memory itself, with all of its complexities, and using individual and collective memories to create a medicinal historical narrative. Like Levins Morales, she connects individual experiences of trauma to the collective experiences of Puerto Rican women. She (re)constructs a poetic truth about Puerto Rican women's history that accounts for both their experiences during historical events and the affective impact of these events in their everyday lives.

Through this poetic truth she creates a medicinal historical narrative. She centers the voices of women in her accounts of events such as the Korean War and the Cuban Missile Crisis. She (re)inscribes agency to women whose historical roles might remain either invisible or prescribed as submissive. The oral dimension provided by poetry, in addition to her use of storytelling, serves to ground her memoir in a sense of collectivity. Using both poetry and prose in her memoir "allow[s] for a space of play, of disguise, of deception, of hiding and revealing, that enables one to speak the 'unspeakable'" (Glunta 85). Ortiz Cofer uses both poetry and prose to speak about that Puerto Rican migrant experience that has been virtually unspoken, the experiences of women.

She not only fills historical gaps but goes a step further, challenging historical methodologies. She juxtaposes questions about the reliance of memory with doubts about the reliability of documented evidence such as photographs. She provides multiple perspectives on events like "the incident" or on the binary definitions of women's roles such as the virgin and whore, and thus engages the reader in the process of interpretation leaving it up to us to decide which perspective to believe. Through these multiple perspectives she also makes evident the subjective role of the historian in their construction of their narratives, challenging any claims to objectivity. These methods of centralizing the voices of women, providing agency, and inserting multiple perspectives, are consistent with the methods of the curandera historian. Ortiz Cofer thus constructs a medicinal historical narrative, not only bearing witness to the experiences of Puerto Rican women but also "making the private public and situating her own traumatic experiences and those of her community within a larger context, as chapters in American history" (Doyle 217). Haunted by the dangers of "El Olvido," she rescues those whose experiences would otherwise have fallen into the abyss of forgetting.

Chapter 4

"DEGREES OF PUERTORICANNESS"

A Gendered Look at Esmeralda Santiago's *When I Was Puerto Rican*

In an interview with Carmen Dolores Hernandez, Esmeralda Santiago claims that her role as a Puerto Rican writer is "to document Puerto Rican culture, to convey a sense of that culture and of the Puerto Rican experience in the United States from many different angles" (168). She is interested in representing what she calls "degrees of Puertoricanness," a variety of ways in which Puerto Rican culture is expressed which considers how race, class, and gender identities influence ones' understanding and expression of Puerto Rican culture. Similar to Nicholasa Mohr, Santiago's impetus for writing was inspired by the lack of representation of Puerto Rican experiences in the literature she'd grown up reading. "There were no books about Puerto Rican girls living in Brooklyn struggling with language, a single mother, lots of sisters and brothers having dreams that people kept trying to squelch" (Santiago, "Conversations" 126). She sets out to create narratives centered on the lives of characters that are typically silenced in our national history. "It's one thing to feel that you don't belong. . . . But there's a whole segment of our population, of our humanity, that feels like they don't exist. That's what I felt when I came to the United States" (Kevane and Heredia 133). She thus aims in her work to make visible and vocal the experiences of Puerto Rican migrants like herself. However, given the critical debates about her autobiographical text, *When I Was Puerto Rican*, as an assimilationist text, what does it mean for Santiago, to assume the role of a Puerto Rican cultural historian?

Many critics have interpreted Santiago's memoir, with its past tense title and an ending that seemingly adopts the American dream tenet of lifting oneself by one's bootstraps, as evidence of the text's assimilationist narrative. Julia Watson offers a concise and effective summary of these critics' arguments.

> Some critics have questioned whether Santiago's autobiographical story can be representative of Puerto Rican experience and identity when the island-born author's assimilation to the mainland middle-class identity betrays the poor working-class women from whom she came. The sharpest criticism has come from feminists who assert that Santiago is a class-traitor for disavowing ethnicity in her narrative's title and for her success as a writer. The implication is that, because of education and authorship, Santiago cannot 'authentically' represent 'brown-and-down' Puerto Rican women faced with the issues of large families headed by unmarried women, sexual promiscuity, and harsh patriarchal rule. (131)

However, in this chapter, I illustrate how reading the text through the lens of a medicinal historian makes visible her critiques of hegemonic definitions of Puerto Rican culture that her own critics appear to ascribe to in their interpretations of her work.[1]

Santiago's approach in (re)presenting Puerto Rican culture as embodying a multiplicity of identities is a response to her cultural trauma and rejection by other Puerto Ricans living on the island. This occurs after retuning as an adult years after leaving the island as a teenager. Having her authenticity questioned, and thus her experiences as a Puerto Rican woman undermined through this questioning, she turned to her literary skills to create a medicinal cultural historical narrative that documents the intersectional reconstruction of Puerto Rican culture both on the island during the historical period of political and economic transition in the early 1950s, and in the United States as migrants begin to arrive in significant numbers. In both the island and New York, Puerto Ricans during this time period were experiencing the influence of Americanization as U.S. corporations industrialized the island and Puerto Rican migrants came into contact with American culture(s) in the belly of the beast.

Santiago problematizes the notion of a Puerto Rican authentic culture by demonstrating that the influence of Americanization doesn't begin upon migration, but that given the colonial status of the island, this influence is always already present in the island experience as well. As Lorna Perez explains, "Puerto Ricans are not Puerto Rican or American. They are always already Puerto Rican and American" (5). Through her culturally historical narrative she challenges the binary constructions of Puerto Rican culture between island and the United States mainland. Furthermore, she picks up Judith Ortiz Cofer's critique of the virgin/whore dichotomy discussed in the previous chapter and adds to her critique of Puerto Rican cultural construction a gendered lens by also problematizing binary constructions of Puerto Rican womanhood. As she has clearly asserted, she is "really interested in women's lives. . . . I write for women. . . . I'm very deliberate about that" (Hernandez 160). She parallels the tensions the virgin/whore binary creates for constructions of Puerto Rican womanhood to the cultural binary Puerto Rican migrants are subjected to between an "authentic" island identity or an Americanized Puerto Rican identity, and dismantles both by documenting and representing a more nuanced experience of Puerto Rican womanhood, where women have agency. She offers a spectrum of cultural and gendered identities offering alternative models than those posed by these binaries including models such as the *jamona*, the spinster, and the influence of media on the construction of Puerto Rican womanhood. I suggest that along the same lines as other Latina feminist writers and theorists such as Gloria Anzaldúa, Cherrie Moraga, Aurora Levins Morales, and Rosario Morales, Santiago offers a hybrid[2] and multi-positional definition of Puerto Rican womanhood, which accounts for how gender identity is mediated through culture. In this manner, she creates a medicinal historical narrative that transcends binary definitions, accounts for localized experiences, and centralizes the experiences of women.

Puerto Rican Culture

Puerto Rican cultural history has long been a source of contention among historians, politicians, and cultural anthropologists as a result of Puerto Rico's colonial relationship with the United States. Debates surrounding the definition of Puerto Rican culture have existed since the turn of the twentieth century as scholars as well as laymen and women have questioned "What is Puerto Rican culture?[3] Where does Puerto Rican culture end and American culture begin given American cultural infiltration in the island?" Moreover, as a marginalized and minoritized group in the United States, which consistently finds itself in between both U.S. and island culture, Puerto Ricans on the mainland have also engaged in the debate and question what exactly is "DiaspoRican" (Flores, "From Bomba") or Puerto Rican mainland culture. Since the 1970s Nuyorican cultural movement, DiaspoRicans have explored cultural definitions that account for their experiences in this interstitial space between the island and the mainland, particularly after experiencing rejection by islanders who accused them of being too Americanized. For instance, in "Nuyorican," the poet Tato Laviera shares his own experience of return and rejection stating,

> Ahora regreso, con un corazon boricua, y tú,
> Me desprecias, me miras mal, me atacas mi hablar,
> Mientras comes mcdonalds en discotecas americanas . . . [4] (qtd in Flores, "Divided Borders" 102)

He returns to the island feeling authentically Puerto Rican, expecting to be embraced by his brethren and instead is met with critiques about his authenticity. In the meantime, his critics succumb to the influence of commercial and cultural Americanization missing the irony entirely.

In a similar vein, Esmeralda Santiago explains her reaction in 1976 when, after receiving her degree from Harvard University, she returns to the island with the intent to stay. She finds that not only had Puerto Rico drastically changed in the thirteen years she had been away, but also islanders who questioned her Puerto Rican identity now rejected her. "Home was no longer home: Puerto Rico was so Americanized. That threw everything off for me, especially since Puerto Ricans kept telling me I was Americanized. I thought, how can puertorriqueños who have never left the island accuse us when they allow the American contamination I was seeing all around? There were McDonald's, Pizza Huts, and so on. I used to think this was not our culture. Big Macs are not our cultural legacy. We in the States at least have an excuse for being Americanized" (Hernandez 163). It was this experience where her now hybrid cultural self was coming into contact with the island culture that led to her eventual writing and titling of *When I Was Puerto Rican*. The title was a tongue and cheek response to the many islanders who rejected her for not being "Puerto Rican enough": "It was devastating to be denied an identity I had struggled so hard to uphold. It was especially difficult to understand why my own people challenged my sense of a self that was the only source of comfort when things were rough. When I titled my book in the past tense, I was answering those who disputed my right to call myself Puerto Rican" (Kevane and Heredia 131). The title was therefore meant as an invitation to the reader to look at her story and assess for themselves whether she was really Puerto Rican or not. The writing of the text was an exercise in trying to understand who she was as a Puerto Rican woman and who she has become as a hybrid "North American jíbara" (Santiago, "Cuando era" xviii).

Nicholasa Mohr described the separation between islanders and mainlanders as one "beyond language." As a response to those who question her writing in English she explains that the separation between islanders and mainlanders is not just in the different languages they write in but also in the differences of culture and experience. In a more recent interview she was asked if she thought that the relationship between island and mainlanders had changed. Mohr responded, "I think it's changing, but I don't think it has totally changed. It still goes beyond language. Last year when I went to Puerto Rico I was at a taller in the Ateneo [a cultural center on the island], when we brought up racism. The response was, what racism? People were not going to own up to the racism and the classism in Puerto Rico" (Kevane and Heredia 93). It is not just the difference in language but also a lack of understanding on the part of islanders of the experiences, culture, and history of those from the diaspora, in addition to the different class and racial identifications of islanders and DiaspoRicans, which separates the experiences of islanders from mainlanders.

Puerto Rican scholars such as Juan Flores, Frances Negrón-Muntaner, Ramón Grosfoguel, and Jorge Duany, have suggested more nuanced definitions of Puerto Rican culture which account for the cultural hybridity found in the island as a result of the cultural encounters and clashes among Taínos, Africans, and European immigrants, the historical relationship of colonization and its consequent addition of American culture to the already hybrid cultural mix, and the racialization of Puerto Ricans in the United States. As a result of these continued debates and mutual frustrations concerning the many facets of and influences on Puerto Rican culture, Puerto Rican cultural critics have expanded earlier cultural paradigms to account for the Diasporic experience. In *Puerto Rican Jam*, Frances Negrón-Muntaner, Ramón Grosfoguel, and Chloe Georas proposed "ethno-nation" as a more inclusive paradigm of Puerto Rican culture. As the authors explain, "it can be argued that to the extent that Puerto Ricans make political (territorial) claims on behalf of Puerto Ricans, Puerto Ricans constitute a national formation. At the same time, to the extent that a political claim is made on behalf of Puerto Ricans formally relinquishing state power, Puerto Ricans constitute a partially territorialized ethnic group" (17). Puerto Ricans oscillate between the two sides of the hyphen negotiating when to claim nationality and when to claim ethnicity. The authors have combined the ambiguous and dual identification of Puerto Rico (the island) as a nation and Puerto Ricans as an ethnicity in the United States to reimagine a diasporic Puerto Rican nation and its history without ignoring the actual colonial situation.

Juan Flores in *From Bomba to Hip-Hop*, expands on his earlier work and more precisely engages the hybrid nature of Puerto Rican culture, focusing on the musical and literary expressions of Puerto Ricans both from the island and the mainland. He establishes historical continuity between the various cultural elements of Puerto Rican culture from both the island and the United States. He illustrates the continuity for instance from plena and bomba (the African influence) to boogaloo and hip-hop (the Nuyorican influence). Puerto Ricans, in other words, already arrive "Americanized" when they get to the mainland. Rap music and its popularity on the island is one example of this kind of transnational cultural influence. Throughout his essays he alludes to several terms that could capture the more complex cultural construction of Puerto Rican identity such as the "diasporic transnation" (162) or one he borrows from poet Mariposa, "DiaspoRican" (187).

Jorge Duany has suggested the image of "la nación en vaivén," or "the nation on the move" to capture what he sees as a shift from political nationalism to cultural nationalism which includes the Puerto Rican Diaspora as a significant component of the Puerto Rican "nation." "I approach the construction and representation of Puerto Rican identity as a hybrid, translocal, and postcolonial sense of peoplehood" (Duany 5). Duany's work illustrates a change also in the way in which island intellectuals think about Puerto Ricans on the mainland and their place in the discourse on Puerto Rican culture. Although all of these scholarly works are significant interventions in creating a more inclusive conceptualization of Puerto Rican culture, they nonetheless leave many questions unanswered about the specific role of women in passing on and redefining Puerto Rican culture.

Virginia Sanchez-Korrol, for instance, briefly explored how the women who migrated prior to the Second World War, had a prominent role in maintaining Puerto Rican culture and ensuring that the children born and/or raised in New York were aware about their cultural identity. Turning to literary texts, such as those by Esmeralda Santiago, we can take Sanchez-Korrol's historical work further and explore how Puerto Rican culture is not just passed on as a whole by migrant women or received as a whole by their daughters, but how renegotiations and redefinitions occur during the transmission of culture from one to the other. Santiago's work, when looked through a feminist lens, can expand the discussion of Puerto Rican cultural history as it illustrates and theorizes Puerto Rican cultural experience from a particular gendered perspective. As seen in the case of Chicano history, the theorizing available in Anzaldúa's hybrid literary work provides the unique historical perspective of Tejana women, which has not been captured or documented by Chicano historians. In her poem, "We Call Them Greasers," Anzaldúa documents the gendered effect of lynch laws in nineteenth century Texas, where the white narrator rapes a Mexican woman in front of her husband in order to further humiliate and terrorize the Mexican man who he then lynches. As Saldivar-Hull states, Anzaldúa "finds the words that acknowledge the history of violence against the Tejana. This history includes rape as institutionalized strategy in the war to disempower Chicano men" (215). Feminist critics like Anzaldúa have proposed more complex paradigms for understanding how Latino culture(s) are defined, lived, and expressed within and against mainstream hegemonic culture. She counters oppositional and binary options with more hybrid and multivocal paradigms. Through her theory of the "new mestiza consciousness" she suggests that the answer to cultural empowerment and cross-cultural healing and understanding lies in leaving "the opposite bank, the split between the two mortal combatants somehow healed so that we are on both shores at once" (Anzaldúa 378). For Latina women who must negotiate their gender identities through their hybrid cultures this means, "break[ing] down the subject-object duality that keeps her a prisoner and to show in the flesh and through the images in her work how duality is transcended" (Anzaldúa 379).

Similarly, Santiago approaches the Puerto Rican cultural divide by suggesting a transcending of boundaries constructing a healing historical narrative that proposes a more holistic cultural identity for DiaspoRicans. In the same manner in which she suggests that Puerto Rican cultural hybridity begins from the island and does not occur only with migration, she also demonstrates that Puerto Rican womanhood transcends the dual gender roles culturally ascribed to it and offers a (re)construction that is more nuanced and complex, "merging ... the woman she was supposed to be [the protagonist] and the woman she has become [the author/narrator]" (Morales-Diaz 136).

Esmeralda Santiago's Puertoricanness

According to Peter Burke, a cultural historian is concerned with "the symbolic and its interpretations" which can be "found everywhere, from art to everyday life" (3). While histories of culture from art to literature have always existed within the historical field, the interest in culture was significantly galvanized by the anthropological concept of "thick description" by Clifford Geertz. The role of the ethnographer according to Geertz is to present his or her interpretations of the meaning of the various cultural symbols they study. Thick descriptions of these symbols, where multiple meanings and possible interpretations of the same symbol are presented, result in more nuanced and fuller understandings of different cultures. Historians turned to studies of everyday life and cultural symbols as a way to gain such fuller historical understandings about a people, country, or time period. This cultural turn by historians was also their "reacting, consciously or unconsciously, to changes in the wider world, including the loss of faith in progress and the rise of anti-colonialism and feminism" (43). Thus, cultural histories are narratives that problematize universalist histories not only by turning the historical lens onto those cultural groups that have been excluded, but also by expanding the definition of the historical archive to include elements of everyday life such as customs and traditions. In Santiago's autobiography, we see elements of the cultural historian at work in both her meticulous descriptions of cultural traditions, but also in her documenting of the cultural transitions experienced by Puerto Ricans in the 1950s as the island endured its modernist transition from an agricultural to an industrialized economy and the consequent migrations to the United States.

Operation Bootstrap entailed the rapid industrialization of the island creating a tax haven for American corporations on the island with the promise of a significant increase in jobs. This economic shift resulted in internal migration in Puerto Rico from the rural parts of the island to the urban areas as workers sought opportunities in these new factories. As Gina Perez discusses in the *Near Northwest Side Story*, this economic shift also resulted in a devaluing of agricultural work in favor of industrial work. Architects of this economic plan however understood that industrialization alone would not address the economic problems of the island. A simultaneous reduction in the work force was necessary in order for the economic plan to be successful resulting in a massive migration to the United States. Concerns over the cultural impact of these economic shifts led to the creation of Operation Serenity, where cultural administrators endeavored to (re)construct a folkloric definition of Puerto Rican culture centered around the image of the *jíbaro*, the peasant dweller whose livelihood was in actuality being undermined by the economic modernization of the island. Santiago's work documents these economic and cultural shifts in ways that no other historical narrative has been able to capture, depicting the everyday impact of these changes on Puerto Ricans both on the island and in New York after her family migrates. As Marisel Moreno explains, "one of the greatest contributions of Santiago's text is that it offers a window into the life of a rural family precisely during a period in which rural communities were not only undergoing significant transformations as a result of Operation Bootstrap but were also being model into the icon of puertorrqueñidad through Operation Serenity" (118). She incorporates both a desire to uphold customs and traditions while problematizing static notions of Puerto Rican culture. While on the one hand she seems to uphold a romantic notion of the jíbaro, critiquing the modernization of the island that slowly dismantles the jíbaro way of life, she also expands the image of the jíbaro through her gendered and hybrid (re)construction of a North American jíbara identity for herself. By taking a masculinist cultural icon and (re)inscribing it as a woman, she follows the medicinal methodology of centering women into national narratives.

Santiago's thick descriptions begin with her prologue where she describes coming upon a guava, a fruit from her youth, in a suburban supermarket in the United States, which leads to her memories of picking and eating these fruits in the countryside of Puerto Rico. "A ripe guava is yellow, although some varieties have a pink tinge. The skin is thick, firm, and sweet. Its heart is bright pink and almost solid with seeds. The most delicious part of the guava surrounds the tiny seeds, if you don't know how to eat a guava, the seeds end up in the crevices between your teeth" (3). She establishes herself as the cultural expert and proceeds to provide tips and tricks on how to appropriately eat a guava, whether it's a sweet ripe one or a more sour and hard green guava. She shares knowledge that only an insider would know. "The narrator's 'authenticity' as a representative Puerto Rican is thereby asserted: she embodies knowledge of the island's sensory richness that those born on the mainland, even Boricuan [sic] descendants, cannot access" (Watson 133). However, instead of purchasing the guavas at the supermarket she instead replaces the guava with "its sisters under the harsh fluorescent lights of the exotic fruit display. I push my cart away, towards the apples and pears of my adulthood, their nearly seedless ripeness predictable and bittersweet" (4). This prologue, along with the past tense of her title, has been used as evidence of her narrative being assimilationist. She rejects the guava of her youth for the American fruit of her adulthood. However, instead I believe that the prologue previews the cultural critiques in the rest of her narrative where the guava's appearance in the American supermarket as an "exotic fruit" removed from its natural environment of the island serves as metaphor for the experience of Puerto Rican migrants who have been uprooted from the island. The guava in the supermarket cannot be known in the same way that she knew it while on the island because it is now removed from its cultural history, in the same manner that Puerto Ricans cannot be completely understood without first knowing the historical narrative that explains their contemporary (re)constructed cultural selves. Furthermore, her description of the American fruits of her adulthood as "predictable and bittersweet" alludes to her experience of Americanization after migration one that we learn by the end of the narrative, was filled with bitter moments regardless of the apparent success she achieves.

Throughout the text Santiago prefaces her chapters with traditional Puerto Rican sayings first in Spanish and then translated into English. This is one of the many methods she employs in documenting Puerto Rican cultural traditions.

She prefaces her opening chapter with the saying "Al jíbaro nunca se le quita la mancha de plátano," meaning that a jíbaro, no matter how much he or she may change, always has some residue of their jíbaro roots attached to them. This chapter tells the story of her family's first move to the rural town of Macún, where she first learns about and embraces a jíbara identity for herself. Thus, she insinuates with the prefacing saying that however much she may change throughout the rest of the narrative her roots are those of the Puerto Rican country dwelling jíbaro.[5] She learns from her father what it means to be a jíbaro, listening to the traditional music played on his radio as he worked on their modest rural home. "Although the songs and poems chronicled a life of struggle and hardship, their message was that jíbaros were rewarded by a life of independence and contemplation, a closeness to nature coupled with a respect for its intractability, and a deeply rooted and proud nationalism. I wanted to be a jíbara more than anything in the world, but Mami said I couldn't because I was born in the city, where jíbaros were mocked for their unsophisticated customs and peculiar dialect" (12). In this passage young Negi asserts her agency claiming for herself an identity as a jíbara. However, she immediately experiences what will become the first of many cultural denials and rejections of her agency, as her mother denies her claim because she was born in the city, where the customs of the jíbaro are disparaged. Perhaps it is this denial of her identity that inspires Santiago to want to document the customs and traditions of the jíbaro in her text, to counter and critique the internalization in the island of modernist ideals that would define the jíbaro as backward in the progressive narrative of industrialization of the time.

Another critique imbedded in her depiction of the jíbaro, is her definition of the jíbaro's livelihood as one filled with a sense of independence and patriotism, something that she later argues in her previously quoted interviews, is missing in the contemporary modern Puerto Ricans who would in a sense sell out the island to American consumerism represented by global corporations, like McDonalds. Thus, in her documenting of jíbaro traditions, her text functions both as "a counter-narrative to official histories of the island and a record of a pre-consumerist kind of ethnic culture now vanished from an island where McDonald's and Subway fast-food stores abound" (Watson 131). She therefore, follows the medicinal tenet of providing alternative narratives to the existing ones.

In contrast to the impending fast-food stores that would soon begin to appear throughout the island, Santiago's text offers detailed descriptions of fruits and vegetables growing in abundance in her rural surroundings as well as in-depth illustrations of food preparations including traditional Christmas meal of pasteles, pig roasts, and homemade rum (40). When one of the local jíbaros (Don Berto) dies, she portrays the customary Puerto Rican wake and funeral procession where the whole community contributes to the event. "Most of the barrio's women had put in some time dusting, washing the floors and walls, sprinkling agua florida all over, positioning wreaths, bathing Don Berto and laying him out in his box" (50). While her father served as the rezador, who leads the mourners in the rosary prayers and the children lead the procession to the cemetery where Don Berto is finally laid to rest. She also depicts traditional superstitions such as the belief that bathing in the first May rain brings good luck as her mother rushes all of the children outside singing the schoolyard song "Que llueva, que llueva!" (59).

Following the many break ups between her mother and father, the family would move to the urban area of Santurce, "which by the early fifties, had become as much a metropolis as the capital" (37). It is during these momentary periods in urban spaces that Santiago most clearly critiques the complicity of islanders in the modernization of the island, juxtaposing how Negi is perceived and experiences the urban spaces against her preferred environment of the rural area of Macún. While they lived in poverty in their rural home, their economic condition wasn't necessarily improved through urbanization. In the city they live in small cramped spaces, surrounded by the filth of poorly built sewer systems and the noises of overcrowded city streets (37). In school she was singled out "for my wildness, my loud voice, and large gestures better suited to the expansive countryside but out of place in concrete rooms where every sound was magnified and bounced off walls for a long time after I'd finished speaking" (39). Although her behavior and demeanor in the city are perceived as backward and indicative of her jíbara status, as a girl, to have a loud voice and the freedom of expression of her body that her rural experience has afforded her is significant for these are the seeds that will allow her later to question and challenge the prescribed gendered norms of a proper Puerto Rican woman. The school children would hurl the label "jíbara" at her as an insult when she hadn't heard about Santa Claus, or didn't know how to use a pencil sharpener, or when she wasn't able to do fractions because her rural school had not covered the subject yet. As she stands in front of her classroom while being admonished by the teacher for coming from one of those "jíbaro schools" whose curriculum is "always so far behind. That's why we have so many ignorant jíbaros" (139), she employs the common method we saw used in *Nilda* whenever a traumatizing embarrassment was experienced, she left her body. "I sent the part of me that could fly outside of the window to the flamboyán tree in the yard" (139). She craves the solace that she could always find outdoors in her rural environment.

Through Negi's experience in the city, Santiago also illustrates the class differences urbanization was creating between those from the cities and those from the countryside. As Negi walks home she passes by cement houses with enclosed porches and gardens, so different from her wooden house in Macún or her one room house on stilts in the city. "Girls from my school walked in groups ahead of me, and one by one they went into these nice homes where mothers, dressed in simple skirts and blouses, with hair neatly combed, no paint on their faces, waited by the door and closed it lovingly after their daughters. Once one of them smiled at me, and I was so grateful I wanted to run into her arms and be swallowed by the ruffles on her blouse. Another gave me a dirty look, as if I had no right to walk on her neat street" (140). In contrast, in her home, no one waited for her. Her mother had to work to provide for her children. When she couldn't find employment, she improvised ways to earn income while caring for her children including taking in laundry, cleaning others homes, or cooking meals to be sold at a nearby bar. Thus, "Santiago's story reveals the hardships that the poor, rural, working classes faced as they tried to make a living under deplorable economic conditions. The poverty faced particularly by female single-headed households, as Santiago's texts illustrates . . . serves to demythify life on the island (rural and urban)" (Moreno 125). Santiago challenges the mythified version of the jíbaro created by political and economic administrators who sought to uphold a hegemonic and masculinist version of Puerto Rican culture portraying the jíbaro as a white male peasant. While some critics, such as Lorna Perez, have argued that Santiago upholds a similar romanticized version, I join other critics such as Marisel Moreno, who instead argue that Santiago is positing a more nuanced version through her gendered portrayal. She instead depicts the jíbaro lifestyle as that of a community of men and women who navigated shifting economic and cultural changes during a time of significant uncertainty and posits the jíbaro lifestyle as one of the many degrees of Puertoricanness. Her more nuanced representation of the jíbaro lifestyle as well as of class differences among Puerto Ricans serves both to fill historical gaps as well as challenges linear historical narratives of progress and modernization, two strategies of the medicinal historian.

The impending threat of Americanization on the island and on the way of life of the jíbaro is most evidently depicted in the chapter entitled "The American Invasion of Macún." The "invasion" comes in the form of the community center where American government officials would conduct workshops on various subjects such as health, hygiene, and nutrition "so that we would grow as tall and strong as Dick, Jane, and Sally, the Americanitos in our primers" (64). As Marisel Moreno explains in her analysis of this chapter, Santiago's childhood years overlap with the active years of the División de Educación de la Comunidad (DIVEDCO), which launched educational programs including publications, posters, and community meetings, targeting rural populations to teach "about hygiene, eliminate superstition, and create a new democratic citizenry" (118). The use of white American role models as those depicted in their school primers is just part of the Americanization imbedded in their education as seen in the opening of the chapter where Negi is learning English phonetically in her rural school. It is in her English class where the announcement regarding the communal center workshops is made, making evident the connection of the center to the broader Americanization project on the island.

Women arrive on the day of the workshops with their children in tow, much to the surprise of the government officials who had not prepared for the presence of children, illustrating the disconnection between the officials and the realities of the community. The first lesson was about proper teeth brushing. In response to the elaborate demonstration where the official illustrated how to clean and polish each tooth, one of the women exclaimed "If I have to spend that much time on my teeth. . . . I won't get anything done around the house" (65). Her response demonstrates the lack of relevance of the lessons to their everyday realities. While the government official uses his paternalistic tone suggesting he knows what is best for these women and their families, her response asserts her localized and gendered knowledge of her everyday reality. "The condescending attitude of the American delegate reflects the dominant posture adopted by the U.S. government over Puerto Rican internal affairs. At the same time, the presence of Puerto Rican men from San Juan . . . conveys the ideology of paternalism" of the existing government and its collusion with the Americanization and colonial project (Moreno 123).

During the nutrition lesson, presenters illustrated an American chart of appropriate nutrition with images of fruits and vegetables that were nonnative to the island, as well as appropriate portions of each type of food they should be having at each meal. They fail to address however structural issues such as availability and affordability of such foods for these rural families. Women once again express this disconnect as they question the presenters about local substitutes that could be used instead of those depicted on the charts. Flustered by their questions one of the officials responds, "it is best not to make substitutions for the recommended foods. That would throw the whole thing off" (67). He failed to realize that the system was already "thrown off" by its imposition of an irrelevant definition of good nutrition. Through these scenarios of the women's resistance Santiago "gives us a group portrait of women who question North American preconceptions about the universality or indeed the desirability of the 'dream' they are attempting to export for the benefit of the underprivileged in their Caribbean colony" (Stephens 37). Similar to Mohr, Santiago refuses to depict these women as passive victims to their circumstances, but instead demonstrates their agency, unwilling to be intimidated by the authoritative presence of these men, juxtaposing their own knowledge as experts in their everyday lives.

At the end of the meeting each family is given a sack of canned and processed foods, samples of those presented in the nutritional chart, whereas a sack of rice and beans would've been preferred and would have actually made more of a difference, keeping "this family fed for a month" (68). Back at home the mother placed each item, "two boxes of cornflakes, cans of fruit cocktail, peaches in heavy syrup, beets, and tuna fish, jars of grape jelly and pickles," on a high shelf as emergency food. They would eat "like Americans when hunger cramped our bellies" (68). One by one eventually the items made their way off the shelf as their poverty, which was ironically dictated by the impact of American economic infiltration on the island, would require the family turn to these emergency foods from time to time.

Schools would continue to function as venues for Americanization, this time through the vaccination program. Children lined outside the new school nurses' room, apprehensively waiting their turn as they saw children coming out of the nurses' office in tears, holding a wad of cotton to their arms. It is in this line where Negi first hears the word "imperialist." One of the other children, clearly repeating adult conversations he's overheard, tells Negi that the reason for all of these new programs was political because it was an election year and as soon as the election was over the programs would end. Speaking about the president of the United States, the child uses the word "imperialist" to describe him "just like all the other gringos" (71). Shocked by the use of such a loaded word, Negi turns to her father for an explanation. Her father explains that imperialists means, "they want to change our country and our culture to be like theirs" (73). Connecting the dots between all of her recent experiences she realizes that the English lessons she's learning in school, the lessons at the community center, and the food she's being offered through the new free breakfast and lunch programs, are all part of the imperialist project of Americanization. We see how from an early age Negi not only understood the cultural shifts being imposed on the island but was also resistant to them, as becomes evident in her final encounter with American food. The quality of the food offered at the community center had begun to diminish and by her final breakfast meal they were merely serving a lump of peanut butter in a glass of milk. When Negi attempts to drink it she gags, drops the glass and spills the disgusting concoction all over herself and the floor. When one of the workers reprimands her for criticizing the food as repugnant and says "I suppose you'd find it less repugnant to go hungry every morning," Negi makes her anti-imperialist stance screaming "My Mami and Papi can feed us without your disgusting gringo imperialist food!" (82). She runs home and proceeds to spend the following days sick "throwing up, racked by chills and sweats" (83). Her body's violent reaction metaphorically rejects its invasion by the repugnant imperialist food that as we've seen throughout the chapter is unnatural to the Puerto Rican social and physical environment. Her bodies reaction is an embodiment of the agency and resistance that we have seen throughout this chapter emanating from the father's explanations of imperialism, to Ignacio's young and seemingly innocent repudiation of the political interests behind the various programs offered, to the women's spoken challenges against the Americanization lessons. Santiago illustrate in this chapter that migration isn't necessarily when the Americanization of Puerto Ricans begins, but is instead, as a direct impact of the island's colonial status, always already taking place on the island. She also demonstrates pockets of resistance to this Americanization and in this manner calls into question those that would now critique her for her supposed Americanization for their own lack of resistance to the Americanization evident on the island itself.

The Americanization of Puerto Ricans is further problematized when the family moves to New York City. Santiago has described her departure from Puerto Rico as a traumatic experience, an abrupt uprooting, or a "psychological violence," as Marisel Moreno argues, where who she understood herself to be changed seemingly overnight (120). In interviews she has recounted one of the earliest experiences she has after arriving to New York where she learns from another Latina child that she is now Hispanic, that all Latinos regardless of where they come from are Hispanic in the United States. "It was a shock to me that just by coming over from Puerto Rico to Brooklyn I had ceased being who I was" (Santiago, "Conversations" 122). In trying to determine who she was now becoming culturally she navigates through the multiple cultures she encounters in the city, while simultaneously trying to hold on to remnants of her jíbara self. As she states at the end of the chapter as she's about to embark in her new journey, "[f]or me, the person I was becoming when we left was erased, and another one was created. The Puerto Rican jíbara who longed for the green quiet of a tropical afternoon was to become a hybrid who would never forgive the uprooting" (209). This process of becoming a cultural hybrid is what she documents in the last chapters of her memoir.

The rejections she experiences when she moves in the island from her rural home to the urban town of Santurce, are exacerbated in New York as soon as she arrives. Rejections in New York are not only based on regional or class-based differences, but become racialized as well, as she immediately experiences racism. As the family tries to find transportation to their new home in Brooklyn, multiple taxi drivers reject them. "The first one looked at us, counted the number of packages we carried, asked Don Julio where we were going, then shook his head and drove along the curb toward a man in a business suit with a briefcase who stood there calmly, his right hand in the air as if he were saluting. . . . The second driver gave us a hateful look and said some words that I didn't understand, but I knew what he meant just the same" (216). Her family is dismissed in favor of a business man, whose privileged social position allows him a calm demeanor, sure of his entitlement to speedy transportation, whereas the family appears as the semblance of excess, too many people, too many packages. Along with the hateful look and disparaging words of the second driver, Negi experiences viscerally her othering in New York as a Puerto Rican female migrant child.

Living conditions lack improvement over those experienced in Puerto Rico. Small, crowded, and "stifling" living quarters along with the "steady roar" of the cacophony of city noises outside only adds to her sense of isolation and confinement. A sense of settling eludes the family as they constantly move from apartment to apartment either in search of slightly better conditions or more affordable livelihood. In addition, the family also shifts from a nuclear one consisting of, either both parents or just the mother and the multiple children, to an extended family model that at different moments includes the maternal grandmother, her partner Don Julio, and an uncle.

Attending a school whose demographics include Puerto Ricans, African Americans, Italians, and other whites, Negi soon realizes that there is no one hegemonic American culture to learn, but a multiplicity of cultures and cultural hierarchies through which to navigate. "There was a social order that, at first, I didn't understand but kept bumping into. Girls and boys who wore matching cardigans walked down the halls hand in hand. . . . They were Americanos and belonged in the homerooms in the low numbers" (16). The "bold girls" who wore makeup and short skirts were the Italian girls. Opposing the Italian section of the school cafeteria sat the African American students. She'd learned from her mother that these morenos were not like black Puerto Ricans. "They dressed like Americanos but walked with a jaunty hop that made them look as if they were dancing down the street" (225). In school, the tensions between Italians and African Americans was one Negi tried to avoid, fearful of the repercussions if she was assumed to be allying herself with either side. Among the Puerto Rican students she also deciphered the existing divisions between those that were recent arrivals from the island and those that were born and raised in the United States. Among the recent arrivals there was also a split between "the ones who longed for the island and the ones who wanted to forget it as soon as possible" (230). The cultural hybrid she evoked earlier begins its formation as she navigates through these multiple cultural groups. She tries on the hairstyles of the Italian girls, practiced walking like the African American kids, while guiltily enjoying learning English and "liking pizza" (230). Negi's Americanization experience is not a hegemonic one. She tries on cultural elements from all of the groups she encounters, picking and choosing those that best fit into the hybrid self she is actively constructing.

In addition to broadening the definition of the Americanization process experienced by Puerto Rican migrants in a diverse city such as New York City, she also challenges the narrative of progress attached to migration. As explained earlier, in order for the industrialization plan to be successful in Puerto Rico, massive migration from the island was also encouraged. This entailed creating a narrative that emphasized the many economic opportunities available in the United States, which promised a better economic future. As Gina Perez explains, the prevalence of this narrative of progress through migration created a *fiebre*, or "migration fever," where many islanders abandoned their homes and jobs in search of a better future. Yet, as we see through Negi's experience, conditions do not improve significantly beyond what they were when they lived on the island. Her mother finds employment in a garment factory, based on her experience in this type of work on the island. However, in New York she had to start at a lower level as a "thread cutter, even though in Puerto Rico she had been a machine operator" (245). She carried her scissors for her garment work in her coat pocket for protection as she walked through dangerous parts of her neighborhood. In New York there were threats to their wellbeing as well as humiliations suffered that did not exist for them in Puerto Rico. When the mother was laid off from work, she would go to the welfare office, where she, along with many other women, sat in waiting rooms for multiple hours, many times without money to purchase lunch for themselves or their children, to plead with unsympathetic social workers for economic assistance, reminiscent of the experiences represented by Mohr in *Nilda*. At times, fights broke out as women expressed their despair and frustration when social workers refused to help them, including her mother. "They treat us like animals,' she cried after she'd been restrained. 'Don't they care that we're human beings, just like them?'" (250). These continuing experiences of isolation and poverty now further exacerbated with racialized humiliations and consistent threats to their physical and economic safety belies the better future that the narrative of progress promised these migrants. As Negi herself concludes, "Sometimes I lay in bed, in the unheated room full of beds and clothes and the rustle of sleeping bodies, terrified that what lay around the corner was no better than what we'd left behind, that being in Brooklyn was not a new life but a continuation of the old one" (247). Nonetheless, by the end of the book we fast-forward to an adult Santiago, a recent Harvard graduate, whose life ultimately does appear to have significantly altered from her experiences as a child. As a result of a rare opportunity to attend the elite Performing Arts High School in Manhattan, educational achievement has afforded her to leap forward into a life remarkably different than the one narrated throughout the rest of the memoir.

This ending of her individual success and advancement has further served as evidence for those critics who deem her as assimilationist. As Lisa Sánchez-González argues ending with her individualistic successes embraces the "assimilationist tenets of the 'American dream,'" and suggests "that the life this protagonist saves is exclusively her own," instead of being interested in the collective improvement of the Puerto Rican community (158). Her critique assumes that Puerto Rican culture is inherently collectivist and is in binary contrast to American culture as individualistic. She prescribes hegemonic definitions of both American and Puerto Rican culture that we've seen Santiago's work problematize. Instead of embracing the American dream, her depictions of their living conditions in Brooklyn instead illustrate the "disillusionment with the 'American dream'" (Rivera 5). Santiago's depiction of "U.S. neo-colonial exploitation" of Puerto Rico along with portrayals of her protagonists' difficulty settling into the mainstream United States, "challenge[s] America's promise of Freedom and thus question[s] . . . the concept of U.S. democracy" (Schultermandl 4). Sánchez-González's analysis of the ending ignores the prefacing Puerto Rican, saying of the Epilogue, "Same *jíbaro*, different horse." Santiago acknowledges that while she's experienced cultural changes as a result of her multiple migrations and her consequent encounters with various cultures, these have not resulted in a total erasure of those foundational cultural elements of the Puerto Rican jíbaro. She has achieved the cultural hybridity she alludes to when she enters the airplane on her journey to New York. As Carmen Torres-Robles asserts, "Empieza como jíbara y termina como jíbara. La jíbara que 'era' concluye sus memorias de niñez y adolescencia, y la que 'es' es la jíbara adulta en Harvard. Es una jíbara con una envoltura diferente"[6] (211). She's a jíbara with a wrapping or envoltura that includes the cultural influences of the urban experiences of Santurce in Puerto Rico and New York City, as well as those of the various ethnic groups she encounters in Brooklyn. As Lorna Perez argues "*When I was Puerto Rican* wrestles with different registers of hybridity that are negotiated across various spaces within the diaspora, including rural Puerto Rico, urban Puerto Rico, and finally urban New York City, with each location having a different sense of what being Puerto Rican means" (2). Santiago's work, thus "represents the latest in a series of literary texts written by authors more comfortable embracing a different brand of puertorriqueñidad, one that typically represents a stronger identification with ethnicity than nationality" (Torres-Padilla 89). Through her cultural history she documents this historical cultural shift Puerto Rican migrants have experienced from one solely identifying with the island to a more hybrid ethnic one influenced by the impact of Americanization that begins on the island and continues in more complex ways upon migration. Yet she refuses to depict this process as one where Puerto Ricans are merely the subjects of the colonizing power upon which the oppressors impose their culture, but instead have agency and consciously participate in the creation of their new hybrid self. She thus creates a medicinal (re)envisioning of Puerto Rican culture where she gives subject's agency, centers women's experiences in the debates on culture and Americanization and fills historical gaps.

(Re)Constructions of Puerto Rican Womanhood

Santiago further problematizes Puerto Rican cultural history by analyzing Puerto Rican culture through a gendered lens. In particular, she takes on the patriarchal elements of the culture that prescribe particular gendered roles for women. The autobiographical form itself allows for this kind of critique as Carmen Rivera explains, "Santiago appropriates the apparently straightforward discourse of autobiographical narrative to underline the contradictions of the social expectations of women" (6). Susan Stanford Friedman has also argued that autobiographies by women and people of color subvert the traditional western autobiography defined as the universal story of an individual. This "emphasis on individualism does not take into account the importance of group identity for women and minorities. Second, the emphasis on separateness ignores the difference in socialization in the construction of male and female gender identity" (Smith and Watson 72). Autobiographical narratives by women, thus, allow for both a collective and gendered construction of the self.

Autobiographies by women of color in particular engage constructions of the self that are multiply voiced. As Lourdes Torres asserts about Latina autobiographies, "Latin[a] autobiographers do not create a monolithic self, but rather present the construction of the self as a member of multiple oppressed groups, whose political identity can never be divorced from her conditions. The subject created is at once individual and collective" (278). She further explains, "their project is to integrate the various parts of their individual experiences and collective histories to create a new self" (285). Thus far we have seen how Santiago engages various elements of Puerto Rican culture including the jíbaro, island urban, and

New York urban experiences and how she incorporates elements of these various "degrees of Puertorricanness" into her construction of her Puerto Rican cultural self. In this section, I focus on how she adds constructions of Puerto Rican womanhood into this process of her self-construction.

As discussed in the previous chapter, Latina womanhood and sexuality has consistently been defined within the parameters of the virgin/whore dichotomy. This dichotomy stipulates women's roles in relation to men's roles and desires as dictated by *machista* ideologies. Many scholars have discussed the ideologies of *machismo* and *marianismo* and how these serve to uphold gender roles and divisions within Latino families. In addition to being linked to concepts of respect, dignity, and honor, machismo also defines Latino manhood through his dominance over women both physically and sexually. Men are believed to have a stronger sexual drive and are therefore allowed to express these desires with both wives and extra-marital lovers.[7] Marianismo is the counter ideology to machismo. *Marianas* are to be submissive wives who take care of their home, children, and husband. They must accept their husband's extramarital affairs as a natural aspect of married life. Women are then divided between those who are wives and those who are lovers (i.e., the virgin vs. whore).[8] As Oliva Espín explains, Latina women "receive constant cultural messages that they should be submissive and subservient to males in order to be seen as 'good women.' To suffer and be a martyr is also a characteristic of a 'good woman'" ("Cultural and Historical" 150). This division between the virgin and the whore influences Santiago's gender construction.

Negi is first introduced to the virgin/whore or puta/wife distinction through her parent's constant arguments, where her mother repeatedly accuses her father of having extramarital affairs. As she overhears her mother's conversations and arguments she begins to understand the distinction between her mother and the puta and their respective role in defining her own womanhood. Her mother's role as the wife is to experience the pain of her husband's adulterous adventures while still fulfilling her wifely duties. For instance, during one of their arguments, Negi's mother cooks and serves her husband his dinner with a chilling silence (22). On another occasion she throws all of his clothes in the yard, drenches them with water, only to pick them back up the next day, to wash and iron them before he got home (25). Although she expresses her anger she does so in a still muted manner as she removes all evidence of it before he returns to the home, thus falling back into the appropriate role of the dutiful wife.

Negi comes to better understand her mother's position when she personally experiences her father's betrayal. After her father fails to pick her up from her grandparents' home after an extended visit, she wonders about her mother's role as wife and mother and her suspicions of her husband's infidelity.

> Perhaps the person he had to see the Sunday before needed him again, and he went there, and maybe that person needed him so much that he had forgotten about us, just like he sometimes forgot about Mami chasing after babies in Macún. . . . I wondered if Mami felt the way I was feeling at this moment on those nights when she slept on their bed alone, the springs creaking as she wrestled with some nightmare, or whether the soft moans I heard coming from her side of the room were stifled sobs, like the ones that now pressed against my throat, so that I had to bury my face in the pillow and cry until my head hurt. (99–100)

In this moment Negi's response to her father's apparent betrayal mimic's her mother's usual responses as the dutiful wife. She also endures her pain in quiet isolation, stifling her sobs so that no one else will know her pain. She appears destined to follow her mother's role as the Mariana, learning at an early age through the betrayal of the father.

Part of Negi's socialization into the role of the Mariana also entails learning about the prescribed role for Puerto Rican men. From the women in her family she learns that men are all *sinverguenzas*, who are expected to stray from their promises of honor and loyalty to their wives. As her young body begins to develop and she enters the transitional phase of being "casi señorita" or almost a woman, she also finds herself subject to male sinverguenza behavior. When she shows interest in learning the piano, her parents sign her up for lessons with her principal Don Luis who one day during her lessons hovers over peeking down her dress which "puffed out for a clear view, to anyone standing above, of the slight mounds, like egg yolks, that had recently begun to ache on my chest" (179). When she realizes what he's doing she screams "Filthy old man," in a "voice and tone borrowed from my mother," turning to her mother's role modeling of the appropriate response to a sinverguenza's offensive behavior (179). During one of her exchanges with her cousin Tato where they would show each other their private parts, Tato tries to touch her, attempting to convince her that it would feel good. Once again, she responds as her mother has taught her. "'Men are such Pigs!' The words flashed into my head like the headline on a newspaper, only I heard it too, in the voices of Mami and Doña Lola, Gloria and Doña Ana, Abuela, bolero singers, radio soap opera actresses, and my own shrill scream into Tato's face" (117–118). Her voice joins the collective of women who have experienced pain and abuse of sinverguenza men.

Cultural values of dignity and respect further solidify the distinctions between men and women for Negi. Describing the definition of dignidad, she states, "It meant men could look at women any way they liked but women could never look at men directly, only in sidelong glances, unless they were putas, in which case they could do what they pleased since people would talk about them anyway.... It meant men could say things to women as they walked down the street, but women couldn't say anything to men, not even to tell them to go jump in the harbor and leave them alone" (30). In other words, maintaining their dignity required women to allow their bodies to become targets of sexual harassment, silence themselves, and constrain any urges they may have to respond, even if in self-defense. In her attempt to understand the gendered definitions of these cultural terms she acknowledges the contradictions imbedded within them and as Ellen C. Mayock explains, struggles "with how to best interpret the words of others and how to incorporate" these terms into her "evolving sense of expression" (228). A similar struggle continues as Negi is introduced to additional models of womanhood.

Although she appears to be following in her mother's footsteps as the dutiful wife, Santiago challenges the "virgin" as the only acceptable option for Negi's womanhood. While Negi learns that putas are bad women, for instance, who keep husbands away from their families, she is nonetheless fascinated and at times admires these women. "I wanted to see a puta close up, to understand the power she held over men, to understand the sweet-smelling spell she wore around the husbands, brothers, and sons of the women whose voices cracked with pain, defeat, and simmering anger" (30). She does not have the intended reaction to the puta that the lessons about the martyred wife are meant to evoke. Instead of automatically perceiving these women as her eventual enemies, she sees them as women who are not only powerful over men, but also present a more powerful alternative to the martyred wife. Her curiosity and awe of the puta also appears when her Uncle Cucho brings his girlfriend Rita to her home, who according to her mother's reaction, appears to be a puta. "I could tell Mami didn't like Rita by the way she screwed up her nose when Rita walked by or looked away when Rita bent over to rub her leg and her breasts almost tumbled out of her blouse" (41). Negi, on the other hand, likes Rita and hopes that she is a puta. Rita is a potential teacher through whom she hopes to learn about the bewitching power of these women over men.

Women like Rita however, are not the only role models she has for challenging the constraints of the martyred wife role. Her Aunt Generosa, for instance, models a type of behavior that appears free from the prescriptions of proper womanhood. "She spoke her mind in the most crude language I'd ever heard, as if there were nothing shameful in it, as if calling a woman a puta were not embarrassing. I loved that about her and wished for the courage to express myself in the hard language she used" (182). Auntie Generosa's carefree dismissal of cultural and societal rules about female decorum implies a certain level of freedom that Negi senses is unavailable to women like her mother who fulfill the roles ascribed to them. While under Auntie Generosa's care, Negi was able to roam through the city without a chaperone or male escort. Although this behavior "set me apart from any friends I might have had at the time" (183), she takes on Auntie Generosa's attitude and enjoys this short-lived freedom. Negi's reactions to women like Rita and Aunt Generosa illustrate how Santiago "works with and against the gendered scripts she experiences as a child" (Rosario 109). Instead of demonizing and sharing the hatred for women like Rita and Auntie Generosa, Negi admires these women who seem to diverge from the behaviors of the "good woman" or the wife. She sees these women as powerful and courageous, but recognizes that through their questionable behavior, they fall into the realm of "bad women." However, this doesn't dissuade her from seeing them as role models. Negi's options for constructing her own womanhood are expanding into more of a spectrum of options than a strict binary choice.

Another option in the spectrum of womanhood Santiago offers is the jamona. The jamona is the Puerto Rican term for old maid, that is, a woman who never marries. She learns about the jamona with her father during one of their trips to the city together. While eating at a local establishment, a woman selling religious figurines approaches them, "plaster heads of Jesus crowned with thorns" (88). The counterman shoos her away from his establishment stating, "That's what happens to women when they stay jamona" (88). Her father explains the jamona never marries because she's found undesirable by men. When Negi innocently asks what is the term for the male equivalent, their taxi driver interjects and jokingly says, "lucky." From this exchange she learns that becoming a jamona is a punishment for women who fail to conform to the role of the wife. She is a sad individual to be pitied or mocked. Yet, given the pain she witnesses and endures herself as a consequence of men, Negi considers being a jamona a more appealing option than becoming a wife. Her reclaiming of the jamona appears as she witnesses her mother's continued suffering over her father's adultery. After her father fails again to pick her up after another extended stay with her grandparents, her mother finally arrives to take her home. She overhears her mother's conversation with her grandmother, where through stifled cries once again, she expresses her dismay at her husband's philandering ways. "It seemed to me then that remaining jamona could not possibly hurt so much. That a woman alone, even if ugly, could not suffer as much as my beautiful mother did. . . . I would just as soon remain jamona than shed that many tears over a man" (104). Negi thus begins "to grapple self-consciously with her identity as a woman in patriarchal culture and with her problematic relationship to engendered figures of selfhood" (Rivera 10). Santiago adds the jamona as another viable option to the construction of Puerto Rican womanhood.

Santiago further problematizes the binary of the virgin/whore and the static definitions of each of these, by demonstrating how defining characteristics of each are always changing and one's membership in either category is never fixed. After their town of Macún is destroyed by a hurricane, the family endures even harsher economic conditions, pushing Negi's mother to work outside of the home and join the needle trade industry. This inevitably leads to her having a dual shift, rising early to care for the children and preparing the days meals, before going to the factory for a full day's work. Working outside of the home however, marks her as different from the other women in the neighborhood who, in order to earn extra money, would take in laundry or cook for unmarried men. Her job opens her to scrutiny and insinuations such as the one made by Negi's schoolmate who told her that, "Mami was not getting her money from a factory but from men in the city" (122). By leaving the space of the home, that is the realm of the virgin/wife, Negi's mother enters the space of the puta. The neighborhood women now "turned their backs on her when they saw her coming, or, when they talked to her, they scanned the horizon, as if looking at her would infect them with whatever had made her go out and get a job" (122). Instead of succumbing to these social pressures, Negi's mother resists them, feeling pride in her work instead of the expected shame for daring to deviate from her role as virgin/wife. As Virginia Sanchez-Korrol has noted, economic necessity forced Puerto Rican women both on the island and the mainland to redefine the role of wife and mother to include income-generating labor, which is perceived as another way in which they provide and nurture their families. While, on the one hand, the mother's enhanced role as mother and wife role models for Negi a more empowered version of the Mariana, the mother's participation in the labor force however, demands a more domestic role for Negi in the household as her mother recruits her as a girl and the oldest to help with the childcare and household chores. Negi, on the other hand, continues to resist the roles forced upon her. Every night her mother would admonish her on how she had "failed in my duty as a female, as a sister, as the eldest" (125). As Watson asserts, "by performing domesticity poorly . . . [Negi] resists the gendered imperative of female caretaking" (140). Even though by working outside of the home, her mother becomes a living example of how to go beyond the limits prescribed to women, she nonetheless insists on passing these on to her daughter. Oliva Espín has noted that, "[m]others provide the core of cultural messages for women through what they say about men and other women, and what is allowed and what is forbidden to a 'good woman' in the culture of origin" ("Cultural and Historical" 175). Negi is constantly bombarded by these conflicting messages and negotiates the apparent contradictions by resisting her mother's spoken lessons and instead learning from her mother's actions.

Santiago problematizes the binary between the whore and the wife by blurring the lines between the two and adding more options creating instead a spectrum or what she might call "degrees" of Puerto Rican womanhood. Through Negi's experiences she refutes the seemingly pure and distinct opposition and definition of the virgin/wife and the whore. Instead she suggests that in women's real lives there are multiple experiences and thus influences, which affect their definition and experience of womanhood. Stuart Hall has argued that cultural identity "is a matter of becoming as well as of being" (212). By problematizing the virgin/whore dichotomy Santiago suggests the same point about gender identity. Puerto Rican womanhood is not strictly defined by these two poles but is in actuality in flux, subject to numerous influences and ever changing and therefore, always in a state of "becoming." Presenting multiple perspectives on womanhood correlates with the medicinal historian's tenet of presenting multiple historical perspectives, allowing Negi as well as her readers to free themselves from binary constructions of womanhood and destabilizes the wife/puta categories as static ones representing the differences between good and evil.

In addition to the words and behavior of the women in her family, Negi's womanhood is also influenced by the media messages about women's roles. As Julia Watson explains, "Machismo is also reinforced through social media—in newspaper articles of men shooting their wives in crimes of passion, in romantic soap operas on the radio portraying women's suffering over men's dalliances, and in melodramatic jukebox songs of lost love" (139). Negi's understanding of romance in particular is filtered through the images she hears or sees in soap operas. From these she learns that men are to be gallant and heroic, while women are to be graceful and demure. Yet, these images are constantly coming into conflict with her real-life experiences with boys and men. The first boy to notice her in school was Johannes Velez. Although she was interested in him and thought about approaching him as gracefully as her soap opera heroines, whenever she found herself in his presence all she could come up with were either rude or blunt remarks. She tries once more to follow the soap opera model when on another occasion she sits at her balcony and notices a handsome man coming out of the neighbor's house. When the man looks her way, she "felt dangerous, bold, older by years, inspired by all the Marianas and Sofías whose emotional ups and downs had fed my romantic fantasies. I looked at him . . . then stuck the stem of the gardenia in the open buttonhole, where it flopped in the wide space between my soon-to-be-breasts" (230). Even though in this case she is actively trying to emulate a particular model on gender roles and women's behavior, she doesn't receive the effect that modeling this behavior is supposed to produce according to the media. The model in essence fails when put into practice, which suggests that the other models (i.e., virgin and whore) that are to guide her in the construction of her own womanhood, are also flawed.

When she migrates to New York she laments the jíbara she is leaving behind and hints at the hybrid she will become. However, the hybrid cultural self she becomes in New York is really just a continuation of the hybridization process that was already taking place on the island. A similar process occurs with the construction of her gendered self. While on the island she was casi señorita, on the mainland she fully enters into womanhood as she becomes a *señorita*, with the arrival of her menstrual flow. Until this point in the narrative we are seeing how a pre-pubescent or casi señorita girl is witnessing and digesting various (and at times, contradictory) models of Puerto Rican womanhood. In New York, there are multiple cultural models for being and performing womanhood, which influence her own gendered construction. For instance, to the repertoire of romantic gestures learned from Spanish soap operas, she now adds the seductive behavior and images of Marilyn Monroe.

One day as she sits at her window looking at all the activity across the street, a white man sitting in a truck across from her window masturbates as he notices that she is watching him. Ashamed and flustered, yet with a growing curiosity Negi, goes back and forth to the window always finding the man at his task. Having watched Marilyn Monroe on television staring directly into the camera lens, actively seducing her viewers, Negi follows her example, and takes agency in the situation, becoming an active participant in the sexual exchange, by smiling at the truck driver. The man seems confused, ceases his performance, and doesn't look at her anymore. "Whatever he'd wanted from me he didn't want anymore, and I was certain it was because I'd been willing to give it to him" (240). In this instance, Negi experiments with several cultural models of women's roles and sexuality. She appropriates the male gaze that the Puerto Rican cultural values of *dignidad* allow men but not women, encouraged by the example of this white American woman who uses her gaze in very direct ways.[9] Yet, once again the models don't work as they are supposed to. Instead of getting the same response Marilyn Monroe receives for her expression of desire, Negi gets rejected and blames herself for being too forthcoming. She does not realize at this point that returning the gaze is a way to empower herself sexually because it suggests her own agency in the sexual encounter. As bell hooks has argued about the oppositional gaze of black female spectators, "the ability to manipulate one's gaze in the face of structures of domination that would contain it, opens up the possibility of agency" (116). At this point in her development she interprets the man's reaction to her gaze as a rejection because her apparent intention was to become an active participant in the sexualized exchange. However, in a situation where the man was evoking his masculinist power to force a sexual voyeuristic exchange onto a young woman, the fact that her gaze interrupted his pleasure is quite powerful. In all of her attempts to employ multiple models proposed by the media however, none function to her desired intention when put into practice. Negi instead begins to negotiate these models, experimenting with all of them until she can achieve a balance that feels comfortable and fulfilling to herself.

This is the phase she has entered when her Uncle Chico molests her. This supposedly harmless alcoholic who comes in and out of their apartment in New York, offers her a quarter in exchange for a peek at her breasts. Although she refuses and threatens to tell her mother, she keeps the incident to herself. On the following day, while she's combing her hair, her uncle passes by, pinches her nipple, and whispers in her ear not to tell anyone. On the way back from the kitchen he tosses a dollar at her. Although at first she feels humiliated, she keeps the dollar and treats herself to her first sundae. She turns to none of the roles or any other examples of how to deal with this situation. Nor does she appear to be affected in any negative way, as far as the author has illustrated in the text. Negi decides not to follow any one prescribed role because clearly none of them lead to adequate results. Behaving in a virginal or proper way does not protect her from the kind of abuse perpetuated by her uncle, nor does the whore paradigm for instance help her digest what has just occurred to her. Is she a puta for not having told her mother about her Uncle's behavior? Does her use of the dollar to buy herself a sundae mean that she enjoyed the sexual advance? Further still, does her reaction suggest that she has internalized the blame and guilt for her uncle's impropriety? I believe Santiago is suggesting a more complex answer, one that would allow for both the recognition of the trespass committed upon her body while at the same time giving Negi agency in how she digests the incident and allows it or not to define her sexuality and womanhood in any demeaning way.

Negi's negotiation through multiple models of womanhood is evident in the scene where her mother is screaming at her for arriving late from school. She wonders whether her mother has found out about all the ways in which she breaks the prescribed roles of the proper señorita, hitching up her skirt, wearing eye make-up, and letting boys walk her home from the library (251). She has reached the point where she no longer attempts to fit into any one model, but is instead carving out a space of her own, outside of her mother's view, where she can come to her own definition of her Puerto Rican womanhood. The Puerto Rican womanhood she ultimately constructs is a culmination of both the effects "the labels and identities she inherits have on her" and her own opposition to these identities (Rosario 122).

The cultural paradigm of Puerto Rican womanhood Santiago proposes accounts for the constant flow of culture and multiplicity of experience. She illustrates how Puerto Rican culture defines and dictates the roles of women and how these women negotiate these cultural definitions in order to create a new hybrid understanding of their own womanhood, thus centering their agency. As Anzaldúa states, "the new mestiza copes by developing a tolerance for contradictions, a tolerance for ambiguity. . . . She learns to juggle cultures. She has a plural personality, she operates in a pluralist mode. . . . Not only does she sustain contradictions, she turns the ambivalence into something else" (379). In a similar vein, Santiago juggles through the contradictory messages she receives about womanhood and turns the ambivalence among the contradictions into "something else," alternative possibilities for constructing Puerto Rican womanhood.

Conclusion

In *When I Was Puerto Rican*, Santiago offers an intersectional cultural history of Puerto Ricans both on the island and the United States. Like Levins Morales's curandera historian, Santiago provides agency to those whose history has been silenced. However, she does so without glossing over the internal and internalized power dynamics within Puerto Rican cultural history. She problematizes the binary between island culture as authentic Puerto Rican culture and migrant culture as Americanized, documenting not only how there are multiple forms of Puerto Rican culture within the island as represented by the jíbaro and urban culture of Santurce, but also how the Americanization process is already experienced by the migrant before they leave the island as a result of the historical colonial relationship between the United States and Puerto Rico. In this manner, she illustrates how individual constructions of the self take place within and against social structures (Eakin). She also challenges hegemonic notions of "American" culture as well, illustrating how regional ethnic cultures as those found in New York City, are all diverse versions of "American" culture to which Puerto Ricans are exposed and from which Puerto Ricans pick and choose to create their own version of a DiaspoRican culture.

Added to this already complex vision of Puerto Rican cultural history is the gendered experience of Puerto Rican women. Puerto Rican women navigate not only the multiple "degrees of Puertoricanness," but also the multiple models of Puerto Rican womanhood. Santiago also challenges the gendered binary of the virgin/whore dichotomy as the only models for constructing Puerto Rican womanhood. She makes visible the multiple models and influences available to Puerto Rican women, such as the jamona, the working wife, and the heroines of soap operas and romantic ballads. By portraying Negi's active questioning and negotiating of the multiple cultural and gendered models, Santiago suggests Puerto Rican women have agency in the construction of their gendered cultural selves. By centering the voices of women, giving them agency, and representing multiplicity, Santiago turns her seemingly cultural ambivalence into a healing and empowering self-definition of Puerto Rican womanhood.

Conclusion

WHO TELLS YOUR STORY?

Situating DiaspoRican Women's Literature

In the Fall of 2015, I had the distinct pleasure of watching fellow DiaspoRican Lin-Manuel Miranda's *Hamilton: An American Musical*. Overwhelmed by the layers of significance of what I was watching I could not even cry, although it was incredibly moving, for fear of missing something in the blur of tears. Listening to the story of a white male founding father, told through hip-hop, the music born in the streets of the Bronx as storytelling language of poverty and racism, embodied by a cast of black and brown bodies, reimagined as an immigrant story, I sat mesmerized by the genius before me. To top it off I sat next to my brown-skinned, fifteen-year-old daughter who could now see herself within this national history and imagine the possibility of belonging.

Similar to that moment of recognition years before when I found Nicholasa Mohr's novel *Nilda*, seeing *Hamilton* felt like a balm over the many wounds of exclusion I've experienced in my life as a Puerto Rican woman. Seeing black and brown bodies on that stage, telling that story, playing the roles of those white historical figures, some of whom I imagined rolling in their graves if they knew black men were portraying them, was a loud affirmation that this history is our history and our history is national history. In this regard, Miranda's historical narrative is not only a medicinal one, but also fulfills the kind of therapeutic purpose Beverley Southgate (2005) argues history should be striving for. In his discussion of the various purposes history has served, Southgate asks "What should the continuing purpose of history be in our contemporary times?" Instead of creating narratives that confirm the stories that we already believe about ourselves, "historians can play a therapeutic, hope-inspiring role" by telling the stories of those who have challenged established power dynamics and acted "in defiance of what seems to be the habitual or the inevitable" (125). Through *Hamilton*, Miranda portrays not just Alexander Hamilton, but a generation of men and women who spoke up against the imperial powers of the time and challenged the status quo. By telling the story in an unexpected manner, Miranda also challenges the established and accepted methods for telling national history.

The closing song of *Hamilton* suggests that there's no control over who lives, who dies, or who tells your story. Aaron Burr asks, "But when you're gone, who remembers your name? Your flame?" These are the same kinds of questions that inspired the Puerto Rican women authors I have analyzed in this text to create narratives that represented their stories. While Miranda has turned to the world of theater to create his counter historical narratives, Puerto Rican women writers have turned to their literary works to write histories countering the kinds of national discourses that aim to erase them. Through their own educational experiences, Nicholasa Mohr, Judith Ortiz Cofer, and Esmeralda Santiago were socialized to believe in the hegemonic history of the nation where white men were the heroes, and their stories of migration, poverty, racism (as well as resilience, activism, and achievement) did not exist. They sought to remedy this absence by creating their own narratives portraying their varied experiences as Puerto Rican women coming of age in the United States.

The colonialist erasure of the histories of the colonized inspired Aurora Levins Morales to create her own historical methodology, resulting in healing historical narratives that, not only fill in historical gaps, but aim to heal the trauma resulting from historical erasure. Using her medicinal analytical lens, we can see how other Puerto Rican women authors like Mohr, Ortiz Cofer, and Santiago, have also undertaken the task of creating medicinal historical narratives through their varied texts. Their focus on the experiences of women, thus centering one of many marginalized voices, is just one of the many medicinal strategies they use in their texts. In Mohr's text she displaces the mainstream narrative about the Second World War and focuses on this time period and its effects on the everyday struggles of a Puerto Rican woman and her family in New York City. Mohr uses her literary text to create her own archive, documenting the experiences of the war from the perspective of a mother whose sons are fighting in the war front, while she fights the everyday battles for survival in an environment filled with hostility against poor Puerto Rican women.

Judith Ortiz Cofer not only fills multiple historical gaps including the experiences of Puerto Ricans in the Korean war and labor migrations to farm lands in the United States, but she self-reflexively takes on the complexities of memory to describe "poetic truth," the kind of truth that includes not just the facts of an event, but the affective experiences and memories attached to those events. She purposely juxtaposes memory against archival evidence such as photographs in order to complicate the validity of the latter. As we saw in her revisiting of "the incident," although there are several versions of that particular event, including documentary evidence in the form of the photograph of the day, no one source has more validity than the other. All that can be reconstructed is a poetic truth about that day that incorporates all versions, however conflicting they might be. In this manner, Ortiz Cofer not only writes a medicinal historical narrative that fills the gaps of mainstream history, but also challenges historical methodologies.

Finally, Santiago takes on binary constructions of both Puerto Rican cultural and gender identities and creates more nuanced representations encapsulated by the idea of "degrees of Puertoricanness." Santiago challenges the cultural binary between Puerto Rico and the United States, which assumes the existence of Puerto Rican cultural purity on the island and Americanization as only existing within the borders of the United States. Instead, she demonstrates how the colonial history between the United States and Puerto Rico has resulted in the Americanization process always already existing within the island itself. The process is further complicated as Puerto Ricans migrate to the United States and are further immersed, not only in American culture, but also with other ethnic cultures as well. She takes a similar approach to binary constructions of Puerto Rican womanhood, which define women within the virgin/whore dichotomy. She challenges this binary by not only problematizing the good vs. evil depictions of each side of the dichotomy (for instance, by depicting the life of the "whore" or "puta" as a potentially desirable one), but by also adding other models for womanhood such as the *jamona*, who although she might never be married, at least does not have to experience the disappointments of heterosexual romance. Santiago thus adds a gendered lens to her medicinal approach.

In addition to filling in historical gaps and centering women in their narratives, all of these authors resist depicting their characters as victims of historical circumstance, instead they are represented with full agency. While social workers, teachers, and police officers may constrain how much freedom women like Lydia in Mohr's *Nilda*, can have, she still uses her *jaibería* tactics to have some control over the fate of her family. Ortiz Cofer demonstrates how the spiritual skills of her grandfather combined with her grandmother's resourcefulness bypassed the limitations of government officials in finding the location of their lost son. Finally, Santiago depicts young Negi's struggles over sexual agency as she navigates through the multiple models of womanhood at her disposal. Through their representations of agency and everyday resistance they challenge depictions of Puerto Ricans as passive victims and create healing and empowering historical narratives.

Discourses of Unbelonging

The narratives created by these Puerto Rican women authors are a response to a sense of unbelonging in this country, affirmed by a national discourse where Latinos/as are always imagined as foreign and un-American. Leo Chavez calls this discourse the "Latino Threat Narrative," which posits that "Latinos are not like previous immigrant groups, who ultimately became part of the nation. According to the assumptions and taken-for-granted 'truths' inherent in this narrative, Latinos are unwilling or incapable of integrating, of becoming part of the national community. Rather, they are part of an invading force from south of the border that is bent on reconquering land that was formerly theirs (the U.S. Southwest) and destroying the American way of life" (2). The pervasiveness of this narrative has manifested itself in the last few years in such cases as the banning of Mexican American studies in Arizona and in the controversy over historical textbooks with the Texas Board of Education. The fact that these two incidences have taken place within the educational system solidifies the points made by Mohr, Ortiz Cofer, and Santiago concerning their own educational experiences and how these contributed to their silencing.

In 2010, the state of Arizona passed a law banning Mexican American studies, making evident the anxiety felt by conservative whites over the continued increase in the Latino/a population and ongoing immigration from Latin America. Proponents of the law argued that Mexican American studies courses, by telling the stories of oppression and exclusion experienced by Mexican Americans in this country, created resentment toward whites and encouraged the overthrow of the United States government. The law affirmed individualist ideology stating that these courses advocated "ethnic solidarity instead of the treatment of pupils as individuals." In essence, what was found most threatening about these courses was their telling of a national history that challenged the mythic narrative of the ethnic immigrant who arrives as an individual to this country, works hard, assimilates, and becomes an American. Instead, Mexican American courses expose the ways in which the proposed paths to American belonging have failed those that are racialized and othered in this country. The response to this threat was to silence and erase the historical experiences of Mexican Americans from the curriculum, thus upholding the role of the educational system as Loewen argued, to create passive, compliant, and patriotic citizens.

In Texas, advocates asked the State Board of Education to provide more representation of Latino/as in their textbooks. The response was the proposal of a new textbook that significantly revises the historical experiences of Mexican Americans. In this version of Chicano/a history, written by non-experts and published by Momentum Instruction, a company that is owned and operated by a right-wing conservative former member of the Texas State Board of Education, Mexican Americans are consistently depicted as illegal immigrants, who refuse to assimilate into American culture, and pose a threat to American national identity and security. When discussing the Chicano movement of the 1960s, the text states "Chicanos . . . adopted a revolutionary narrative that opposed Western civilization and wanted to destroy this society" (Wang). Furthermore, the text argues that Mexican pride as expressed by Chicano youth in colleges and universities during this time period created divisions in our society. "College youth attempted to force their campuses to provide indigenismo-oriented curriculum, Spanish-speaking faculty and scholarships for poor and illegal students. . . .

During the Cold War, as the United States fought Communism worldwide, these kinds of separatist and supremacy doctrines were concerning. While solidarity with one's heritage was understood, Mexican pride at the expense of American culture did not seem productive" (Wang). By contextualizing the Chicano student's advocacy for curricular and faculty representation and expressions of Mexican pride during the nation's fight against communism, the authors portray the movement and the Chicanos themselves as anti-American and threatening to the nation's agenda of fighting the evil of communism. Such a portrayal suggests Mexican Americans are unassimilable and thus untrustworthy, not just in the past, but in our own contemporary times. Not only do Mexican Americans pose a threat to our national political agendas, but as a population, they are fraught with social problems that threaten the economy. As Oliva P. Tallet explains in the *Houston Chronicle*, according to the textbook, "illegal immigration has 'caused a number of economic and security problems in the United States,' the textbook notes. 'Poverty, drugs, crime, non-assimilation, and exploitation are among some of these problems. Studies have shown that the Mexican American community suffers from a significant gap in education levels, employment, wages, housing, and other issues relating to poverty that persist through the second, third, and fourth generations.'" The text fails to explain the systemic structures that have contributed to the poverty conditions found among some members of the Mexican American population. Furthermore, while the authors identify these social problems as characteristics of illegal immigrants, they suggest these as inherent characteristics when they extrapolate these into the second, third, and fourth generations, the presumably now American citizens. Thus, they assert the notion that all Mexican Americans, whether immigrant or fourth generation American, are always foreign, suspect, and a threat to the nation.

The ultimate power of this discourse of perpetual foreignness or unbelonging has most recently been made manifest in the presidential election of 2016, where Donald Trump's campaign overtly and successfully employed the "Latino Threat Narrative" to galvanize support among anti-immigrant voters. His promises of constructing a wall along the Mexican border, strict deportation enforcements, and withdrawal of temporary protection status for Central American and Haitian immigrants who have lived in the United States for decades, have all relied on this discourse to justify political viewpoints and immigration policies (Hohmann).

For Puerto Ricans, the discourse of unbelonging became most evident in the aftermath of Hurricane Maria, a Category 4 hurricane that devastated the island in September of 2017. The administration's response resulted in political leaders both on the island and the United States, as well as multiple media outlets, describing the treatment of Puerto Ricans as "second-class citizens." The delayed visit to the island by the President, along with his condescending and insulting comments on social media, and the limited financial response to the devastation on the island, have acted as salt in the open colonial wound of perpetual neglect experienced by people on the island. Waiting two weeks before visiting the island, his visit was punctuated by self-congratulatory comments responding to critics such as San Juan mayor Carmen Yulin Cruz, who continuously argued that the situation on the island was dire and that not enough support was being provided by the federal government. He rated himself a "10 out of 10" in his government's response to the situation, while those on the ground painted a significantly different picture (Bump). The image of the President tossing paper towels at Puerto Ricans who'd gathered to meet him at a local community church, juxtaposed against images of the mayor of San Juan wading through flooding waters to provide assistance to people stranded in their homes, confirmed the administration's condescending attitude toward Puerto Ricans, which had already been expressed through social media comments. In these comments the President complained that Puerto Ricans "were not doing enough to help themselves," and consistently reminded his audience of the financial burden the island was now posing, commenting, "I hate to tell you, Puerto Rico, but you've thrown our budget a little out of whack" (Landler). The financial difficulties that the island was experiencing were further exacerbated however, by colonial policies such as the Jones Act, which requires that all goods shipped to the island must arrive on American ships. This archaic regulation prevented nearby countries eager to send assistance from being able to do so. Instead, islanders had to petition the government for a waiver of the regulation, which was granted after considerable advocacy and only allowed for ten days.[1]

The economic effects of Puerto Rico's colonial relationship with the United States had already reached a breaking point prior to the hurricane, something the President also reminded the storm victims (Whack). The island economy had been suffering for years as tax incentives, which had drawn U.S. companies to the island, were faded out and these companies began to leave, leading to increases in unemployment and migration. The government turned to debt as a way to keep the economy afloat, a debt that they were not able to withstand. Because of its colonial situation as a non-incorporated territory, Puerto Rico was unable "to seek relief in a federal bankruptcy court, [as other U.S. cities have been able to do], but is also ineligible for aid or debt restructuring from the International Monetary Fund because it is not a sovereign nation" (Moore 503). The result was the creation of a government oversight board through the passage of the Puerto Rico Oversight, Management, and Economic Stability Act (PROMESA). While the bill protected the island from being sued by its debtors, it continues to perpetuate a colonial relationship, taking agency away from local leaders in creating economic solutions, and instead created a board of outsiders, which are responsible for "overseeing negotiations with creditors, the creation of a fiscal plan . . . and the restructuring of debt" (White). The members of this board are appointed by the President of the United States, harkening back to earlier times when the governor and other cabinet administrators were appointed by the U.S. president.

The PROMESA legislation and the current administration's response to the humanitarian crisis on the island are just two recent examples of the many ways in which Puerto Ricans both on the island and the diaspora, receive consistent messages of unbelonging. The persistent reminder by Puerto Rican legislators in the U.S. Congress such as Luis Gutierrez and Nydia Velasquez of the fact that Puerto Ricans are American citizens underscores the position of Puerto Ricans always being "foreign in a domestic sense." As one poll conducted after the hurricane found, almost half of Americans were unaware that people born in Puerto Rico are U.S. citizens (Dropp and Nyhan). It is precisely this lack of recognition of their American citizenship that justifies their treatment as second-class citizens. In this context, the work of authors such as Levins Morales, Santiago, Ortiz Cofer, and Mohr, becomes more urgent in order to inscribe Puerto Rican belonging into our national history and resist the colonial erasure of our experiences.

Literature and the (Re)Claiming of Belonging

These discourses of unbelonging have defined the Puerto Rican experience within the United States. While some Latino/a writers have responded to their experiences of unbelonging by seeking belonging in their countries of origin, for most of these authors, including those in this study, their attempts of "return" with assumptions that they would be accepted with welcomed arms have been disappointing at best. As referenced earlier, Puerto Rican writers have written or expressed in interviews the hypocritical critiques they've endured on the island where they've been rejected for being too Americanized or not Puerto Rican enough. These writers therefore have turned their lens to their experiences within the United States. Attempts by literary critics to incorporate their writings into the literary canon of the island in a noble pursuit to be inclusive of the diaspora, miss this point.[2] Some of the authors themselves have expressed a desire to have their literary works achieve recognition as part of the American (meaning U.S.) literary canon. As Judith Ortiz Cofer states when asked what canon she feels her work belongs in, "basically what I hope will happen, and I may not be around to confirm it, is that someone eventually will say, 'well you can look for her work somewhere in mid to late twentieth-century American literature'" (Crompton 104). In other words, "for these puertorriqueñas, writing becomes the tool, the weapon, the magic wand enabling them to authorize themselves in a literary tradition that up until the second half of the twentieth century denied them access. It is through writing that these women can create a space of their own, can rescue themselves from the borderlands of literary canons and stand at the epicenter of their own imaginary community" (Rivera 149). They are not necessarily vested in staying in interstitial literary spaces somewhere between Puerto Rican and American literary history,[3] but instead are demonstrating through the stories they tell, that their experiences and the literary works that portray them, belong within a redefined and inclusive American literary canon.

In this respect my analysis coincides with critics such as Maya Socolovsky and Jose Saldívar, who have posited broadened definitions of the American nation that stretches beyond the United States borders into Latin America. In her work, Socolovsky approaches Latina literature as imagining "a collective geographical, political, and cultural presence, where Latin America becomes part of, not apart from, the political and national identity of the United States," thus imagining "the United States as part of a broader 'Americas'" (3–4). Similarly, in *Border Matters*, Saldívar remaps the borderlands and its cultural production into the center of the American cultural imagination and thus challenges hegemonic definitions of the nation. Instead of situating Latino/a literary and cultural productions within their respective supposed countries of origin, by incorporating Chicano/a, Puerto Rican, or Cuban American writers and artists into the canons of Mexico, Puerto Rico, or Cuba, these critics broaden the definition of the United States, of what entails American cultural identity and expression that legitimates "Latino belonging within the United States" (Socolovsky 4). Furthermore, by including writers like Ortiz Cofer and Santiago who do depict parts of their experiences on the island and attest to constructions of hybrid identities into the U.S. American literary canon, we further broaden the definition of American experiences to include experiences of cultural hybridity.

Situating Puerto Rican women's literature as belonging within the United States allows for comparative work that has yet to be achieved within both Puerto Rican and Ethnic Literary Studies. Juan Flores, for instance, has raised the cultural connections between Puerto Ricans and African Americans. By the time Puerto Rican literature in the United States develops into Nuyorican literature of the 1970s, it "comes to share the features of 'minority' or noncanonical literatures of the United States. Like them, it is a literature of recovery and collective affirmation, and it is a literature of 'mingling and sharing,' of interaction and exchange with neighboring, complementary cultures" (*Divided Borders* 152). He thus suggests that Puerto Rican literature turn toward a "minority literature" that incorporates the cultural influences of those other minoritized communities these authors have come of age sharing space with. How do these interactions with other minoritized groups influence the historical and cultural self-understanding of DiaspoRicans? In the chapter on Esmeralda Santiago, we see for instance how her interactions with Italians, African Americans, and Jews impact her acculturation process "mingling" into the construction of her new Puerto Rican identity characteristics of these various ethnic/racial groups. In what ways do Puerto Rican writers expand the definitions of the nation, citizenship, and belonging as colonized subjects writing within the belly of the beast? How do they (re)imagine what "American" means? These are the kinds of research inquiries that situating Puerto Rican literature within the United States literary canon could allow for.

This desire for inclusion in the U.S. literary canon, however, is not an indication of assimilation as other critics have asserted accusatorily. While much of Latino/a Studies takes on a tone inclusive of our respective differences while exploring our similarities, when it comes to defining who it is that we include when we use either umbrella terms such as Latino/a or particular Latino ethnic terms such as Chicano/a, Puerto Rican, or Cuban American, we can still find discourses around authenticity. Some critics continue to reify a particular class position as emblematic of authenticity, particularly when speaking of Chicano/a or Puerto Rican experiences. If the Latino/a experiences portrayed or historicized are not those of the working class then one must relate to the proverbial "people," otherwise one's motivations and even cultural identity are brought into question. For example, Ignacio García, in his assessment of Chicano historiography, lamented what he saw as the negative effects of feminist and lesbian theoretical influence in Chicano Studies. He critiqued the younger generation of Chicano scholars whom he argues "have no ideological connection with the original premises of Chicano Studies" (I. Garcia 181). In other words, these younger scholars are part of the middle-class or lower middle-class and "were not weaned politically or intellectually in a Chicano working-class environment" (I. Garcia 192). He, therefore, defines the authentic Chicano experience and community as that of the working-class barrio.[4] Similarly, the work of Richard Rodriguez had long been dismissed as "assimilationist" among Chicano/a literary circles. Randy Rodriguez, however, has approached his work through a queer lens and raised some interesting questions about the motivations behind dismissing Rodriguez's literary work. He argues that Rodriguez's work was not rejected by Chicano critics solely because of its assimilationist politics, but because of its effeminate style and content. Through a gender and queer theoretical analysis of Rodriguez's work, Randy Rodriguez offers a more nuanced reading of *Hunger of Memory* and of his critics. Brilliantly, this critic argues that Chicano critics' own response to Richard Rodriguez's work demonstrates their fears of seeing themselves in Rodriguez's own Mexican identity. So, Rodriguez argues, Chicano critics either "chain" him or "expel" him:

> Chain Rodriguez—contain him in our understanding of him as a conservative Hispanic and he will not threaten our radical, progressive, ethnic self-conception. Expel Rodriguez—define him and the content and style of his writing as nonconforming (as inauthentic, fabrication, tainted, calculated, fluff) in order to maintain our authentic cultural identities free from contamination, and most importantly, as inapplicable to our lives. To see (any part of) ourselves reflected in his tragic visage would be to view our own repressed desire and self-knowledge and challenge our sacred cultural and ideological beliefs of authentic, organic, integrated communities. (406)

In the case of Puerto Rican women writers, the work of Esmeralda Santiago and Judith Ortiz Cofer has also been dismissed by some literary critics as assimilationist as evidenced in previous chapters. Significantly Lisa Sanchez Gonzalez has argued that Santiago and Ortiz Cofer's works uphold the capitalist narrative of individual success at the expense of collective uplift by creating narratives highlighting the protagonist's upward mobility. She argues that these narrative conclusions of individualistic success are indicative of the marketability to a mainstream audience of these particular writers. "It is as if this literature's narrative politics have migrated toward the conservative epistemological center in tandem with its academic and industrial institutionalization" (135). She suggests that the mainstream acceptance of these writer's narratives in and of itself dilutes their authority to speak of "authentic" Puerto Rican women's experiences. Is it necessary then to stay somewhat marginalized in order to be "authentic"? Furthermore, she questions feminist critics' assertion that the act of writing or "print articulation connotes not so much an individualist will to power as a counterhegmonic will to a collective and collectivizing empowerment" (137). Instead she argues, "these mainstreamed Latina feminist texts narrate personal experiences of the feminine condition to the near total exclusion of a collective predicament that entails growing problems with racism, poverty, reproductive rights, education, and colonial maldevelopment" (140). As the previous chapters have demonstrated however, writers such as Santiago and Ortiz Cofer not only depict their individual experiences with poverty and racism, for instance, but incorporate into their narratives the stories of other women in their families and communities.

Sanchez Gonzalez fits into the anticolonialist group of Latino/a literary critics determining the Latino/a canon as described by Dalleo and Machado Saez. This type of Latino/a critic "is defined by a concern with a politics of social justice; thus its focus on oppositionality in the service of a fairer distribution of resources leads to a distrust of market success as a form of political betrayal" (6). While I too share a politics of social justice, my approach to writers such as Santiago and Ortiz Cofer in this study follows Dalleo and Machado Saez's posited strategy of demonstrating the connections between these contemporary writers and those writers of the 1970s who are hailed by critics such as Sánchez-González as anti-colonialist, but building on that past in a way that is relevant to contemporary times. "Addressing the contemporary situation as distinct from the past means rethinking culture's relation to the market and reimagining the possibilities of the popular" (8). The relationship between the market and the cultural producer is a more nuanced one than simply one of either assimilation or resistance (10). As the analysis included in the previous chapters on Ortiz Cofer and Santiago demonstrate, a more nuanced reading of their texts through a gendered lens illustrates the possibilities of marketably successful Puerto Rican women's texts that nonetheless include critical assessments of the historical exclusion of Puerto Rican women's voices.

As cultural critics, who are part of the academic institutional establishment, holding our respective numerous degrees, we now belong to the middle-class. We therefore need to ask ourselves "What do we fear?" when we so feverishly and vociferously critique the works of writers such as Richard Rodriguez and Esmeralda Santiago for embracing not just upward class mobility, but reconciling their cultural identities with U.S. American mainstream culture. Randy Rodriguez's persuasive analysis of Chicano critics in relation to Richard Rodriguez's work, I think, can be expanded and applied to those Puerto Rican cultural critics who, in a similar vein, create an authenticity hierarchy when analyzing the works of Puerto Rican Diaspora writers. This is not to suggest that critiques of these works as assimilationist should not be done. The purpose is not to replace one type of politically correct reading with another. What I am positing is that we become more self-reflexive in our positions as critics as we analyze the literary works of Puerto Rican writers. Even if we believe that an author's work is assimilationist, we should employ medicinal strategies, raising questions that can get us to a more nuanced understanding of the authors' perspective. We should take that analysis further by asking why an author would create such a narrative? What possible critiques of Puerto Rican culture and cultural theories and paradigms would assimilation suggest? Is there a gender- or class-based critique that can enlighten her presumably assimilationist stance about culture? These are the kinds of questions that I believe works such as Santiago's contribute to our understanding and continued exploration into Latino/a and Puerto Rican history. We may not be comfortable with some of Santiago's apparent ambivalences, as some of her critics would describe her cultural positions. But there is a lot to learn by taking a second look at her text through a feminist lens as I've done in this study.

Using emerging theories and methods, such as Levins Morales's medicinal historical methods, allows us to reintroduce texts such as those analyzed here into the larger discourse on Puerto Rican cultural history. Puerto Ricans as a marginalized group in a society that professes equality as one of its values, suffer from a dual trauma. On the one hand they suffer the traumatic effects of multiple oppressions. On the other their marginalized position is exacerbated by their erasure from the nation's historical imaginary. Authors like Santiago and Ortiz Cofer who are dismissed as assimilationist however seemed to have suffered from one more source of trauma—exclusion from their own ethnic/cultural group.

If we are to follow Levins Morales's defined role of the medicinal historian as socially committed, then as historians and cultural critics we cannot perpetuate the traumatic exclusions that Puerto Ricans as a group have experienced in this country. We must adhere to the tenets of the curandera historian: giving agency and voice to those whose stories are undertold (if at all); broaden our sources and definitions of historical evidence; create complex narratives that allow for multiple and diverging perspectives; and contextualize our histories locally and globally while crossing not only national borders but social location borders of race, class, gender, and sexuality. Writers such as Nicholasa Mohr, Ortiz Cofer, and Santiago have given us examples of how to create healing historical narratives. They have demonstrated that literary works can serve as spaces for creating historical narratives. They have wrestled with their memories to fill in historical gaps while self-reflexively questioning the veracity of these memories. They have challenged hegemonic masculinist histories centering the experiences of Puerto Rican women.

In this study I have attempted to employ some of the medicinal historians methods in my analysis of the narratives by Nicholasa Mohr, Aurora Levins Morales, Judith Ortiz Cofer, and Esmeralda Santiago. Using these works, I have posed challenges and questioned definitions of historical evidence. I have demonstrated the vast knowledge available when we look at historical experiences from multiple perspectives. I have crossed disciplinary borders merging literary works and historical methods. And, most importantly, I have given precedence to the voices and subjective experiences of the writers since it was within these works that I found knowledge that helped me in my own search for a better understanding of my multiple identities as a Puerto Rican woman positioned in the educated middle-class, but with roots in the working-class.

We have seen that the histories about Puerto Ricans and other Latino/a groups have been consistently excluded from our national imaginary. Instead we have what has become a hegemonic discourse of unbelonging that is persistently repeated and upheld, whether it's by policies that aim at silencing alternative historical curriculums (like in Arizona), the creation of revisionist histories that affirm the image of Latino/as as a national threat, or the discourse of the current presidential administration. To counter their historical erasure, Puerto Rican women writers have, in the same vein as Lin-Manuel Miranda, turned to their creative talents, in their literary works, to create historical narratives that not only fill the historical gaps, but bring into question the historical narrative process. They refuse to give their agency up and let others tell their stories for them. They may not be able to control who lives or who dies, but they will control who tells their story. In creating their histories they offer the potential for healing from the traumas of exclusion and silencing that continue to plague our communities. They create histories that are not only healing for themselves, but for the rest of us who through their narratives, can see ourselves, perhaps for the first time. We can finally see ourselves as more than bodies to be labor and labored upon and then discarded when no longer needed, but as significant contributors and creators of our national future. Thus they create a hope-inspiring, healing history.

NOTES

Introduction. "La Cultura Cura"

1. See Vega, Colón (1961, 1993), Sánchez Korrol, Whalen, Morales (1986), Perez, G. (2004), and Padilla.
2. See Falcón, Cruz, Flores (2000, 1993), and Glasser (1995).
3. See Acosta-Belen (1986), Matos Rodriguez and Delgado, and Ortiz (1996).
4. See Matos Rodriguez, and Ortiz (1998).
5. The second-class citizenship of Puerto Ricans was most recently made evident by the treatment of the United States in the aftermath of Hurricane Maria. I'll address this more in depth in the conclusion chapter.
6. A similar project in search of the historical experiences of Latinos as documented through literary works, is found in the Recovering the Hispanic Literary Heritage project by Arte Público Press (https://artepublicopress.com/recovery-project/).
7. Loewen's text serves as a correction on some of the misrepresentations and/or absences found in traditional history textbooks.
8. In 1937 the Nationalist Party organized what was expected to be a peaceful march and rally in the southern town of Ponce in Puerto Rico. They had acquired all legal permissions for such an event, however at the last minute permission was denied. The marchers decided to go ahead and march without the permission. They were surrounded by mounted police who proceeded to shoot into the crowd when they refused to obey the police's orders. Several were killed and wounded.
9. By "stories" I mean experiences that are passed on orally among women and between generations. I am not using the term in its literary definition of a particular genre.
10. On the term Nuyorican and Nuyorican literature see Flores (1993) and Algarin and Piñero.
11. For an in-depth, critical analysis of Marisel Moreno's text, see my book review (Garcia 2013).
12. Although Rosario Ferré began to write in English in the 1990s with her novel *The House on the Lagoon*, becoming marketable, her writing career was established in Puerto Rico, starting in the 1970s writing in Spanish and had become internationally known prior to crossing over into writing in English. The subject matter of her novels also focuses on the island elite and not on the lived experiences of migrant Puerto Ricans.

13. This debate continues in the work of Rafael Dalleo and Elena Machado Saez, where they analyze more contemporary works by Latino writers and problematize the notion that these works no longer have a social justice focus and are merely compromising their politics to market forces. As they argue, "recent Latino/a literature imagines creative ways to rethink the relationship between a politics of social justice and market popularity—a combination that the critical reception denies by either rejecting one of these elements or articulating them as binary opposites" (3).

Chapter 1. The Making of a Curandera Historian

1. Lisa Lowe explains hybridity "refers to the formation of cultural objects and practices that are produced by the histories of uneven and unsystematic power relations" (67). This includes here the uneven power relations that have defined Puerto Rican history through its various colonial experiences, first with Spain and now with the United Sates. Multiplicity, Lowe suggests, designates "the ways in which subjects located within social relations are determined by several different axes of power" (67) such as race, class, and gender. Here I invoke her definitions when speaking of Puerto Rican experiences as being both culturally hybrid (a result of encounters of uneven power relations between Africans, Tainos, Europeans, and Americans on the island and mainland) and multiple as these experiences are defined along race, class, and gendered axes of power relations.

2. For further discussion on the challenges by postmodernist historians see Jenkins (1997), Southgate (1996), Trouillot; and White H.

3. For critical work on *This Bridge Called My Back*, see Alarcón (1990).

4. For additional discussion and analysis on these polarizing distinctions between different Latino/a literary works, see Dalleo and Machado Saez.

5. Although within the individual pieces the name of the author is not identified, they are identified within the table of contents.

6. For other analyses of *Getting Home Alive*, see Rojas, Benmayor, and Wadman.

7. For an in-depth discussion of this trend, see Haslip-Viera.

8. In his analysis of *Remedios*, Efraín Barradas makes a similar point about Levins Morales's text as well, arguing that the author constructs a narrative that is both steeped in personal and collective history, Barradas (2011).

9. See, for example, Ortiz (1998, 1996).

10. For an in-depth discussion of population control policies in Puerto Rico, see Briggs.

Chapter 2. Double Victory for Puerto Rican Women Too

1. See Honey, Brandt, and Escobar.

2. For more on how some of these authors tell history in their narratives, see Kim, Shostak, and Saldívar-Hull.

3. Ismael Muñiz also demonstrates the ways in which the bildungsroman format is redefined in the hands of Puerto Rican authors where "the bildungsroman tradition become not just stories of individual evolution, sold as statements of survival in the margins or perimeters of society for the singular tastes of middle America, but also stories of cultural identity in which the conflicting polarities are worked out in the reformulation of the self" (84).

4. In earlier readings of *Nilda* by critics, such as John Miller, the interaction of the Puerto Rican community with these institutions were presented as merely Mohr's representation of whites as villains, as "others," to the community, without a critical analysis of the power dynamics between these institutions and communities of color. See Miller (1979).

5. Incidents of police brutality and hostile encounters between Puerto Ricans and police officers are discussed by Carmen Whalen who discusses the 1954 study by the Commission on Human Relations which found that "one-third of Puerto Ricans felt the police treated them worse than other Americans." In their 1962 study, the Migration Division reported "police mistreatment" as a problem in Puerto Rican communities. See Whalen (2001).

6. The Supreme Court declared Puerto Rico during the insular cases as being "foreign in a domestic sense" as a way to define Puerto Rico's status as an unincorporated territory.

Chapter 3. "Mending Broken Memories"

1. For a critical discussion on the limitations of claiming Virginia Woolf for women of color writers, see Doyle (2009). She argues that Ortiz Cofer doesn't wholeheartedly follow Woolf, but instead she reappropriates Woolf's arguments and methodologies to suit her own needs in the construction of her narratives.

2. For further discussion on the symbolism of the silent dancing, see Lara-Bonilla.

3. See Whalen, Bonilla Santiago, and Glasser 1997.

4. For more discussion on race and Puerto Ricans, see C. Rodriguez, 2000.

5. See Briggs.

6. For additional critiques of *Silent Dancing*, see Grobman and Sandin.

Chapter 4. "Degrees of Puertoricanness"

1. The following are some examples of works that see Santiago's work as assimilationist: Sánchez-González, Barradas, and Szadiuk. Critics who argue the opposite include Torres-Robles and C. Rivera (2002).

2. Here I invoke Lisa Lowe's definition of hybridity as "the formation of cultural objects and practices that are produced by the histories of uneven and unsynthetic power relations" (67).

3. See Pedreira, 1942, and more recent works Duany (2002) and Davila (1997).

4. Tato Laviera, "Nuyorican" as quoted in Juan Flores, *Divided Borders*, 102: "Now I return, with a Boricua heart, and you/ reject me, look at me badly, and attack my way of speaking/ while you eat McDonalds at American discotheques" (my translation).

5. For additional readings of the representation of the jíbaro icon in Santiago's work, see Soto-Crespo and Acosta Cruz.

6. "She begins as a jíbara and ends as a jíbara. The jíbara she 'was' concludes her memories of childhood and adolescence, and the jíbara she 'is' is the adult one in Harvard. She is a jíbara with a different wrapping" (my translation).

7. While many critics have challenged the limitations of definitions of machismo, as well its attribution to Latino cultures exclusively, arguing "[t]he components of machismo are better treated as products of the relationship between masculinity and power than as unique Latino cultural attribute. Our understanding of Latino traditional gender roles, however, is [nonetheless] heavily influenced by the concept of machismo" (Asencio 1 09). It is in this vein that I use the term "machismo" in my analysis.

8. For definitions of machismo and marianismo, see Asencio, Andrade, and Ramírez.

9. For a full reading on the appropriation of the male gaze in Santiago's work, see Morales-Díaz.

Conclusion

1. For coverage of the Trump Administration's handling of the crisis in Puerto Rico following Hurricane Maria, see J. Rivera, Varela, Hand, Whack, and E. Morales.

2. Marisel Moreno's *Family Matters* for instance is such an attempt that fails in its application of an island ideology, "la gran familia puertorriqueña," onto a diaspora context and experience.

3. Sánchez-González talks about Boricua literature as a literature that doesn't seek to be part of the island canon or the mainstream American canon, but one that is distinctly DiaspoRican.

4. In response to his critiques, the anthology *Voices of a New Chicana/o History* compiles various articles which debunk Garcia's claims and posit the great contributions that not only feminist and lesbian theorists have made to the field, but also expand the definition of Chicano culture, community, and historical experience as including Mexican American communities outside of the American Southwest, and Chicanos who are not from "the barrio," who represent various class experiences.

WORKS CITED

Acosta-Belen, Edna. "Beyond Island Boundaries: Ethnicity, Gender, and Cultural Revitalization in Nuyorican Literature." *Callaloo* 15.4 (1992): 979–98. Print.
Acosta-Belen, Edna, ed. *The Puerto Rican Woman*. Santa Barbara: Praeger, 1986. Print.
Acosta-Belen, Edna. "Conversations with Nicholasa Mohr." *Revista Chicano-Riqueña* 8.2 (1980): 35–41. Print.
Acosta Cruz, Maria. "Esmeralda Santiago in the Marketplace of Identity Politics." *Centro Journal* 18.1 (Spring 2006): 170–87. Print.
Acuña, Rodolfo. *Occupied America: A History of Chicanos*. New York: Harper and Row, 1988. Print.
Alarcón, Norma. "The Theoretical Subject(s) of *This Bridge Called My Back* and Anglo-American Feminism." *Making Face, Making Soul: Haciendo Caras*. Ed. Gloria Anzaldúa. San Francisco: Aunt Lute Books, 1990. 356–69. Print.
Alarcón, Norma. "Chicana's Feminist Literature: A Re-vision through Malintzín/or Malintzín: Putting Flesh Back on the Object." *This Bridge Called My Back*. Ed. Cherríe Moraga and Gloria Anzaldúa. Kitchen Table: Women of Color Press, 1983. 182–90. Print.
Algarin, Miguel, and Miguel Piñero, eds. "Introduction: Nuyorican Language." *Nuyorican Poetry: An Anthology of Puerto Rican Worlds and Feelings*. New York: Morrow, 1975. 9–20. Print.
Andrade, Rolando A. "Machismo: A Universal Malady." *Journal of American Culture* 5 (1992): 33–41. Print.
Anzaldúa, Gloria. "La conciencia de la mestiza: Towards a New Consciousness." *Making Face, Making Soul: Haciendo Caras*. Ed. Gloria Anzaldúa. San Francisco: Aunt Lute Books, 1990. 377–89. Print.
Anzaldúa, Gloria. *Borderlands/ La Frontera*. San Francisco: Aunt Lute Books, 1987. Print.
Aparacio, Frances, "Judith Ortiz Cofer, *Silent Dancing: A Partial Remembrance of a Puerto Rican Childhood*." *Reading U.S. Latina Writers: Remapping American Literature*. Ed. Alvina E. Quintana. New York: Palgrave Macmillan, 2003. 61–70. Print.
Aptheker, Bettina. *Tapestries of Life*. Amherst: U of Massachusetts P, 1989. Print.
"Army Set to Assign Non-Puerto Ricans to as Replacements in Famed 6th Reg't." *News from Korean War*, valersos.com. March 3, 1953. Web.

Asencio, Marysol. "Machos and Sluts: Gender, Sexuality, and Violence among a Cohort of Puerto Rican Adolescents." *Medical Anthropology Quarterly* 13 (1999): 107–26. Print.
Baker, Susan S. *Understanding Mainland Puerto Rican Poverty*. Philadelphia: Temple UP, 2002. Print.
Barradas, Efraín. "El Recuerdo Como Remedio: History y Memoria en Aurora Levins Morales." *La Nueva Literatura Hispanica* 11 (2011): 203–20. Print.
Barradas, Efraín. *Partes de un Todo: Ensayos y notas sobre literatura puertorriqueña en los Estados Unidos*. San Juan: Editorial de la Universidad de Puerto Rico, 1998. Print.
Benmayor, Rina. "Getting Home Alive: The Politics of Multiple Identity." *Americas Review* 17.3–4 (1989): 107–17. Print.
Bold, Christine, "An Enclave in the Wilderness." Review of *Paradise*, by Toni Morrison. *Times Literary Supplement*, 27, March 1998, 22. Print.
Bonilla Santiago, Gloria. "Puerto Rican Migrant Farmworkers: An Untold Story." *Migration World Magazine* 14.4 (1986): 14–8. Print.
Bost, Suzanne. "Transgressing Borders: Puerto Rican and Latina Mestizaje." *MELUS* 25.2 (Summer 2000): 187–211.
Brandt, Nat. *Harlem at War: The Black Experience in World War II*. Syracuse: Syracuse UP, 1996. Print.
Briggs, Laura. *Reproducing Empire: Race, Sex, Science, and U.S. Imperialism in Puerto Rico*. Berkeley: U of California P, 2002. Print.
Brooks Higginbotham, Evelyn. "Beyond the Sound of Silence: Afro-American Women in History." *Gender and History* 1.1 (1989): 50–67. Print.
Bucchioni, Eugene. "The Daily Round of Life in the School." *The Puerto Rican Community and its Children on the Mainland*. Ed. Francisco Cordasco and Eugene Bucchioni. Lanham: Scarecrow Press, 1973. Print.
Bump, Philip. "Trump Rates his Puerto Rico Handling a 10 out of 10. America rates it a 4." *Washington Post*, washingtonpost.com. October 19, 2017. Web. Accessed January 9, 2018.
Burke, Peter. *What is Cultural History?* Cambridge: Polity Press, 2008. Print.
Butler-Evans, Elliott. *Race, Gender and Desire*. Philadelphia: Temple UP, 1989. Print.
Cade Bambara, Toni. "Foreword." *This Bridge Called My Back*. Ed. Cherrie Moraga and Gloria Anzaldúa. Kitchen Table: Women of Color Press, 1983. vi–viii. Print.
Chang, Sucheng. "Asian American Historiography." *The History and Immigration of Asian Americans*. Ed. Franklin Ng. New York: Garland Publishing, 1998. 1–37. Print.
Chavez, Leo. *The Latino Threat: Constructing Immigrants, Citizens, and the Nation*. Palo Alto: Stanford UP, 2013. Print.
Cheung, King-Kok. "'Don't Tell': Imposed Silences in The Color Purple and the Woman

Warrior." *Reading the Literature of Asian Americans*. Ed. Shirley Geok-Lim and Amy Ling. Philadelphia: Temple UP, 1992. 163–90. Print.

Chow, Rey. *Writing Diaspora*. Bloomington: Indiana UP, 1993. Print.

Clark, VéVé. "Performing the Memory of Difference in Afro-Caribbean Dance: Katherine Dunham's Choreography, 1938–87." *History and Memory in African-American Culture*. Ed. Genevieve Fabre and Robert O'Meally. New York: Oxford UP, 1994. 188–204. Print.

Colón, Jesus. *The Way It Was and Other Writings*. Arte Público Press, 1993.

Colón, Jesus. *A Puerto Rican in New York and Other Sketches*. New York: Mainstream Publishers, 1961. Print.

Crumpton, Margaret. "An Interview with Judith Ortiz Cofer." *Meridians* 3.2 (2003): 93–109. Print.

Cruz, Jose. *Identity and Power*. Philadelphia: Temple UP, 1998. Print.

Dalleo, Rafael, and Elena Machado Saez. *The Latino/a Canon and the Emergence of Post-Sixties Literature*. New York: Palgrave Macmillan, 2007. Print.

Dasgupta, Sayantani, and Marsha Hurst, ed. *Stories of Illness and Healing: Women Write Their Bodies*. Kent, OH: Kent State UP, 2007. Print.

Davila, Arlene. *Sponsored Identities: Cultural Politics in Puerto Rico*. Philadelphia: Temple UP, 1997. Print.

Dehay, Terry. "Narrating Memory." *Memory, Narrative and Identity: New Essays in Ethnic American Literature*. Ed. Amritjit Singh, Joseph T. Skerrett, Jr., and Robert E. Hogan. Boston: Northeastern UP, 1994. 26–44. Print.

De Roman, Josefina. "New York's Latin Quarter." *Inter-American* 5.1 (1946): 10. Print.

Derrickson, Teresa. "'Cold/Hot, English/Spanish': The Puerto Rican American Divide in Judith Ortiz Cofer's *Silent Dancing*." *MELUS* 28.2 (Summer 2003): 121–37. Print.

Doyle, Jacqueline. "Thinking Back Through her Mothers: Judith Ortiz Cofer and Virginia Woolf." *Woolf Studies Journal* 15 (2009): 91–111. Print.

Doyle, Jacqueline. "The Stories Her Body Tells: Judith Ortiz Cofer's 'The Story of My Body.'" *Auto/Biography Studies* 22.1 (2007): 46–65. Print.

Dropp, Kyle and Brendan Nyhan, "Nearly Half of Americans Don't Know Puerto Ricans are Fellow Citizens." *New York Times*, nytimes.com. September 26, 2017. Web. Accessed January 8, 2018.

Duany, Jorge. *The Puerto Rican Nation on the Move*. Chapel Hill: U of North Carolina P, 2002. Print.

Eagleton, Terry. *Literary Theory: An Introduction*. Minneapolis: U of Minnesota P, 2008. Print.

Eakin, Paul. *Living Autobiographically: How We Create Identity in Narrative*. Ithaca: Cornell UP, 2008. Print.

Escobar, Edward. *Race, Police, and the Making of a Political Identity: Mexican Americans and the Los Angeles Police Department, 1900–1945*. Berkeley: U of California P, 1999. Print.

Escobedo, Elizabeth R. *From Coveralls to Zoot Suits: The Lives of Mexican American Women on the World War II Home Front*. Chapel Hill: U of North Carolina P, 2013. Print.

Espín, Oliva. *Latina Realities: Essays on Healing, Migration, and Sexuality*. Boulder: Westview Press, 1997. Print.

Espín, Olivia. "Cultural and Historical Influences on Sexuality in Hispanic/Latin Women: Implications for Psychotherapy." *Pleasure and Danger: Exploring Female Sexuality*. Ed. Carole S. Vance. Pandora, 1989. 149–64. Print.

Espín, Olivia. "Spiritual Power and the Mundane World: Hispanic Female Healers in Urban U.S. Communities." *Women's Studies Quarterly* 16.3–4 (Fall-Winter 1988): 33–47. Print.

Falcón, Angelo. "A History of Puerto Rican Politics in New York City: 1860s to 1945." *Puerto Rican Politics in Urban America*. Ed. James Jennings and Monte Rivera. Westport: Greenwood Press, 1984. 15–42. Print.

Fernandez Olmos, Marguerite. "Growing up Puertorriqueña: The Feminist Bildungsroman and the Novels of Nicholasa Mohr and Magali Garcia Ramis." *Centro Journal* 2.7 (Winter 1989–90): 56–73. Print.

Flores, Juan. *From Bomba to Hip-Hop*. New York: Columbia UP, 2000. Print.

Flores, Juan. *Divided Borders*. Houston: Arte Público Press, 1993. Print.

Foucault, Michel. *The Birth of the Clinic: An Archeology of Medical Perception*. New York: Vintage, 1994. Print.

Garcia, Elizabeth. "Family Matters: Puerto Rican Women Authors on the Island and the Mainland, Review." *Centro Journal* (2013): 208–11. Print.

Garcia, Elizabeth. "Medicinal histories: the future of the past." *Rethinking History* 12.2 (June 2008): 253–62. Print.

Garcia, Elizabeth. "The making of a *curandera* historian: Aurora Levins Morales." *Centro Journal* 17.1 (Spring 2005): 185–201. Print.

Garcia, Elizabeth. "Degrees of Puertoricanness: A Gendered Look at Esmeralda Santiago's *When I was Puerto Rican*." *Latino Studies* 2.3 (December 2004): 377–94. Print.

García, Ignacio M. "Juncture in the Road: Chicano Studies Since 'El Plan de Santa Barbara.'" *Chicanas/Chicanos at the Crossroads*. Ed. David R. Maciel and Isidro D. Ortiz. Tuscon: U of Arizona P, 1996. 181–203. Print.

Geertz, Clifford. *The Interpretation of Cultures*. New York: Basic Books, 1973. Print.

Glasser, Ruth. *Aqui Me Quedo: Puerto Ricans in Connecticut*. Connecticut Humanities Council, 1997. Print.

Works Cited

Glasser, Ruth. *My Music is My Flag: Puerto Rican Musicians and their New York Communities, 1917–1940.* Berkeley: U of California P, 1995. Print.
Glunta, Edvige. "Teaching Memoir at New Jersey City University." *Transformations* 11.1 (2000): 80–9. Print.
Grobman, Laurie. "The Cultural Past and Artistic Creation in Sandra Cisneros' *The House on Mango Street* and Judith Ortiz Cofer's *Silent Dancing*." *Confluencia* 11.1 (1995): 42–9. Print.
Grosfoguel, Ramón, Frances Negrón-Muntaner, and Chloe Georas. "Beyond Nationalist and Colonialist Discourses: The *Jaiba* Politics of the Puerto Rican Ethno-Nation." *Puerto Rican Jam: Essays on Culture and Politics*. Ed. Frances Negrón-Muntaner and Ramón Grosfoguel. Minneapolis: U of Minnesota P, 1997. 1–36. Print.
Hall, Stuart. "Cultural Identity and Cinematic Representation." *Black British Cultural Studies*. Ed. Houston A. Baker, Manthia Diawara, and Ruth H. Lindeborg. Chicago: U of Chicago P, 1996. 210–22. Print.
Hand, Mark. "Trump's Second-Class Response to Hurricane Maria Deepens the Divide with Puerto Rico." *Think Progress*, thinkprogress.org. October 17, 2017. Web. Accessed January 8, 2018.
Haslip-Viera, Gabriel, ed. *Taino Revival: Critical Perspectives on Puerto Rican Identity and Culture*. Princeton: Marcus Wiener, 2001. Print.
Herman, Judith. *Trauma and Recovery*. New York: Basic Books, 1997. Print.
Hernandez, Carmen Dolores. *Puerto Rican Voices in English*. Santa Barbara: Praeger, 1997. Print.
Hohmann, James. "The Daily 202: Trump systematically alienates the Latino diaspora—from El Salvador to Puerto Rico and Mexico." *Washington Post*, washingtonpost.com. January 9, 2018. Web. Accessed January 10, 2018.
Honey, Maureen. *Bitter Fruit: African American women in World War II*. Columbia: U of Missouri P, 1999. Print.
hooks, bell. *Black Looks: Race and Representation*. Brooklyn: South End Press, 1992. Print.
hooks, bell. *Sisters of the Yam*. Brooklyn: South End Press, 1993. Print.
Jenkins, Keith. *Rethinking History*. New York: Routledge, 1991. Print.
Jorge, Angela. "The Black Puerto Rican Woman in Contemporary American Society." *The Puerto Rican Woman: Perspectives on Culture, History, and Society*. Ed. Edna Acosta-Belen. Santa Barbara: Praeger, 1986. 180–8. Print.
Kallet, Marilyn. "The Art of Not Forgetting: An Interview with Judith Ortiz Cofer." *Prairie-Schooner* 68.4 (1994): 68–75. Print.
Kelly, Robin D. G. "'Slanging' Rocks . . . Palestinian Style: Dispatches from the Occupied Zones of North America." *Police Brutality*. Ed. Jill Nelson. New York: W. W. Norton and Co, 2000. 21–59. Print.

Kevane, Bridget, and Juanita Heredia. *Latina Self-Portraits: Interviews with Contemporary Women Writers*. Albuquerque: U of New Mexico P, 2000. Print.

Khader, Jamil. "Subaltern Cosmopolitanism: Community and Transitional Mobility in the Caribbean Postcolonial Feminist Writings." *Feminist Studies* 29.1 (Spring 2003): 63–82. Print.

Kim, Elaine. "Poised in the In-between: A Korean American's Reflections on Theresa Hak Kyung Cha's *Dictree*." *Writing Self/Writing Nation*. Ed. Elaine Kim and Norma Alarcón. Berkeley: Third Woman Press, 1994. 3–34. Print.

Kim, Elaine. *Asian American Literature: An Introduction to the Writings and Their Social Context*. Philadelphia: Temple UP, 1982. Print.

Labarthe, Pedro Juan. *The Son of Two Nations: The Private Life of a Columbia Student*. New York: Carranza & Co., 1931. Print.

Landler, Mark. "Trump Lobs Praise, and Paper Towels, to Puerto Rico Storm Victims." *New York Times*, www.nytimes.com. Oct 3, 2017. Web.

Lara, Irene. "Bruja Positionalities: Toward a Chicana/Latina Spiritual Activism." *Chicana/Latina Studies* 4.2 (Spring 2005): 10–45. Print.

Lara-Bonilla. I. "Getting Home Alive: Urgency and Polyphony in the figuration of the 'Diasporican.'" *Latino Studies* 8.3 (2010): 355–72. Print.

Lara-Bonilla, Inmaculada. "Desarraigos Discursivos: La Narrativa Inconsecuente Como Tercer Espacio Identitario en *Silent Dancing: A Partial Remembrance of a Puerto Rican Childhood*." *Nueva Literatura Hispanica* 15 (2011): 147–78. Print.

Lao Montes, Agustín. "Mambo Montage: The Latinization of New York City." *Mambo Montage*. Ed. Agustin Lao Montes. New York: Columbia UP, 2001. 1–53. Print.

Levins Morales, Aurora. *Remedios: Stories of Earth and Iron from the History of Puertorriqueñas*. Boston: Beacon Press, 1998. Print.

Levins Morales, Aurora. *Medicine Stories: History, Culture and the Politics of Integrity*. Brooklyn: South End Press, 1998. Print.

Levins Morales. "And Even Fidel Can't Change That . . ." *This Bridge Called My Back*. Ed. Cherrie Moraga and Gloria Anzaldúa. Kitchen Table: Women of Color Press, 1983. 53–6. Print.

Levins Morales, Aurora, and Rosario Morales. *Getting Home Alive*. Ann Arbor: Firebrand Books, 1986. Print.

Loewen, James. *Lies My Teacher Told Me: Everything Your American History Textbook Got Wrong*. New York: The New Press, 1995. Print.

Lopez Springfield, Consuelo. "Mestizaje in the Mother-Daughter Autobiography of Rosario Morales and Aurora Levins Morales." *a/b: Auto/Biography Studies* 8.2 (1993) 303–15. Print.

Lowe, Lisa. *Immigrant Acts*. Durham: Duke UP, 1996. Print.

Works Cited

Lugones, Maria. "Playfulness, 'World'-Travelling, and Loving Perception." *Making Face, Making Soul: Haciendo Caras.* Ed. Gloria Anzaldúa. San Francisco: Aunt Lute Books, 1990. 390–402. Print.

Marques, René. *The Docile Puerto Rican.* Philadelphia: Temple UP, 1976. Print.

Matos Rodriguez, Felix V. "Women's History in Puerto Rican Historiography: The Last Thirty Years." *Puerto Rican Women's History: New Perspectives.* Ed. Felix Matos Rodriguez and Linda C. Delgado. Armonk: ME Sharpe, 1998. 9–37. Print.

Matos Rodriguez, Felix V., and Linda C. Delgado, eds. *Puerto Rican Women's History: New Perspectives.* Armonk: ME Sharpe, 1998. Print.

Mayock, Ellen C. "The Bicultural Construction of Self in Cisneros, Alvarez, and Santiago." *Bilingual Review/La Revista Bilingue* 23.3 (1998): 223–29. Print.

McCracken, Ellen. "Latina Narrative and Politics of Signification: Articulation, Antagonism, and Populist Rupture." *Critica: A Journal of Critical Essays* 2.2 (1990): 202–7. Print.

Miller, Carol T. and Branda Major. "Coping with Stigma and Prejudice." *The Social Psychology of Stigma.* Ed. Todd F. Heatherton, Robert E. Kleck, Michelle R. Hebl, and Jay G. Hull. New York: Guilford Press, 2000. 243–72. Print.

Miller, John C. "Nicholasa Mohr: Neorican Writings in Progress 'A View of the Other Culture.'" *Revista/Review Interamericana* 9.4 (December 1979): 543–49. Print.

Mohanty, Satya. *Literary Theory and the Claims of History.* Ithaca: Cornell UP, 1997. Print.

Mohr, Eugene. *The Nuyorican Experience: Literature of the Puerto Rican Minority.* Westport: Greenwood Press, 1982. Print.

Mohr, Nicholasa. "Freedom to Read." *The New Advocate* 12.1 (1999): 11–20. Print.

Mohr, Nicholasa. "The Journey Towards a Common Ground: Struggle and Identity of Hispanics in the USA." *Americas Review* 18.1 (1990): 81–85. Print.

Mohr, Nicholasa. "Puerto Rican Writers in the U.S., Puerto Rican Writers in Puerto Rico: A Separation beyond Language." *Breaking Boundaries: Latina Writing and Critical Readings.* Ed. Asuncion Horno-Delgado, Eliana Ortega, Nina M. Scott, and Nancy Saporta Sternbach. Amherst: U of Massachusetts P, 1989. 111–16. Print.

Mohr, Nicholasa. *Nilda.* Houston: Arte Público Press, 1986. Print.

Montilla, Patricia. "Gathering Voices: Storytelling and Collective Identity in Judith Ortiz Cofer's *Silent Dancing: A Partial Remembrance of a Puerto Rican Childhood.*" *Bilingual Review/La Revista Bilingue* 27.3 (2003): 205–20. Print.

Moore, Colin D. "American Political Development: Expansion and Sovereignty Beyond the States." *PS: Political Science & Politics* 50.2 (2017): 501–5. Print.

Moraga, Cherrie. *Loving in the War Years: lo que nunca paso por sus labios.* Brooklyn: South End Press, 1985. Print.

Moraga, Cherrie. "La Guera." *This Bridge Called My Back*. Ed. Cherrie Moraga and Gloria Anzaldúa. Kitchen Table: Women of Color Press, 1983. 27–34. Print.

Moraga, Cherrie and Gloria Anzaldúa, eds. *This Bridge Called My Back*. Kitchen Table: Women of Color Press, 1983. Print.

Morales, Ed. "Puerto Rico in Crisis." *Nation*, thenation.com. September 27, 2017. Web. Accessed January 8, 2018.

Morales, Julio. *Puerto Rican Poverty and Migration: We Just Had to Try Elsewhere*. Santa Barbara: Praeger, 1986. Print.

Morales Carrion, Arturo. *Puerto Rico: A Political and Cultural History*. New York: W. W. Norton, 1983. Print.

Morales-Díaz, Enrique. "Catching the Glimpses: Appropriating the Female Gaze in Esmeralda Santiago's Writing." *Centro Journal* 14.2 (Fall 2002): 130–47. Print.

Moreno, Marisel. *Family Matters: Puerto Rican Women Authors on the Island and Mainland*. Charlottesville: U of Virginia P, 2012. Print.

Moreno, Marisel. "'More Room': Space, Woman and Nation in Judith Ortiz Cofer's *Silent Dancing*." *Hispanic Journal* 22.2 (2001): 437–46. Print.

Morrison, Toni. "Sites of Memory." *Inventing the Truth: The Art and Craft of Memoir*. Ed. William Zinsser. Boston: Houghton Mifflin Company, 1995. 103–24. Print.

Moya, Paula. *Learning from Experience: Minority Identities, Multicultural Struggles*. Berkeley: U of California P, 2002. Print.

Moya, Paula and Michael Hames-Garcia. *Reclaiming Identity: Realist Theory and the Predicament of Postmodernism*. Berkeley: U of California P, 2000. Print.

Muñiz, Ismael. "Bildungsroman written by Puerto Rican Women in the United States: Nicholasa Mohr's Nilda: A Novel and Esmeralda Santiago's When I was Puerto Rican." *Atenea* 19.1-2 (June 1999): 79–101. Print.

Negrón-Muntaner, Frances, and Ramón Grosfoguel. *Puerto Rican Jam*. Minneapolis: U of Minnesota P, 1997. Print.

Nieto, Sonia. "Puerto Rican Students inn U.S. Schools: A Brief History." *Puerto Rican Students in U.S. Schools*. Ed. Sonia Nieto. Mahwah: Lawrence Erlbaum Associates, 2000. 5–38. Print.

Nora, Pierre. "Between Memory and History: Les Lieux de Memoire." *History and Memory in African-American Culture*. Ed. Genevieve Fabre and Robert O'Meally. New York: Oxford UP, 1994. 284–300. Print.

Ocasio, Rafael. "The Infinite Variety of the Puerto Rican Reality: An interview with Judith Ortiz Cofer." *Callaloo* 17.3 (1994): 730–42. Print.

Ocasio, Rafael. "Speaking in Puerto Rican: An Interview with Judith Ortiz Cofer." *Bilingual Review/Revista Bilingue* 17.2 (1992): 143–46. Print.

Ocasio, Rafael. "Puerto Rican Literature in Georgia: An Interview with Judith Ortiz Cofer" *The Kenyon Review* 14.4 (1992): 43–50. Print.

Ortiz, Altagracia. "Puerto Rican Women Workers in the Twentieth Century: A Historical Appraisal of the Literature." *Puerto Rican Women's History: New Perspectives*. Ed. Felix Matos Rodriguez and Linda C. Delgado. Armonk: ME Sharpe, 1998. 38–61. Print.
Ortiz, Altagracia. *Puerto Rican Women and Work: Bridges in Transnational Labor*. Philadelphia: Temple UP, 1996. Print.
Ortiz Cofer, Judith. *Silent Dancing: A Partial Remembrance of a Puerto Rican Childhood*. Arte Público Press, 1990. Print.
Padilla, Felix. *Puerto Rican Chicago*. Notre Dame: U of Notre Dame P, 1987. Print.
Pedreira, Antonio. *Insularismo*. Puerto Rico: Biblioteca de Autores Puertorriquenos, 1942. Print.
Perez, Emma. *The Decolonial Imaginary: Writing Chicanas into History*. Bloomington: Indiana UP, 1999. Print.
Perez, Gina. *The Near Northwest Side Story: Migration, Displacement and Puerto Rican Families*. Berkeley: U of California P, 2004. Print.
Perez, Gina, ed. "Special Issue on Puerto Ricans in Chicago." *Centro Journal* 13.2 (2001). Print.
Perez, Lorna. "Multiple Hybridities: Jibaros and Diaspora in Esmeralda Santiago's *When I was Puerto Rican*." *Label Me Latina/o* 4 (Summer 2014): 1–15. Print.
Pérez-Firmat, Gustavo. *Life on the Hyphen*. Austin: U of Texas P, 1994. Print.
Perez y Gonzalez, Maria. *Puerto Ricans in the United States*. Westport: Greenwood, 2000. Print.
Pesquera, Beatriz, and Adela de la Torre. "Introduction." *Building with Our Hands: New Directions in Chicana Studies*. Ed. Beatriz Pesquera and Adela de la Torre. Berkeley: U of California P, 1993. 1–14. Print.
Peterson, Nancy J. *Against Amnesia: Contemporary Women Writers and the Crisis of Historical Memory*. Philadelphia: U of Pennsylvania P, 2001. Print.
Pietri, Pedro. "Puerto Rican Obituary." *Boricuas: Influential Puerto Rican Writings-An Anthology*. Ed. Roberto Santiago. New York: Ballantine, 1995. 117–25. Print.
Phippen, J. Weston. "How One Law Banning Ethnic Studies Led to Its Rise." *The Atlantic*, theatlantic.com. July 19, 2015. Web. Accessed July 13, 2016.
"Puerto Ricans Now in Korea," *News from the Korean War*, valerosos.com. October 8, 1950. Web.
"Puerto Rico Officer Cites Island's Role in Korea." *News from the Korean War*, valerosos.com. November 29, 1952. Web.
"Puerto Rico Raiders Make Exposed Dash to Save Harassed." *News from the Korean War*, valerosos.com. February 15, 1952. Web.
Ramírez, Rafael L. *What It Means to be a Man: Reflections on Puerto Rican Masculinity*. New Brunswick: Rutgers UP, 1999. Print.

Rebolledo, Tey Diana. "The Politics of Poetics: Or, What Am I, A Critic, Doing in This Text Anyhow?" *Making Face, Making Soul: Haciendo Caras*. Ed. Gloria Anzaldúa. San Francisco: Aunt Lute Books, 1990. 346–55. Print.

Rich, Adrienne. *On Lies, Secrets and Silence, Selected Prose, 1966–1978*. New York: Norton, 1979. Print.

Rivera, Carmen S. *Kissing the Mango Tree: Puerto Rican Women Rewriting American Literature*. Houston: Arte Público Press, 2002. Print.

Rivera, Jose. "Hurricane Relief or Abandonment? Independence or Statehood? Puerto Rico Waits, Like Always." *Los Angeles Times*, latimes.com. October 1, 2017. Web. Accessed January 8, 2018.

Roche Rico, Barbara. "'An Island Like You': Representing the Puerto Rican Diaspora in the Short Stories of Nicholasa Mohr and Judith Ortiz Cofer." *Short Fiction in Theory & Practice* 1.2 (2011): 201–15. Print.

Roche Rico, Barbara. "'Rituals of Survival': A Critical Reassessment of the Fiction of Nicholasa Mohr." *Frontiers* 28.3 (2007): 160–79. Print.

Rochin, Refugio I., and Dennis N. Valdes. *Voices of a New Chicana/o History*. East Lansing: Michigan State UP, 2000. Print.

Rodriguez, Clara. *Changing Race: Latinos, the Census, and the History of Ethnicity in the United States*. New York: New York UP, 2000. Print.

Rodriguez, Clara. *Puerto Ricans: Born in the US*. Boulder: Westview Press, 1991. Print.

Rodriguez, Randy. "Richard Rodriguez Reconsidered: Queering the Sissy (Ethnic) Subject." *Texas Studies in Literature and Language* 40.4 (Winter 1998): 396–423. Print.

Rodriguez, Richard. *Hunger of Memory*. New York: Bantam Books, 1983. Print.

Rodriguez Vecchini, Hugo. "Cuando Esmeralda 'era' puertorriqueña: Autobiografia etnografica y autobiografia neopicaresca." *Nomada* 1 (1995): 145–60. Print.

Rojas, Lourdes. "Latinas at the Crossroads: An Affirmation of Life in Rosario Morales and Aurora Levins Morales' Getting Home Alive." *Breaking Boundaries: Latina Writing and Critical Readings*. Ed. Asuncion Horno-Delgado, Eliana Ortega, Nina M. Scott, and Nancy Saporta Sternback. Amherst: U of Massachusetts P, 1989. 166–77. Print.

Root, Maria. "Reconstructing the impact of trauma on personality." *Personality and Psychopathology Feminist Reappraisals*. Ed. L.S. Brown and M. Ballou. New York: Guilford, 1992. 229–66. Print.

Rosario, Jose. "On the Ethics and Poetics of How We Make Our Lives: Esmeralda Santiago and the Improvisation of Identity." *Centro Journal* 22.2 (Fall 2010): 106–27. Print.

Rushin, Donna Kate. "The Bridge Poem." *This Bridge Called My Back*. Ed. Cherrie Moraga and Gloria Anzaldúa. Kitchen Table: Women of Color Press, 1983. xxi–xxii. Print.

Saldívar, Jose D. *Border Matters: Remapping American Cultural Studies*. Berkeley: U of California P, 1997. Print.

Saldívar, Ramon. *Chicano Narrative: The Dialectics of Difference.* Madison: U of Wisconsin P, 1990. Print.
Saldívar-Hull, Sonia. "Feminism on the Border: From Gender Politics to Geopolitics." *Criticism in the Borderlands: Studies in Chicano Literature, Culture, and Ideology.* Ed. Hector Calderon and Jose David Saldívar. Durham: Duke UP, 1991. 203–20. Print.
Sánchez-González, Lisa. *Boricua Literature: A Literary History of the Puerto Rican Diaspora.* New York: New York UP, 2001. Print.
Sánchez Korrol, Virginia. *From Colonia to Community.* Berkeley: U of California P, 1994. Print.
Sandin, Lyn di Iorio. "Torn Between Two Cultures: *Silent Dancing* by Judith Ortiz Cofer." *Sojourner: The Women's Forum* 16.4 (1990): 43–5. Print.
Sandoval, Chela. "Feminist Forms of Agency and Oppositional Consciousness: U.S. Third World Feminist Criticism." *Provoking Agents: Gender and Agency in Theory and Practice.* Ed. Judith Kegan Gardiner. Champaign: U of Illinois P, 1995. 208–26. Print.
Santiago, Esmeralda. "Conversations with Ilan Stavans." *Latina Writers.* Ed. Ilan Stavans. Westport: Greenwood Press, 2008. 122–8. Print.
Santiago, Esmeralda. *Cuando era Puertorriqueña.* New York: Vintage, 1994. Print.
Santiago, Esmeralda. *When I was Puerto Rican.* New York: Vintage, 1993. Print.
Scarry, Elaine. *The Body in Pain: The Making and Unmaking of the World.* New York: Oxford UP, 1985. Print.
Schultermandl, Silvia. "Rewriting American Democracy: Language and Cultural (Dis)Locations in Esmeralda Santiago and Julia Alvarez." *Bilingual Review/La Revista Bilingue* 28.1 (2004): 3–15. Print.
Sheehan, Susan. *A Welfare Mother.* New York: New American Library, 1976. Print.
Shostak, Debra. "Maxine Hong Kingston's Fake Books." *Memory, Narrative, and Identity,* Ed. Amritjit Singh, Joseph T. Skerrett, Jr., and Robert E. Hogan. Boston: Northeastern UP, 1994. 233–60. Print.
Smith, Bonnie G. *The Gender of History: Men, Women, and Historical Practice.* Harvard UP, 2000. Print.
Smith, Sidonie, and Julia Watson. *Women, Autobiography, Theory: A Reader.* Madison: U of Wisconsin P, 1998. Print.
Socolovsky, Maya. *Troubling Nationhood in U.S. Latina Literature: Explorations of Place and Belonging.* New Brunswick: Rutgers UP, 2013. Print.
Sontag, Susan. *Illness as Metaphor.* New York: Farrar, Straus, and Giroux, 1978. Print.
Soto-Crespo, Ramon. "An Intractable Foundation: Luis Muñoz Marín and the Borderland State in Contemporary Puerto Rican Literature." *American Literary History* 18.4 (Winter 2006): 712–38. Print.

Southgate, Beverley. *What is History For?* New York: Routledge, 2005. Print.
Southgate, Beverley. *History: What and Why?* New York: Routledge, 1996. Print.
Stefanko, Jacqueline. "New Ways of Telling: Latinas' Narratives of Exile and Return." *Frontiers: A Journal of Women Studies* 17.2 (1996): 50–69. Print.
Stephens, Gregory. "*When I was Puerto Rican* as Borderland Narrative: Bridging Caribbean and U.S. Latino Literature." *Confluencia* 25.1 (Fall 2009): 30–45. Print.
Szadiuk, Maria. "Culture as transition: Becoming a woman in bi-ethnic space." *Mosaic* 32.3 (September 1999): 109–29. Print.
Tallet, Olivia P. "Mexican American Textbook Incites Controversy." *Houston Chronicle*, chron.com. June 14, 2016. Web. July 13, 2016.
Takaki, Ronald. *Double Victory: A Multicultural History of American in World War II*. Boston: Little, Brown, and Company, 2000. Print.
Taylor, Diana. *The Archive and the Repertoire: Performing Cultural Memory in the Americas*. Durham: Duke UP, 2003. Print.
Thomas, Piri. *Down These Mean Streets*. New York: Vintage Books, 1997. Print.
Torres, Carlos Antonio, Hugo Rodriguez Vecchini, and William Burgos. *The Commuter Nation: Perspectives on Puerto Rican Migration*. San Juan: Editorial de la Universidad de Puerto Rico, 1994. Print.
Torres-Padilla, Jose L. "When 'I' Became Ethnic: Ethnogenesis and Three Early Puerto Rican Diaspora Writers." *Writing Off the Hyphen: New Perspectives on the Literature of the Puerto Rican Diaspora*. Ed. Jose L. Torres-Padilla and Carmen Haydee Rivera. Seattle: U of Washington P, 2008. 81–104. Print.
Torres-Padilla, Jose L., and Carmen Haydee Rivera, eds. *Writing Off the Hyphen: New Perspectives on the Literature of the Puerto Rican Diaspora*. Seattle: U of Washington P, 2008. Print.
Torres-Robles, Carmen L. "Esmeralda Santiago: Hacia una (re) definicion de la puertorriqueñidad." *Bilingual Review/Revista Bilingue* 23.3 (1998): 206–13. Print.
Trouillot, Michel-Rolph. *Silencing the Past: Power and the Production of History*. Boston: Beacon Press, 1997. Print.
Tuttle, William. *Daddy's Gone to War: The Second World War in the Lives of America's Children*. New York: Oxford UP, 1995. Print.
Varela, Julio Ricardo. "Puerto Rico is Being Treated Like a Colony After Hurricane Maria," *The Washington Post*, washingtonpost.com. September 26, 2017. Web. January 8, 2018.
Vasquez, Melba J.T. "Power and Status of the Chicana: A social-psychological Perspective." *Chicano Psychology*. Ed. Joe L. Martinez and Richard Mendoza. Academic Press, 1984. 269–88. Print.
Vega, Bernardo. *Memoirs of Bernardo Vega*. Ed. Cesar Andreu Iglesias. New York: Monthly Review Press, 1984. Print.

Works Cited

Wadman, Monika. "Multiculturalism and Nonbelonging: Construction and Collapse of the Multicultural Self in Rosario and Aurora Levins Morales' Getting Home Alive." *Literature, Interpretation, Theory* 11.2 (2000): 219–37. Print.

Wang, Yanan. "Proposed Texas Textbook Says Some Mexican Americans 'Wanted to Destroy' U.S. Society." *Washington Post*, washingtonpost.com. May 24, 2016. Web. Accessed July 13, 2016.

Watson, Julia. "Strategic Autoethnography and American Ethnicity Debates: The Metrics of Authenticity in When I was Puerto Rican." *Life Writing* 10.2 (2013): 129–50. Print.

Wear, Delese, and Lois LaCivita Nixon. *Literary Anomalies: Women's Bodies and Health in Literature*. New York: SUNY Press, 1994. Print.

Welfare Council of New York City. *Puerto Ricans in New York City*. February, 1948.

Whack, Errin Haines. "'As if Puerto Rico Did Not Exist.' Hurricane Maria is a Reminder of 'Second-Class' Status for Some." *Time*, yahoo.com. September 30, 2017. Web. Accessed January 8, 2018.

Whalen, Carmen. *From Puerto Rico to Philadelphia: Puerto Rican Workers and Postwar Economies*. Philadelphia: Temple UP, 2001. Print.

White, Gillian B. "Puerto Rico's Problems Go Way Beyond Its Debt," *The Atlantic*, theatlantic.com. July 1, 2016. Web. Accessed January 8, 2018.

White, Hayden. *Tropics of Discourse: Essays in Cultural Criticism*. Baltimore: Johns Hopkins UP, 1978. Print.

Wilentz, Gay. *Healing Narratives: Women Writers Curing Cultural Dis-Ease*. New Brunswick: Rutgers UP, 2000. Print.

Willis, Susan. *Specifying: Black Women Writing the American Experience*. Madison: U of Wisconsin P, 1987. Print.

Wolf, Virginia. *Moments of Being*. San Diego: Harcourt, 1985. Print.

Zentella, Ana Celia. *Growing Up Bilingual: Puerto Rican Children in New York*. New York: Blackwell, 1997. Print.

INDEX

Acosta-Belen, Edna, 6
African Americans, 70; discrimination against, 51, 54; Puerto Ricans and, 46–47
agency, 117, 137, 152; girls', 135–36; giving the marginalized, 26, 97; grandparents', 81, 90; negotiating, 59–61; students taking, 67–68; women's, 97–99, 109, 121
Americanization, 84–86, 109; effects of, 110–11, 116–18, 123; in Puerto Rico, 20, 112, 120–22; resistance to, 88, 122
Anzaldúa, Gloria, 12, 113–14, 137
Aptheker, Bettina, 18
assimilation, 82–83, 88, 126; assumptions about, 142–44; criticisms for, 108, 149–51, 150; trauma from pressure for, 87–89
autobiographies, 127; collective *vs.* individual, 76–77; histories as collective, 41–42, 45, 76–77

Barradas, Efraín, 19, 41
Benmayor, Rina, 34
Birth of the Clinic (Foucault), 11
Bonilla Santiago, 90
Border Matters (Saldívar), 147

Boricua Literature (Sánchez-González), 15–16
Bucchioni, Eugene, 64–66, 68
Burke, Peter, 114

Carrion, Arturo Morales, 57
Chavez, Leo, 142
Cheung, King-Kok, 12
Chicano literature, 148–49
citizenship, 21, 65, 74, 146
class, social, 16, 85, 149; discrimination based on, 111, 123; disparities among, 58–59, 94–95, 119; identity and, 35–36; relation to race and gender, 29–31; schools teaching values of middle class, 64, 66
Colón, Jesus, 41
cultural historians, 114–15
cultural hybridity, of Puerto Ricans, 36–38, 111–12, 114, 123, 126
cultural schizophrenia, 88–89
culture, 124; Americanization *vs.* Puerto Rican, 109–11; gender and, 109, 127; hybridity of Puerto Rican, 114, 137; Latino, 113; Puerto Rican, 108, 127, 130; traditional Puerto Rican, 85, 112, 118
curandera handbook, 6–7, 25–29, 38

curandera historians, 137; healing narratives of, 38–48; Levins Morales as, 18–19, 24, 40–41, 101, 140–41; methodology of, 27–29, 44–45, 49, 74, 101, 105, 140–41; tenets of, 42, 152

Dalleo, Rafael, 150
Dasgupta, Sayantani, 11
daughters, and mothers, 31–32, 72–73, 102–4
Derrickson, Teresa, 88–89
DiaspoRicans, 110, 112, 114
discourse of unbelonging: of Latinos/as, 147–48, 152–53; of Mexican Americans, 142–44; of Puerto Ricans, 145–46
discrimination: against African Americans, 51; effects of, 9–10; against immigrants, 35; against Mexican Americans, 51–52; against Puerto Ricans, 31, 55–56, 64–66, 141
División de Educación de la Comunidad (DIVEDCO), 120–22
doctor-patient relationship, 11
Double Victory (Takaki), 54
Down These Mean Streets (Thomas), 31
Doyle, Jacqueline, 86
Duany, Jorge, 112–13

economy, of Puerto Rico, 145–46
education: Americanization through schools, 121–22; discrimination against jíbaras in, 118–19; by División de Educación de la Comunidad, 120–22; importance of, 4, 63, 125–26; in *Nilda*, 4, 63–69; "othering" of Latinas/os in, 142–44; Puerto Ricans' school experiences, 94–95, 124; racism in, 65–67
Escobar, Edward, 69–70
Espín, Olivia, 24, 133
ethnicity, of Puerto Ricans, 112

"False Memories: Trauma and Liberation" (Levins Morales), 6
families, 79; idealization of, 92–93, 103–4; importance of, 56–57, 72, 80; photos supporting narratives of, 91–92, 103
Family Matters: Puerto Rican Women Authors on the Island and the Mainland (Moreno), 14–15
feminists, liberal, 27
Fernandez Olmos, Marguerite, 53
Fiandt, Julie, 40
Flores, Juan, 14, 112, 148
forgetting, danger of, 81–82, 86, 105–6
Foucault, 11
Friedman, Susan Stanford, 127
From Bomba to Hip Hop (Flores), 14, 112

García, Ignacio, 149
Geertz, Clifford, 114
gender: class, and race and, 29–31; mothers and daughters, 72–73; of mothers and daughters, 31–32; spaces for, 97–99
gender constraints, 24, 30–31, 97–98, 131–32

gender differences, in Puerto Rican culture, 130, 131
gender identity: complexity of, 133–34; construction of, 127, 132, 134–36; of Latinas, 113–14; of Puerto Rican women, 109, 137–38
gender roles: in media, 134–36; of Puerto Rican women, 84, 97, 128–29, 137; Puerto Rican women challenging, 80, 98, 131–32
Georas, Chloe, 112
Getting Home Alive (Levins Morales), 33–38, 49
grandfather, as spiritual healer, 79–80
Grosfoguel, Ramón, 112

Hall, Stuart, 133
Hamilton: An American Musical (Miranda), 139–40
Hawaii, migration to, 46–47
healers, 24, 78–79
healing: grandfather's spiritual, 79–81; Levin Morales on, 39–40; through narratives, 38–48, 87, 153
Herman, Judith, 10–11
"The Historian as Curandera" (Levins Morales), 5, 25–26
historians, 25, 43
histories, 45, 63; affective elements in, 76, 96; centrality of women in, 25–26; as collective autobiographies, 41–42, 45; erasure from, 46, 140, 152–53; evidence in, 43–44; exclusion from, 9–12, 43–44, 105; filling gaps in, 17, 34–35, 46–48, 80–81; forgotten, 81–83; healing through narratives, 9–13, 23–24, 29, 87, 140, 153; hegemonic, 10–11, 36, 42; importance of context in, 27–28; importance of naming individuals in, 26, 28; memory as source of, 18–20, 81; methodologies of, 25–29, 32, 96; of migration as progress, 124–25; objectivity in, 7–8; photos supporting narratives in, 91–92, 103; Puerto Rican perspective on, 89–90, 93–94; Puerto Ricans excluded from, 4–7, 17, 77–78, 81; sources of, 7, 18, 76, 77; subjectivity in, 25, 52. *See also* medicinal histories
hooks, bell, 12, 135
Hunger of Memory (Rodriguez), 149
Hurricane Maria, 145
Hurst, Marsha, 11

immigrants, 35, 47, 60, 143–44
independence movement, in Puerto Rico, 9

jaibería, 59–61
Jenkins, Keith, 8, 25
Jews, 27, 35–37, 45–46
jíbaro identity, 115–18, 123, 126

Kallet, Marilyn, 82
Kingston, 12
Korean War, 91

labor, Puerto Ricans', 90
LaCivita Nixon, Lois, 11–12

language, 39, 67–68
Lara, Irene, 41
Latinas/os, 123; discourse of unbelonging, 147–48, 152–53; lacking representation in textbooks, 142–43; as literary critics, 150–51; literature of, 127, 145–48, 150; seen as un-American, 142–44
"Latino Threat Narrative," 142–44
Laviera, Tato, 110
Levins Morales, Aurora, 10; curandera handbook by, 6–7, 25–26; as curandera historian, 18–19, 24, 101, 105, 140–41; filling gaps in histories, 46–48; *Getting Home Alive* by, 33–38; "The Historian as Curandera" by, 5, 25–26; on medicinal histories, 17, 24, 32; *Medicine Stories* by, 23, 38–48, 49; other Puerto Rican women writers and, 49–50; *This Bridge Called My Back* by, 18–19, 24, 29–30, 49
Lies My Teacher Told Me: Everything Your American History Textbook Got Wrong (Loewen), 8
literature: Puerto Rican island *vs.* diaspora, 15–16; scarcity of Puerto Rican women in, 76, 107; truth in, 75–76
Loewen, James, 8
Lopez Springfield, Consuelo, 34

Machado Saez, Elena, 150
Major, Brenda, 10
marianismo, 84, 129
Mayock, Ellen C., 130

McCracken, Ellen, 68–69
medicinal histories, 18, 98; Levins Morales on, 17, 24, 32, 37–48; methods of, 78–81; Mohr's, 53, 60, 74; by Puerto Rican women, 140–41; *Silent Dancing* as, 75, 78, 89, 106; tenets of, 91, 134; used in literary criticism, 151–52
medicine, Western, 11
Medicine Stories: History, Culture, and the Politics of Integrity (Levins Morales), 23, 38–48, 49
memoirs, of Puerto Rican women, 76–78
memory, 89, 96, 152; danger of forgetting and, 81–82, 86, 105–6; discrepancies in, 102–4; photos and, 81–82, 142; as source of history, 18–20, 76, 81; traumatic *vs.* narrative, 86–87
Mexican Americans, 54; "othering" of, 142–44; police brutality against, 69–70
Mexican American studies, ban on, 142–43
Mexico, U.S. relations with, 12
migration: effects of, 34, 123, 126; hardships of, 46–47; to Hawaii, 46–47; internal, 115; between island to mainland, 78, 88, 94–95; pressures for, 9, 115, 125; Puerto Rican women's experience of, 17, 78
Miller, Carol T., 10
Miranda, Lin-Manuel, 139–40
Mohr, Eugene, 13–14
Mohr, Nicholasa, 3–4, 14, 60, 111, 140–41; Levin Morales and, 49–50;

Index

school experiences of, 64–66, 69. *See also Nilda*
Montilla, Patricia, 98
Morales, Rosario, 33–38
Moreno, Marisel, 14–15, 76–77, 120
mothers, 4, 77; daughters and, 31–32, 72–73; discrepancies with memories of, 102–4
Moya, Paula, 20–21

Native Americans, 43
Near Northwest Side Story (Perez), 115
Negrón-Muntaner, Frances, 112
New York City: lonely deaths of Puerto Ricans in, 81–82. *See also* Nuyoricans
Nieto, Sonia, 69
Nilda (Mohr), 3–5, 19, 94; education in, 63–69; jaibería in, 59–60; police brutality in, 70–72; as semi-autobiographical, 52, 54–55; set in WWII, 52–55, 141; welfare in, 59–61
The Nuyorican Experience: Literature of the Puerto Rican Minority (Mohr), 13–14
"Nuyorican" (Laviera), 110
Nuyoricans, 30, 88, 110; literature of, 12–14, 148; police brutality against, 70–72; poverty of, 57–60; in WWII, 55–57

objectivity, 7–8, 104, 106
Operation Bootstrap, 115
oppression, 26, 58; healing through historical narratives, 23–24, 29; by oppressed, 39–40, 44; patriarchy as, 99–100; relation of race, gender, and class in, 29–31, 73
origin myths, 5
Ortiz Cofer, Judith, 15–16, 19–20, 96, 142, 147; assimilation and, 82–83, 150; on danger of forgetting, 81–82, 86; medicinal histories methodologies of, 78–81, 98; memory as source of histories and, 77, 81, 102–4; motives for writing, 97, 140; on patriarchy, 99–100; on Puerto Rican soldiers, 90–92; school experiences of, 94–95; on silencing of Puerto Ricans, 83–84; on truth in literature, 75–76; on virgin *vs.* whore dichotomy, 85, 98–102. *See also Silent Dancing: A Partial Remembrance of a Puerto Rican Childhood*

patriarchy, 99–100, 127
Perez, Emma, 9
Perez, Gina, 115, 125
Perez, Lorna, 109, 126
Perez y Gonzalez, Maria, 84
Peterson, Nancy, 12
photos, 84; memory and, 81–82, 91, 142; supporting narratives, 91–92, 103
Pietri, Pedro, 82
police brutality, 69–73
population, Puerto Rico's, 48, 115
postmodernism, 43
poverty, 144; of Nuyoricans, 57–60; of Puerto Ricans, 31, 35–36, 42; in

Puerto Rico, 118–21; of Santiago's family, 118–20, 125
power, 11, 37, 80; histories and, 25, 44, 46; language in, 68–69; women's, 131. *See also* agency
propaganda, 55–56, 65
Puerto Rican Jam (Negrón-Muntaner, Grosfoguel, Georas), 112
Puertoricanness, 116; degrees of, 107, 110–11, 128, 137
Puerto Ricans: assumptions about, 62–63, 65–66, 88, 98–99; as authors, 145–51; citizenship of, 21; class of, 35–36; cultural hybridity of, 36–38, 111–12, 114, 123, 126; cultural schizophrenia of, 88–89; discourse of unbelonging, 65–66, 72, 145; exclusion from histories, 4–6, 14, 81; island *vs.* diaspora, 15, 30, 109, 111, 123–26; Jews and, 27, 35–37; limited options for, 87–88; lonely deaths of, 81–82; migration of, 9, 46–47, 126; national identity of, 56–57, 74, 109, 112, 123, 126; oppression of, 12, 31, 90, 123, 152; as other, 85, 123; "others" of, 88–89; schools training as good citizens, 64–65; silencing of, 83–84, 85–86; in WWII, 56, 90–93. *See also under* culture
"Puerto Rican Students in US Schools: A Brief History" (Nieto), 69
Puerto Rican women, 21, 34, 41, 96, 107; agency of, 26, 120–22, 137–38; dichotomous roles of, 20, 84–85; gender roles of, 97–98, 137; histories and, 4–7, 17, 78, 90, 140–41; identities of, 24, 109, 133–34, 137–38, 152; income for, 47, 132–33; island *vs.* mainland, 20, 39; memoirs of, 76–78; oppression of, 73, 141; sexuality of, 98–102; as writers, 5, 49–50, 140; in WWII, 53, 73–74
"Puerto Rican Writers in the U.S., Puerto Rican Writers in Puerto Rico" (Mohr), 14
Puerto Rico, 27, 42; Americanization in, 20, 110–11; economy of, 145–46; independence movements in, 9; industrialization/modernization of, 115, 118–19, 125; Jews in, 45–46; migration and, 78, 115, 147; overpopulation in, 48; race and class divisions in, 94–95; rural *vs.* urban life in, 118–19; U.S. relations with, 20, 91, 109, 145
Puerto Rico Oversight, Management, and Economic Stability Act (PROMESA), 146

race, 37; class, and gender and, 29–31; Puerto Ricans', 38–39, 42, 46–47, 94–95
Race, Police, and the Making of a Political Identity (Escobar), 69–70
racism, 111, 123; in schools, 63, 65–67, 94–95
Rebolledo, Tey Diana, 24–25
Remedios: Stories of Earth and Iron from the History of Puertorriqueñas, 40–49, 79

representation: importance of, 3–4, 139; Latinas/os lacking, 142–43
Rivera, Carmen, 127
Roche Rico, Barbara, 60
Rodriguez, Randy, 149, 151
Rodriguez, Richard, 149, 151
Root, Maria, 9–10
Rothberg, Michael, 46, 86–87

Saldívar, Jose, 147
Saldivar-Hull, Sonia, 113
Sanchez Gonzalez, Lisa, 150
Sánchez-González, Lisa, 15–16, 56, 126, 150–51
Sanchez-Korrol, Virginia, 112, 133
Santiago, Esmeralda, 16, 20, 50; on Americanization, 110–11, 123; criticisms of, 150–51; on Industrialization/modernization of Puerto Rico, 115–16; learning about imperialism, 121–22; life on island *vs.* mainland, 123–26; motives for writing, 107–8, 111, 140; on parents' marriage, 128–29, 132; on patriarchy in Puerto Rican culture, 127; on rural *vs.* urban life in Puerto Rico, 117–18, 123; school experiences of, 118–19, 124; on sexuality, 129–30, 134–36; on virgin *vs.* whore dichotomy, 109, 137–38. See also *When I Was Puerto Rican*
Scarry, Elaine, 11
self, construction of, 12, 48, 127–28
sexuality: of Puerto Rican women, 98–102; Santiago on, 128–30, 134–36

Sheehan, Susan, 61–63
silencing, 60; of Puerto Ricans, 83–86; trauma from, 86–87, 105
Silent Dancing: A Partial Remembrance of a Puerto Rican Childhood (Ortiz Cofer), 19–20, 75, 85, 94, 105–6
Sisters of the Yam (hooks), 12
Socolovsky, Maya, 147–48
Southgate, Beverly, 8, 140
"Spiritual Power and the Mundane World: Hispanic Female Healers in Urban U.S. Communities" (Espín), 24
storytelling, 79, 96; healing trauma through, 12–13, 89. See also medicinal histories
subjectivity, 25, 43, 52

Takaki, Ronald, 54
Taller, Oliva P., 144
Tapestries of Life (Aptheker), 18
Taylor, Diana, 7–8, 81–83
This Bridge Called My Back (Levins Morales), 18–19, 24, 29–30, 49
Thomas, Piri, 31
Torres, Lourdes, 127
Torres-Robles, Carmen, 126
trauma, 23; definitions of, 6; healing through narratives, 9–13, 24, 29, 76, 78, 87; sources of, 9–10, 58, 87–89, 105, 123, 140, 152; traumatic memory and, 86–87
Tropics of Discourse (White), 7, 25
Trump, Donald, 145
truth: in literature, 75–76; poetic, 79–80, 94, 142

United States: relations with Mexico, 12; relations with Puerto Rico, 8–9, 91, 109, 120–22, 145–46

Vasquez, Melba J. T., 10
Vega, Bernardo, 41
virgin *vs.* whore dichotomy, 20, 84–85; challenges to, 98–102, 109, 137–38; girls socialized in, 99–100; in *When I Was Puerto Rican,* 128–34, 136

Walker, Alice, 52
wars: children's perspective on, 53–55; impact on women, 47–48
Watson, Julia, 108, 134
Wear, Delese, 11–12
welfare, 4, 59–61, 125
A Welfare Mother (Sheehan), 61–63
When I Was Puerto Rican (Santiago), 20, 107–8, 137; on degrees of Puerto-ricanness, 126–27; gender roles in, 128–29; virgin *vs.* whore dichotomy in, 128–34, 136. *See also* Santiago, Esmeralda
White, Hayden, 7, 25
Wilentz, Gay, 12
women, 43, 112; as authors, 76, 140; centrality in history, 25–26, 42; wars and, 47–48, 90–91. *See also* Puerto Rican women
Woolf, Virginia, 19–20, 76–77
World War II, 141; *Nilda* set in, 52–55, 72; people of color participating in, 51–52, 55–57, 72–73, 90; propaganda in, 55–56

Yulin Cruz, Carmen, 145

Zentella, Ana Celia, 67

www.ingramcontent.com/pod-product-compliance
Lightning Source LLC
Chambersburg PA
CBHW020110020526
44112CB00033B/1128